CULTURE, TECHNOLOGY, A
THE CREATION OF AMERIC.
NATIONAL PARKS

Richard Grusin's innovative study investigates how the establishment of national parks participated in the production of American national identity after the Civil War. The creation of America's national parks is usually seen as an uncomplicated act of environmental preservation. Grusin argues, instead, that parks must be understood as complex cultural technologies for the reproduction of nature as landscape art. He explores the origins of America's three major parks – Yosemite, Yellowstone, and Grand Canyon – in relation to other forms of landscape representation in the late nineteenth century. He examines such forms as photography, painting, and mapping, plus a wide range of travel narratives, scientific and nature writing, and fiction. Grusin shows that while establishing a national park does involve preserving an area of land as a "natural" rather than economic asset, a ranch or mine for instance, it also transforms the landscape into a culturally constructed object called "nature."

RICHARD GRUSIN is Professor and Chair of the Department of English at Wayne State University. He is the author of *Transcendentalist Hermeneutics: Higher Criticism and the Institutional Authority of the Bible* (1991) and co-author (with Jay David Bolter) of *Remediation: Understanding New Media* (1999).

CAMBRIDGE STUDIES IN AMERICAN LITERATURE AND CULTURE

Editor
Ross Posnock, *New York University*

Founding editor
Albert Gelpi, *Stanford University*

Advisory board
Sacvan Bercovitch, *Harvard University*
Ronald Bush, *St. John's College, Oxford University*
Wai Chee Dimock, *Yale University*
Albert Gelpi, *Stanford University*
Gordon Hutner, *University of Kentucky*
Walter Benn Michaels, *University of Illinois, Chicago*
Kenneth Warren, *University of Chicago*

CULTURE, TECHNOLOGY, AND THE CREATION OF AMERICA'S NATIONAL PARKS

RICHARD GRUSIN

Wayne State University

CAMBRIDGE
UNIVERSITY PRESS

CAMBRIDGE UNIVERSITY PRESS
Cambridge, New York, Melbourne, Madrid, Cape Town, Singapore, São Paulo

Cambridge University Press
The Edinburgh Building, Cambridge CB2 8RU, UK

Published in the United States of America by Cambridge University Press, New York

www.cambridge.org
Information on this title: www.cambridge.org/9780521826495

First published 2004
This digitally printed version 2008

A catalogue record for this publication is available from the British Library

ISBN 978-0-521-82649-5 hardback
ISBN 978-0-521-08168-9 paperback

For Ann, Sarah, and Sam

Contents

Illustrations

Preface and acknowledgments

This book was a long time in the making. Its "germ," in a Jamesian sense, can be traced to the summer of 1985, at the School of Criticism and Theory at Northwestern University in Evanston, Illinois. While still in the process of revising my dissertation for publication, I began to look around for another project. My dissertation had examined the role of the higher criticism of the Bible in shaping the anti-institutionalism of the self in New England Transcendentalism. In it I had argued that the intuitive authority of the Transcendentalist self was not independent of institutional authority but in fact produced by the hermeneutic authority generated by the higher criticism of the Bible. Although this project had engaged me professionally and intellectually, it had no further connection to my personal interests. I began to think about a project that might have such a connection.

In large part it had been Transcendentalist ideas of nature to which I was initially attracted (indeed, another of the project's germs can be traced to the summer of 1977 and one particularly lengthy inter-species exchange with a wood thrush in the post-glacial forests of the Canadian Rockies during my graduate school years at Berkeley). Consequently I began to consider a project on the institutionalization of nature in national parks. In the simplest sense I started to think about what kind of action it was for the federal government to legislate a boundary and declare that on one side of it is "nature" or "wilderness," while on the other side is "culture" or "civilization." Not unlike my interest in looking at the institutional formation of Transcendentalist anti-institutionalism, I soon became intrigued by the question of where the idea of institutionalizing nature came from, particularly as it was manifested in the formation of America's national parks. In researching various histories of how the United States developed the "national park idea," I began to think that just as the Transcendentalist distinction between intuition and institutions could be better understood by examining the hermeneutic practices and institutionalization of biblical criticism, so the logical and rhetorical opposition between nature and culture that motivates America's national parks might also be better understood by placing it in relation to a series of mid-nineteenth-century aesthetic practices of representing nature.

In the West, thinking about nature or the environment has developed within the context of a series of powerful logical and rhetorical antinomies between nature and culture, wilderness and civilization, preservation and use – or more recently between biocentrism and anthropocentrism or (in more weakened form) sustainability and development. These dichotomies are themselves rooted in some of the fundamental antinomies of liberal thought. This book is an attempt to think about the origins of America's national parks without adhering to these antinomies. Rhetorically those who would seek to defend nature or the environment against the depredations of industrial capitalism and Western civilization have employed these antinomies differently from those who would subordinate nature or wilderness to human or economic needs. The logic of capitalism relies upon the assumptions that nature provides the resources or raw material for economic and technological development, and that the protection or preservation of the environment is clearly subordinate to, and can only be understood within, a calculus of economic growth and prosperity; the logic of environmentalism, on the other hand, depends much more centrally on an appeal to the value of nature, wilderness, or the environment as somehow escaping or transcending economic calculation. Thus, even ecologically well-meaning attempts to elide or complicate the dichotomies on which the rhetoric of environmentalism depends can be greeted with hostility and suspicion by many environmentalists. When William Cronon argued in "The Trouble with Wilderness," for example, that wilderness was a cultural construction, he caused an uproar among a segment of the environmentalist community both within and outside of the academy for denying that wilderness escapes or exceeds culture. Such criticism ignores the essay's advocacy of wilderness and environmental values, as well as Cronon's inability to escape the reinscription of some of the very antinomies he sets out to resist.

But to try to resist these logical antinomies is not the same thing as to resist the idea that there is something of nature that exceeds culture, something (which we might even want to call "wilderness") that is not produced by or limited to or contained within cultural or social constraints. In developing the book's thesis that national parks function as technologies for the reproduction of nature, I have not set out to deny the "naturalness" of these parks, but to emphasize the way in which national parks function as heterogeneous cultural formations that help to preserve and reproduce that which resists or exceeds cultural practices. In thinking about the technology of national parks, I have tried to think about the agency of nature, how nature acts. That is, how does nature (as that which is not finally reducible to culture) act within a particular cultural or historical formation like a national park? What kind of natural agency do national parks help authorize and make possible within late-nineteenth-century American culture? For even though a park's natural elements (like mountains, waterfalls, and wildlife, or forests, fields, and flowers) are created by and exert non-human agency, this agency invariably operates within both natural and cultural formations, often in a way that makes national parks very similar to other technologies of representation or remediation. In treating the national parks as technologies for the reproduction of nature I have tried to think of the way in which the "nature" of each of the USA's three major parks has acted within the cultural and historical field of representation in the last half of the nineteenth century.

But what about human action? What are the implications of this line of thought for contemporary environmental issues facing the national parks today? Some readers of this book might be disappointed with my refusal to argue for nature as against culture, or wilderness as against civilization, or preservation as against use. Some may object that I have attempted to strip the national parks of that which makes them most sacred – their tran-scendence of all that is human or that humans have made. Others may object that I have minimized or understated the political significance of the creation of national parks as milestones in the history of environmental activism or protection both in the United States and worldwide. Still others may feel that in focusing on aesthetic and cultural questions I have failed to fulfill the obligation of ecocriticism to use scholarly work as a means of advocacy for environmental protection. And in some sense such objec-tions would not be unfounded. In trying to understand the way in which the creation of national parks emerged from and functioned within late-nineteenth-century American culture, I have not set out to make specific recommendations about how national parks should be managed within the culture of the twenty-first century. Where I have touched on current developments in the national parks, I have confined myself to a couple of emblematic examples of how some of the aesthetic and cultural concerns that informed the creation of America's national parks continue to persist (albeit in significantly different discursive and technological manifestations) today.

My reasons for not using this book to stake out positions on environ-mental issues facing America's national parks at the start of the twenty-first century have less to do with my understanding of the ethical obligations of environmentalism than with my understanding of the professional obliga-tions of academic scholarship. Put differently, I do not consider my scholarly obligations to be identical with my obligations as an environmentally aware citizen of the United States at the start of the twenty-first century. In pursuing the question of how national parks emerged from and functioned within the cultural and technological formations of late-nineteenth-century America, I have acted as a scholar of American cultural studies to investigate the parks as technologies for representing or reproducing nature, not (as has been ably done by numerous scholars before me) to tell the important story of the role the national parks have played in the history of environmentalism in America. Consequently I have tried to make sense of the creation of America's national parks less in relation to questions of environmental policy than in relation to a number of issues, particularly of representation, that have concerned scholars of nineteenth-century American literature and culture more broadly – scholars who may have no sense of the important relationship between the questions informing the creation of national parks and those informing the creation of literary, cultural, or artistic works, for example. Insofar as this book sets out to do ecocritical work, it does so by bringing the concerns of American literary and cultural studies to bear on environmental questions – by being responsible to the field in which I have chosen to work. As a scholar of nineteenth-century American culture, I feel that this is perhaps the most professionally responsible (if indirect) way for my work to advocate for the environment.

In choosing primarily to pursue epistemological rather than ecological issues, I have continued to work in the discourse in which I have been trained and have worked for the past two decades and more. I do so not because I do not have positions on many of the policy issues facing the national parks today, or because my positions would be significantly different from those who see ecocriticism as entailing environmental advocacy, but because my positions on these issues are largely those of the "amateur," and because they belong more to my private life than to my life as an academic. Nonetheless, I originally conceived this project more than fifteen years ago because of my love of the national parks, and of what Thoreau called "wildness," wherever it might be found. Indeed, in the course of writing this book I often found myself wrestling in different ways and at odd moments, in my personal as well as my professional life, with what it is about nature that both distinguished it from and inextricably tied it to culture. Although this question is addressed only obliquely in the book, one stab at a potential explanation (that in some fundamental sense we need to understand the agency of nature as an agency of mediation, to think of nature not only as that which is mediated by culture but as that which actively mediates both culture and nature) emerged from my personal life in the form of the following poem:

natura medians, natura mediata
(composed on the banks of the chattahoochee river, october 8, 2000)

how do you think the agency of matter?

i think i have the beginning of an answer.

you think the agency of matter
by taking mediation seriously.

the large rock
in the middle of the river
or stream
that forces the water
on either side
increasing its strength
its interest
breaking up the un-
interrupted flow
mediates the river.

saying
"you can't go here
go around me
take your way on
either side"
the rock re-
presents the river
as river
acknowledges
stream as stream.

so how do you think the agency of matter?

perhaps now an answer would run:

by thinking of nature as that which mediates
and mediation as what matters.

(*Technical note.* Transmitted from East Palisades Unit of Chattahoochee
National Recreation Area by Powertel digital network to Bell South voice
mail. Broadcast in 361 Skiles Building, Georgia Institute of Technology,
on Meridian speakerphone. Transcribed on Apple G3 running Corel
Word Perfect on MAC OS9.)

If it is true, as I argue explicitly and implicitly throughout this book, that national parks are heterogeneous technologies for the reproduction of nature, technologies that include multiple forms of representation, then in its own way this book is part of the network that works to protect and defend what remains of our natural environment from those human and non-human agents who would work to destroy it. Furthermore, this book was itself dependent upon another network, a personal and intellectual community of humans and non-humans, without which it could never have been completed. After such a long period of time, it will be impossible to remember all the support I received, but I feel obligated to try.

I owe a debt of gratitude to my fellow students at the School of Criticism and Theory in 1985, whose conversations helped to germinate this project, particularly Howard Horwitz, Rob Wilson, and Anne Marie Oliver. At the College of William and Mary, where I began my research, I was encouraged by David Rosenwassser, Walt Wenska, and Kevin McManus. My thinking on matters of environmentalist rhetoric and visual representation was developed largely in the context of my students and colleagues in the Science, Technology, and Culture program at Georgia Tech. In addition to those students in my classes on the rhetoric of environmentalism and the cultural history of the national parks, my work was enriched by the advice and conversation of Blake Leland, Alan Rauch, Sandra Corse, Hugh Crawford, Phil Auslander, Kavita Philip, Rebecca Merrens, Daryl Ogden, Greg Van Hoosier-Carey, and Lance Newman. Other Georgia Tech colleagues from whom I benefited included Bryan Norton, Greg Nobles, Stan Carpenter, and Daniel Kleinman. At a 1988 NEH Summer Institute on Image and Text in the Eighteenth Century at Johns Hopkins University, I learned a tremendous amount about how to look at pictures from my fellow students as well as from the Institute's directors, Ronald Paulson and especially Michael Fried.

The book would never have been completed without the luxury of my time as a visiting fellow at the Robert Penn Warren Center for the Humanities at Vanderbilt University, during the 1999–2000 academic year. Not only did that fellowship year provide me with the time and space to bring the manuscript to completion, but the intellectual stimulation and camaraderie of our seminar on the Construction, Destruction, and Deconstruction of Nature provided me with an incalculable benefit. To my fellow nature seminarians Beth Conklin, Leonard Folgarait, Kathy Gacca, Laurie Johnson, Jay Noller, David Weintraub, and co-directors Michael Bess and David Wood, I owe a debt that will never adequately be repaid. In addition my project was supported by the friendship and collegiality of others at Vanderbilt University, including center director Mona Frederick and members of the English Department, including Jay Clayton, Lynn Enterline, Dennis Kezar, Mark Wollager, and Cecelia Tichi; for weekly (or more frequent) support I gladly acknowledge the companionship and good cheer provided by Jerry Christensen, Sam Girgus, and Deak Nabers.

Over the decade and a half during which I have been working on this book, portions of it have been delivered at various conferences and institutions. Portions of the introduction were delivered at Vanderbilt University and Berry College. Parts of the Yosemite chapter, in various versions, were presented at Columbia University, the Universities of Washington, Oregon, and Nevada, the University of California at Irvine, and at annual meetings of the Modern Language Association. Versions of the Yellowstone chapter were presented at Indiana University, the University of Utah, and at the annual meetings of the Society for Literature and Science, the British Society for the History of Science, and the American Society for Environmental History. Portions of the Grand Canyon chapter have been presented at the Georgia Institute of Technology, Georgia State University, the University of Michigan, the Landscape and Technology Seminar at Odense University, and the annual conferences of the Society for Literature and Science and the American Society for Environmental History. Versions of the conclusion were presented at Berry College and at the Center for North American Studies at Bonn University. I am grateful for the feedback I received on all of these occasions. Earlier versions of the Yosemite and Yellowstone chapters were published in *Cultural Studies* and *Configurations*; I am grateful to both of these journals for permission to incorporate revisions of these articles into the book.

Research for the book was conducted at numerous libraries, archives, and museums across the United States. For their gracious assistance I am grateful to the staffs of the Library of Congress Print and Photographic Division; the National Archives; the United States Geological Survey; the National Park Service; the Gilcrease Museum in Tulsa, Oklahoma; the Cooper-Hewitt Institute of Design; the Huntington Library; the libraries of Montana State University, Georgia Institute of Technology, Emory University, and Vanderbilt University; and especially the Park Service employees at the libraries, museums, and archives of Yosemite, Yellowstone, and Grand Canyon National Parks.

Finally, I could not have completed the book without much generous assistance. My research and writing were supported by release time made possible by the National Endowment for the Humanities, the Georgia

Tech Foundation, and the Robert Penn Warren Center for the Humanities at Vanderbilt University. Wayne State University, particularly Dean Lawrence Scaff, Associate Dean Don Spinelli, and Humanities Center Director Walter Edwards, have helped provide financial support for the costs of bringing the book to print.

The editorial team at Cambridge University Press has been extremely supportive: Ray Ryan, Neil De Cort, Jackie Warren, and Penny Wheeler. I am especially grateful to Ross Posnock, editor of the Cambridge Series in American Literature and Culture, for reading and hearing earlier parts of the manuscript and for supporting it during the publication process. I am also grateful to the two manuscript referees, whose criticisms and suggestions helped make this a better book.

Most important of all are those who read parts or all of the book and those nearest to me who have provided me with the love and emotional support necessary to keep at a project over such an extended period of time. For reading and responding to parts of the manuscript during the long course of its composition, I am indebted to Phil Auslander, Sandra Corse, Stuart Culver, Michael Fried, Howard Horwitz, Irene Klaver, Blake Leland, Greg Nobles, Bryan Norton, and Alan Rauch. For the heroic work of providing a challenging, yet supportive reading of the entire manuscript in its nearly finished form, I owe a tremendous debt of gratitude to Deak Nabers. For preparing and assembling the book's illustrations, and for obtaining permissions to reprint them, I am grateful to my research assistant, Joy Burnett. To my two children, to whom I have tried to pass on my love of the national parks, and to my wife, the person with whom I first fell in love with the parks, this book is dedicated.

Reproducing nature: the technology of national parks

What do we think of when we think of America's national parks? For most of us, national parks are natural parks – evoking images of large tracts of unspoiled wilderness, majestic mountains, spectacular waterfalls, or undisturbed forests. If asked, many of us would acknowledge and embrace the management goal adopted in 1963 by the National Park Service: that "the biotic associations within each park be maintained, or where necessary recreated, as nearly as possible in the condition that prevailed when the area was first visited by the white man."[1] In other words, the origins of America's national parks are usually thought to consist in the desire to withdraw or preserve particularly spectacular natural areas from the threat of social, political, and economic development, at least partly for the purpose of reminding Americans what their country was like when their European predecessors first took possession of it. Indeed it is something of a historical truism that the construction of American national identity has always been inseparable from nature. Unlike European nations, whose identity derived from a common language, ethnic or racial heritage, religion, or cultural history, the identity of the United States of America as "nature's nation" has been grounded in large part in the land itself.[2] Because of this centrality of nature to American self-identity, questions of environmentalism in America have invariably taken on ideological and national significance. In America, the preservation of natural spaces has involved not only the creation of an alternative to the nation's cultural space but also the creation of America itself.

In claiming that nature, wilderness, or the national parks themselves are culturally constructed, I am echoing what in the past decade has become a common refrain among ecocritics and environmental historians.[3] At the 1995 biennial meeting of the American Society for Environmental History in Las Vegas, for example, Susan Flader began her response to a session entitled "Nature Objectified/Nature Commodified: The Defense of Scenery" by noting the general agreement among environmental historians that nature is a cultural construction. Despite what nineteenth- and twentieth-century preservationist ideology might maintain, Flader averred, the preservation of natural scenery works to further, not to oppose, the values of the dominant culture. Speaking in the same conference's two-part headliner session, "Reinventing Nature," William Cronon made a similar point, arguing that the concept of wilderness does not escape the categories of culture – that there is "nothing natural about the concept of wilderness."[4] Contending that wilderness reproduces the cultural values its advocates seek to escape, Flader and Cronon are hardly alone in their indictment of "romantic nature as an instrument of imperial conquest." As Lawrence Buell has noted, citing (among other examples) "The West as America," the 1991 exhibit at the Smithsonian Museum of American Art, it is now almost taken for granted that the "nineteenth-century American romantic representation of the West was built on an ideology of conquest."[5] For each of these three scholars, as for any number of others, the ideology of nature or wilderness preservation has been demystified, has been revealed to harbor within it the very will to power it would set out to escape.

Countering a less critical body of primarily historical scholarship that often took at face value the claims of early preservationists (that nature offered an escape from the ideologies of progress and development that fueled American expansion in the nineteenth and early twentieth centuries), recent work in environmental studies has set the stage for a revaluation of the cultural meanings of the origins of environmentalism in America. Motivated largely by the widespread acceptance of arguments for the social or cultural construction of knowledge, environmental historians have begun to rewrite the story of American environmentalism. No longer a triumphant narrative of the acceptance of concepts like the rights of nature or the intrinsic value of wilderness, the history of environmentalism increasingly tells the story of a deployment of the ideology of nature's intrinsic value to further the social, cultural, or political interests of a dominant race, class, gender, or institutional formation. Compelling as this revisionist narrative is, however, it runs the risk of stripping nature of any particularity or specificity whatsoever – of transforming nature so completely into culture that the preservation of nature as a national park, for example, becomes indistinguishable from its transformation into a ranch or a mine or a private resort.

In defending the particularity of different constructions of nature, my work diverges from this narrative. In so doing, I do not propose that we undo the hard-earned insights of the cultural construction of knowledge, but that we undertake the more difficult task of pursuing these insights more seriously.[6] Granted that nature is inseparable from culture, we need to ask how national parks differ from (and intersect with) other culturally constructed entities. Further, we need to ask both how the cultural construction of nature varies historically and how it remains constant through time and across different geographical locations. In other words we need to pursue locally the more global insights of the cultural construction of nature – perhaps in something like an ecological criticism, which understands that the cultural construction of nature circulates within what could be called a discursive ecosystem. The task of such a criticism would be to trace the connections and interrelations both within the discursive practices of environmentalism and among the scientific, technological, and cultural networks through which environmentalism emerges. For it is only through such connections and interrelations that the particularity of nature can be defined.[7]

In attempting to exemplify such a critical practice, I set out from the premise that the origins of America's national parks can be fruitfully understood not as straightforward instances of the preservation of nature but rather as complex cultural representations or productions. I challenge the notion that "nature" is a self-identical quality, and that the creation of national parks involves establishing a boundary and declaring that inside that boundary is "nature," while outside of that boundary is something else, say, "culture" or some other non-natural quality or essence. To establish a national park is not to put an institutional fence around nature as you would put a fence around a herd of cattle. Rather, to establish a national park is to construct a complex technology, an "organic machine" that operates according to and within a discursive formation, a set or network of discursive practices.[8] Saying this is not to deny the matter-of-fact sense in which establishing a national park involves preserving an area of land as "natural" as opposed to (for example) converting it into a farm, a ranch, a mine, a housing development, a shopping mall, or an amusement park. Nor is it to deny the differences between what goes on inside the boundaries of a park and what goes on outside. But these differences are not intrinsic ones, differences in the essence or "nature" or quality of the land on one side as opposed to the other; rather these differences are the product of a complex assemblage of heterogeneous technologies and social practices, the aim of which is the production or reproduction of a culturally and discursively defined and formed object called "nature." To map out the way in which national parks emerge in the last third of the nineteenth century requires the description of the relations among these parks and the various discursive formations which enable their emergence at a particular historical moment and in a particular cultural formation. It is, in other words, to insist upon the fact that the preservation of nature entailed in establishing the national parks should be seen as the preservation of culture as well – more specifically of the network of scientific, technological, aesthetic, social, economic, and other practices that makes up what we call "culture" at any particular historical moment. For in thinking of the cultural origins of our national parks, I would agree with Bruno Latour that people do not typically think of themselves as actually living in a "culture" until their customary practices are challenged.[9] The origins of the national parks can be understood as instances of a challenge that not only allow us to define America's culture at a particular historical moment, but also reveal or make visible aspects of that culture which might otherwise go unnoticed.

One aspect of nineteenth-century American culture that the national parks makes visible is how nature is persistently identified with landscape. Whereas the turn to landscape painting in early-nineteenth-century France, for example, has traditionally been explained as a move away from the more elevated subjects of historical painting, in antebellum America the representation of landscape by New York School painters was understood as itself a form of historical painting in which the landscape was imbued with culturally rich iconographic and symbolic meaning (see Figure 1). Contending in an "Essay on American Scenery" (1835) that "the most distinctive, and perhaps the most impressive, characteristic of American scenery is its wildness," Thomas Cole exalts American scenery over European, precisely "because in civilized Europe the primitive features of scenery have long since been destroyed or modified."[10] Similarly in "Letters on Landscape Painting" (1855), Asher Durand urges American painters to paint American landscapes, arguing that the persistence of many "forms of nature yet spared from the pollutions of civilization," combined with the "principle of self-government," should furnish the conditions for the American landscape painter "boldly [to] originate a high and independent style, based on his native resources."[11] For both Cole and Durand, although America's untouched wilderness offers the opportunity for a distinctly American landscape painting, the westward "progress" of civilization across the continent suggests that this opportunity will not last forever.

Angela Miller has mapped out the relations among landscape painting, progress, and ideas of nationalism as they evolved in mid-nineteenth-century America, arguing that such painting, particularly in New York and New England, took as its foremost cultural task the representation of the natural landscape's role in constructing American national identity. Cole's critique of American expansion, she argues, his refusal "to accept this emergent definition of 'nature's nation' as an empire," manifests itself in paintings that persistently work through questions of national identity, by persistently dramatizing the conflict between nature and culture in such a way as to emphasize the destructive agency of America's social, cultural, and technological institutions.[12] Largely in response to the political conflicts of the Mexican–American and Civil Wars, Frederic Church takes a different stance towards the destructiveness of America's westward expansion. In his monumental landscapes of Central and South America, for example, nature is depicted as the conceptual and pictorial ground for an allegory of national identity in which human and social agency is erased: "In place of Cole's engagement of the spectator as an actor implicated in the transfomations of nature is a nature that has erased culture's wounds."[13] Where Church's paintings often represented nature as doing away with the evidence of cultural agency (see Figure 2), Durand's most programmatic works "projected a pious belief in wilderness as the basis of national culture," in which "wilderness served as the blank slate ready to receive culture's imprint."[14] In *Progress, or The Advance of Civilization* (1853) (see Figure 3) Durand offers a paradigmatic visual portrayal of the mid-century relation between technology, nature, and American democratic progress, in which "a sense of place gives way almost entirely to an ideal vision of nationhood as it was to be realized in time and space. Here democratic social energies would harness technology to transform wilderness into a productive middle ground where nature and culture were ideally balanced."[15] By 1875, Miller concludes, the shared concern with national landscape, developed (albeit to different ends) in painters like Cole, Church, and Durand, had given way to the vicissitudes of an emerging consumer culture: "While it had one last and glorious gasp following the Civil War in the work of Albert Bierstadt and Thomas Moran, the national landscape eventually collapsed as an anachronism in an age when communal associations were increasingly marketed through new media and choreographed by new urban experiences. In such spaces as the department store, replete with exotica and historical fantasies, American identity was being redefined around private acts of acquisition and possession."[16]

Although landscape painting's role in defining national identity may have diminished in the late nineteenth century, the same is not necessarily true of the natural landscape itself. The creation of national parks in the last third of the nineteenth century, I would argue, entails the reproduction of an American national landscape in light of the redefinition of American national identity that accompanied the rise of consumer culture. Indeed the act of setting aside parks from private acquisition and development

1 Thomas Cole, *Course of Empire: Destruction*

2 Frederic Church, *Cotopaxi*

3 Asher Durand, *Progress, or The Advance of Civilization*, 1853

needs itself to be understood as part of the growth of media, urbanism, and spectacle that marked consumer culture. Although more visibly manifest in urban, industrial centers of the East, consumer culture participated in the postbellum transformation of the United States "from a society of 'island communities' to a modern, urban-industrial nation-state" that included the trans-Mississippi West.[17] This transformation laid the foundation for the establishment of "western tourism" as a "a truly national tourism," in which the national parks played a significant role in helping to define American national identity.[18] But it was not only as a tourist destination and national symbol that the West was brought together with the East after the Civil War; technology-intensive industries like mining and the railroads "made the West an integral element of the industrializing Atlantic economy."[19] Against earlier accounts of Western exceptionalism, the best of the new Western history has portrayed the region as integral to the growth of Eastern, urban America as the hub of a major industrialized nation.[20]

By all accounts the West loomed large in the post-Civil War industrial program: as an investment arena for surplus capital, as a source of raw materials, and as a vast vacant lot to enter and occupy . . . The history of the post-Civil War West – and of the nation at large – is the story of dynamic, reciprocal, and interconnected phenomena. That is especially true of the establishment and evolution of modern capitalism and of the integration of the trans-Mississippi West into national- and international-exchange relationships. To attempt to describe change in the West as an isolated, internally homogenous process falsifies the material world; it ignores important and integral relationships involving the modern capitalist world system.[21]

Insofar as the West as a region participates in "the central technological, economic, and cultural changes that helped to initiate and define this transformation," the origins of the national parks must be understood in the context of "the construction of a national transportation network, the emergence of a national market, and the development of a national print media" which mark post-Civil War America.[22]

To make sense of the way in which national parks participate in the production of American national identity after the Civil War, I argue that nature is not only culturally constructed, but technologically constructed – that national parks function (in the broadest sense) as technologies for the reproduction of nature. Consequently I take up the origins of the three "major" national parks – Yosemite, Yellowstone, and the Grand Canyon – as sites whose particularity and specificity emerge from an affiliation of diverse technological practices and cultural beliefs that each of the book's three chapters traces out. These chapters are not in any strict sense essays in the history of ideas of conservation, preservation, environmentalism, or biocentrism; the history of landscape art, aesthetics, or representation; or the history of the social, technological, economic, or political development of the American West. Rather they are essays in what I have elsewhere called cultural historicism, a way of thinking about cultural history that could claim to be discursively ecocritical.[23] These essays proceed from the assumption that the national parks need to be understood not simply by explaining how they are socially or culturally constructed, but also by looking at how certain fundamental cultural logics or metaphors (like natural agency or fidelity to nature) are worked out through the parks at the same historical moment in different discursive practices. In taking up certain American origin myths as played out across heterogeneous discourses and technologies of representation and reproduction, I hope to illuminate the way in which American cultural origins are simultaneously constructed and destabilized through the act of reproducing nature.

In traditional accounts of the post-Civil War appropriation of undeveloped Western lands by the industrialized East, nature is characteristically defined in opposition to technology in two general senses. On the one hand, nature is understood as the raw material with which or on which technology works, and which is threatened by the industrial development of America as the nation moves westward across the continent (for example, Alan Trachtenberg's idea of the incorporation of America).[24] On the other, nature is often conceived as, or in conjunction with, something like spirit, which provides a refuge or alternative space from which to mount a critique of technology, progress, or industrial capitalism (compare, say, the traditional account of Thoreau or John Muir in American environmental history, or of romanticism generally in the history of Western culture). Given these general assumptions about nature and technology, the creation of national parks in nineteenth-century America has traditionally been seen as the creation of places that are natural as opposed to technological, that are reserved, preserved, or set aside as sanctuaries within which technology (or culture, or capital) is not supposed to hold sway.

Taking issue with this account of the origins of national parks, I argue that national parks are themselves hybrid technologies for the reproduction of nature. In the last third of the nineteenth century, insofar as nature or wilderness (defined either as raw material or as sanctuary) is understood as being transformed into cultural landscape by industrialization and incorporation, or as being threatened by the westward movement of the American nation, national parks need to be understood as technologies for the reproduction of that very nature which is being threatened and destroyed. In characterizing our national parks in this manner, I mean in the first instance that the parks are created by and employ a variety of technologies. That is, I mean to acknowledge the common-sense way in which it takes technologies to create and maintain the parks (particularly technologies of mapping and surveying, of road and trail construction, of communication, of lodging, of commerce, of land and resource management). But I mean more crucially that the parks themselves function as technologies of representation not unlike painting, photography, cartography, or landscape architecture. Constructed of and by a number of different technologies, national parks also operate in alliance with nature as complex and heterogeneous technological apparatuses. Neither gardens in the machine nor machines in the garden, national parks are machines that are made up of gardens, or gardens that function as machines. Like both gardens and machines, national parks are not self-replicating, but need tending and maintenance: trails erode or are blocked by fallen debris; roads require improvement or repair; exotic flora and fauna need to be eradicated or controlled. I am not of course suggesting that the national parks are the only such technologies in nineteenth-century America. Not only are landscape photography, painting, or illustration, for example, technologies for the visual reproduction of nature (often reproducing many of the same geographical areas or natural features that are preserved as parks), but urban parks and rural cemeteries, gardens and farms, hunting reserves and national forests are also technologies that reproduce nature according to the cultural formations and discursive practices of the time.

Granted then that national parks are in some senses like these other cultural formations, why should we think of them as technologies of representation, instead of simply as institutions or discursive formations or cultural constructions? By thinking of the parks as technologies of representation, I would argue, we are reminded that, like all technologies, they participate in a complex, heterogeneous network of social practices, a network that is made up of human, social, and natural actors and attributes. In other words, thinking about national parks as technologies reminds us that, contrary to the way in which they have been romanticized in the varied discourses of environmental studies, national parks do not emerge in isolation from society, culture, and industry, but are part of the network of institutional structures, of discursive and material practices that make up American culture. Furthermore, in characterizing the parks as technologies, I mean to emphasize what Richard White characterizes as the labor (human, natural, cultural, and technological) involved in their reproduction of nature, the sense in which national parks are inseparable from the industrial production of material artifacts or commodities.[25] Indeed in the years following the Civil War, the American West became increasingly embedded not only in the networks of manufacturing, transportation, and media extending from the urban centers back East, but also in the extension of capital both from major Eastern cities and from European, particularly British, sources: "Because of a profitability crisis in Europe by the 1870s where investments in traditional industrializing sectors such as railroads were no longer returning acceptable profit margins, American financial ventures proved especially attractive."[26] It is not accidental, I would argue, that national parks emerge precisely at the moment when the extension of the railroad, as well as the expansion of capital-, labor-, and technology-intensive industries like mining, make the Western landscape more accessible to and exploitable by Eastern, and increasingly European, capital. Because national parks are both natural and American, they appear both necessary and desirable at precisely the moment that nature's appropriation by American capital is being threatened by European investment.

In thinking through the specificity of national parks generally, and of the three "major" parks in particular, I take up the materiality of nature and its representations by considering national parks in relation to various nineteenth-century technologies of representation. My point in so doing is to emphasize that, like photography and painting, national parks are technologies that work in concert with other cultural forces to enmesh the unclaimed and undeveloped wilderness lands of the American West into the social, political, and economic networks of Eastern capitalism. To photograph a Western landscape like Yosemite, for example, is in some direct sense to mark the extension of the industrial, technological, cultural networks of the nation to that very spot that is photographed. Thus, when Fitz-Hugh Ludlow writes in the *Atlantic Monthly* of his travels with Albert Bierstadt to Yosemite, "into the vale whose giant domes and battlements had months before thrown their photographic shadow through Watkins's camera across the mysterious wide Continent, causing exclamations of awe at Goupil's window, and ecstasy in Dr. Holmes's study," what he is identifying (without needing to mention it) is the fact that the commercial, cultural networks of the Eastern art establishment had extended themselves to include the undeveloped wilds of Yosemite Valley and the Mariposa Big Tree Grove. That is, partly because of its ontological dependence on the photographic object, and partly because of the dependence of the photographer on a wagon load of chemicals, glass plates, and other technical equipment to make his picture, the photographic image marks the fact that this particular landscape was in some very real sense connected to those who would walk by Goupil's gallery in New York. While painting also works to appropriate the nation's Western landscape for the Eastern art and cultural establishment, it does so by different means and according to a different logic. Thus, I would argue that Bierstadt's paintings of Yosemite mark a more tenuous possession, a less robust or complex extension of Eastern networks than do Watkins' photographs – partly because a painting is taken as less faithful to nature than a photograph, partly because Bierstadt did not need to rely so intensively on those networks, and partly because his paintings are finished in the studio back East, unlike Watkins' photographs, which are developed and fixed in the mobile photographic studio which he brought with him.[27] National parks, on the other hand, are technologies of reproduction which mark a more heterogeneous connection with the legal, industrial, economic networks of the nation than do photography or painting – a connection which can be seen to include the networks through which painting, photography, and other forms of landscape representation have circulated images of the parks and made them available to the American public.

Or perhaps it would be more precise to say that national parks are not only technologies for incorporating the natural resources of the Western states and territories into the growing networks of an increasingly industrialized nation, but also technologies for simultaneously preserving nature as a purified space free from the very networks that make the parks' creation and continued existence possible.[28] After all, the removal of wilderness or undeveloped land from private acquisition and possession does create a cultural space in which American citizens can experience the private acquisition and possession of nature – not only in the tourist's feeling of owning the landscape in visiting the parks (an experience available to only a small portion of the population in the nineteenth century), but also in the experience of consuming these landscapes in visual and verbal representations far from the parks' geographical locations. Unlike a landscape painting, for example, which can only be owned by a single individual or institution (such as a museum, a corporation, or the government itself), a national park, by not being made available for ownership, reproduces nature as a kind of idealized commodity which could be acquired and possessed, but would never be exhausted or appropriated or used up or consumed.[29]

Indeed national parks are enabled to exist as areas set aside from the cultural and institutional mainstream only by virtue of their circulation within the networks that make up that mainstream. In characterizing national parks in this way, I would identify them as among what Latour describes as the hybrids or quasi-objects that proliferate in modernity.[30]

Neither simply the product of anti-modern sentiments, nor sites for the contestation of modernism, national parks participate in the project of establishing modernity in the United States in the last third of the nineteenth century. Like other modern hybrids, national parks work to produce nature as a purified essence, distinct or separate from culture or society or technology, while simultaneously reproducing it as part of a complex and heterogeneous network of scientific, cultural, social, technological practices. From this perspective, Yosemite, Yellowstone, and Grand Canyon national parks consist not just in the natural objects and artifacts that one finds within the boundaries of the parks, but also in their representation and reproduction in the photographs, stereographs, paintings, prints, maps, illustration, guide-books, laws, and scientific accounts that help to perpetuate the parks and enable them to circulate within the heterogeneous social, cultural, scientific, and political networks that make up America at any particular historical moment. Indeed, ecologists, conservationists, wildlife managers, and other private and public sector environmental professionals have come increasingly to recognize that the natural ecosystems that one finds in the national parks, and the flora and fauna that reside within their boundaries, do not respect park boundaries. This is a problem that has plagued recent attempts to reintroduce wolves into Yellowstone National Park or that led in early 2000 to a decision not to build a plant for the incineration of nuclear waste in Idaho because emissions from the plant would not respect park borders any more than wolves do. Consequently, managing Yellowstone today involves various state, federal, and private agencies in a coalition that takes as its object what has been defined as the Greater Yellowstone Ecosystem. Just as the natural features and creatures of Yellowstone National Park are part of any number of larger natural systems (such as mountain ranges, riparian systems, and seasonal migration routes), so the park itself is part of any number of larger cultural systems. By thinking of the national parks as technologies for the reproduction of nature, we can begin to trace out the way in which, just as the park's natural elements circulate within a heterogeneous network of natural ecosystems, so they circulate within a heterogeneous network of cultural or discursive ecosystems as well. It is precisely this circulation that I set out to trace in the cultural origins of America's three major national parks.

In tracing out these cultural logics, I might in some strict sense be accused of not actually writing a book about the national parks at all. As Michel Foucault suggests in *Archaeology of Knowledge*, "there can be no question of interpreting discourse with a view to writing a history of the referent."[31] From this perspective my book would be seen not primarily as a history of the national parks as referent of the network of discursive practices delineated throughout the book, but rather as an analysis of the national parks as themselves discursive formations, complex technologies for the reproduction of nature – again understood not as referent but as discursive object. In engaging such an archeological practice, Foucault suggests, one is "to dispense with 'things,'" by which he means "To substitute for the enigmatic treasure of 'things' anterior to discourse, the regular formation of objects that emerge only in discourse."[32] Such a practice would not take national parks as cultural or discursive formations for the preservation of "nature" or "wilderness" anterior to discourse, but as discursive technologies that reproduce nature or wilderness only within discourse.

Although I am indebted to Foucault's approach for suggesting how one might trace out genealogical affinities among different discursive formations, in characterizing national parks as complex technologies for the reproduction of nature, I mean to resist the idea that national parks "emerge only in discourse." In looking at the emergence of national parks in relation to a particular discursive formation, I acknowledge that "when one speaks of a system of formation, one does not only mean the juxtaposition, coexistence, or interaction of heterogeneous elements . . ., But also the relation that is established between them – and in a well determined form – by discursive practice."[33] But insofar as I see the emergence of national parks as a discursive "system of formation," I also see them as the technologies for the reproduction of a material nature. That is to say, I am interested not only in the "juxtaposition, coexistence, or interaction of heterogeneous elements" within and among the parks, but more importantly the particular "relation" between these elements that is established in each of the three major parks by the interaction between discursive practice and the distinctive natural characteristics of each of these parks.

In characterizing national parks as technologies for the reproduction of nature, then, I do not mean to say that each park is the same kind of technology, or works in exactly the same way. I am arguing not that national parks are technologies for the reproduction of an abstracted, uniform, homogenous, or undifferentiated essence called "nature," but that national parks always reproduce "nature as." That is, they reproduce nature not as anterior to discourse, but in terms of a particular place, location, or environment. Thus the chapters that follow look in specific detail at the origins of each of the three major national parks – Yosemite, Yellowstone, and Grand Canyon – to try to determine as precisely as possible both how each park functions as a technology and what kind of material and discursive formation each park reproduces nature as. In linking a cultural logic to a particular park, I have sought to avoid arbitrarily imposing a particular logic on a specific natural landscape. The association of questions of natural and aesthetic agency with Yosemite, or of questions of cognitive inaccessibility with Grand Canyon, is not unrelated, for example, to the fact that Yosemite Valley looked to Easterners and Europeans like the urban parks with which they were already familiar, or that Grand Canyon is so immense that it is impossible to perceive it in its entirety from any particular spot on its rim or at any particular moment. At the same time, however, I do not want to suggest that the cultural logic affiliated with a particular park, the technologies by which it reproduces "nature as," grow necessarily from, or emerge as fundamental consequences of, the park's natural features. The cultural and technological logics I trace out in relation to these three parks emerge not only from the particular natural features of a park but also from the contingent historical facts of who was involved in the different parks' discovery, exploration, and formation, and from other cultural issues or practices prevalent at a certain time. Thus the questions of nature's aesthetic agency that I trace out in regard to Yosemite are also the consequences of the historical accident that Frederick Law Olmsted, who was working as superintendent of a mine in California when Yosemite was first preserved, was named chairman of the park's first board of commissioners and that his prior and subsequent work as a landscape architect made questions of natural and aesthetic agency of great interest to him. In discussing each of the parks, I have tried to maintain that while the logic affiliated with a particular park is not founded in nature, the natural conditions of the park are not irrelevant to this logic either. The specificity of each park's origins is due both to the natural features that make up the park and to the historical and cultural circumstances of the park's establishment. While of course there are numerous affinities between the way in which nature is reproduced in all of America's national parks, as well as among other international, national, regional, local, or urban parks (think, for example, of the construction of trails, scenic lookouts, and interpretive markers), each type of park or natural preserve and each park itself has its own cultural, historical, ecological, and geographical specificity. This discursive specificity of the origins of America's national parks is precisely what the book sets out to detail.

I

Recreating Yosemite: landscape, nationalism, and the nature of aesthetic agency

THE YOSEMITE LANDSCAPE

If national parks are technologies for the reproduction of nature, then the preservation of Yosemite in 1864 constitutes the creation of a technology for the reproduction of nature as landscape. While this might appear to go without saying, insofar as all national parks would seem to be landscapes, this is not strictly the case. Because the creation of Yellowstone National Park in 1872, for example, serves to reproduce nature as it appeared prior to its discovery by Europeans – that is, prior to being encountered by the very culture in which the category of landscape provides an influential and pervasive framework for the perception of nature – the aim of preserving Yellowstone, unlike the aim of preserving Yosemite, can be characterized as the reproduction of nature prior to its being perceived as "landscape." Similarly one reason that it took more than fifty years from the first government-sponsored exploration of the Grand Canyon to establish it as a national park is that the canyon could not easily be comprehended within the conventional aesthetic frameworks provided by the European landscape tradition. When the federal government ceded Yosemite Valley to the State of California in 1864, on the other hand, it set the stage for the reproduction of nature according to landscape conventions that had been in force for well over a century. Yosemite's preservation operates according to a logic which recreates nature as landscape through the aesthetic agency of nature itself. In this chapter I trace out this cultural logic as it circulates through a number of different discursive domains in the last third of the nineteenth century, beginning with the events that led up to the federal government's 1864 decision to cede Yosemite Valley to the State of California.

On March 28, 1864, Senator John Conness of California introduced a bill to grant Yosemite Valley and the Mariposa Big Tree Grove to the State of California "for public use, resort, and recreation," to be "held inalienable for all time."[1] The idea for the grant had been suggested to Senator Conness

about a month earlier by Israel Ward Raymond, the California representative of the Central American Steamship Transit company. In a letter of
February 20, with which he had included a copy of Carleton Watkins'
photographic album of Yosemite views, Raymond had provided Senator
Conness with much of the bill's language and the suggestion that the grant
be administered by a board of commissioners appointed by California's
governor. Senator Conness in turn passed on Raymond's letter to J. W.
Edmonds, the Commissioner of the General Land Office, who drew up
the final version of the bill. When the bill was introduced on March 28,
it was referred without discussion to the Committee on Public Lands, as
was a bill to grant additional lands to the State of Kansas to aid in the
construction of the Osage and Cottonwood Valley Railroad.[2]

On May 17 the Committee returned the Yosemite bill to the Senate
with a recommendation that it be passed. Debate on the bill was brief.
Senator Conness assured his colleagues that although the lands "constitute,
perhaps, some of the greatest wonders of the world," they were "for all
public purposes worthless" and "of no value to the Government" (*Globe*
2300–2301). Senator Foster of Connecticut commented that because it was
"a rather singular grant, unprecedented as far as my recollection goes," it
was important to know if the State of California had requested the grant
(*Globe* 2301). Assuring Senator Foster that the measure had originated with
some California gentlemen "of fortune, of taste and of refinement," Senator
Conness agreed that "There is no parallel, and can be no parallel for this
measure, for there is not, as I stated before, on earth just such a condition
of things" (*Globe* 2301). After only a little further discussion, the bill was
passed and sent on to President Lincoln, who signed it into law on June
30, 1864, the same day on which he signed a bill to aid in the settlement,
subsistence, and support of Navajo Indian captives on a reservation in the
Territory of New Mexico.

The summary quality of Congressional debate on the question of ceding
Yosemite to the state of California suggests that if, as Roderick Nash has
argued, "the legal preservation of part of the public domain for scenic and
recreational values created a significant precedent in American history," it
was a precedent the significance of which members of Congress seemed
largely unaware.[3] Traditionally such actions as the construction of railroads and the relocation of Native Americans to reservations have been
explained as instruments of the incorporation of the American West into
the expanding marketplace of industrial capitalism, while the withdrawal
of wilderness lands from the marketplace has just as routinely been understood to stand in opposition to the ideology of westward expansion.[4] The

context in which the Yosemite bill was introduced, debated, and signed into law, however, indicates that – unlike much traditional scholarship on the history of American environmentalism – neither Congress nor President Lincoln appeared to register any ideological discontinuity between preserving Yosemite Valley and the Mariposa Grove, constructing the Osage and Cottonwood Valley Railroad, and relocating Navajo Indian captives to a reservation in New Mexico. Such lack of cognitive dissonance has sometimes been dismissed by noting that the lands to be set aside were, in Senator Conness' words, "worthless" and "of no value to the government." Indeed Alfred Runte has pointed out that well into the twentieth century "there evolved in Congress a firm (if unwritten) policy that only 'worthless' lands might be set aside as national parks."[5] For Runte this unwritten policy reaffirms the fundamental opposition between the preservation and exploitation of nature. He sees environmentalism as running counter to "dominant American purposes," arguing that Congress would support preservation only when it did not conflict with the aims of westward expansion.[6]

If we unpack the logic informing Yosemite's preservation, however, the claim that the beginnings of American environmentalism can be separated from dominant American purposes raises a number of questions, not the least of which is whether such contestatory ideological positions cannot themselves be understood as participating in our sense of what constitutes these dominant purposes.[7] In other words, how can the preservation of nature be seen either as participating in or as opposing the predominant values of American culture? What kind of action was the federal government's cession of Yosemite to the State of California? And why does the preservation of nature become institutionalized at this particular historical moment and in this particular form?[8]

The idea that natural areas should be preserved as public parks was, as environmental historians have noted, not entirely unprecedented in 1864. George Catlin had called for the preservation of a "nation's park" on the Great Plains as early as 1832; Thoreau's claim in "Walking" (1851) that "in Wildness is the preservation of the world" has also been taken as preservationist precedent; and in 1864, George Perkins Marsh proposed in *Man and Nature* that the United States establish and preserve a fixed ratio between woodlands and other lands in order to help stabilize the nation's institutions.[9] Thus, the idea to preserve Yosemite was not in itself unprecedented. And while Yosemite National Park plays a pivotal role in origin stories of American environmentalism, this role stems less from the valley's 1864 preservation than from the heated struggle over Hetch Hetchy Valley in the first decade of the twentieth century. Indeed it is generally accepted that the core beliefs of the environmentalist movement in the twentieth century were forged out of the losing effort to prevent Hetch Hetchy (a smaller yet equally spectacular version of Yosemite Valley) from being converted into a reservoir to supply the municipal water (and eventually power) needs of the populace of San Francisco. More specifically John Muir's spirited defense of Hetch Hetchy put into place the fundamental (and increasingly insurmountable) rhetorical, philosophical, and political distinction between natural preservation and economic development that still defines the shape of contemporary debates over the environment. "These temple destroyers, devotees of ravaging commercialism, seem to have a perfect contempt for Nature, and, instead of lifting their eyes to the God of the mountains, lift them to the Almighty Dollar. Dam Hetch Hetchy! As well dam for watertanks the people's cathedrals and churches, for no holier temple has ever been consecrated by the heart of man."[10] Although the battle to protect the sanctity of the national parks was lost, and Hetch Hetchy dammed, the battle lines had been clearly drawn.[11]

The struggle for Hetch Hetchy was instrumental in polarizing the terms of environmentalist debate in the twentieth century. The story of Yosemite's creation as a national park, however, does not fit so neatly into this history of American environmentalism. If Yosemite was a temple of nature, its consecration occurred only gradually. Yosemite National Park was not created in a single act of Congressional inspiration, but created and re-created over a period of more than forty years. In 1864 Yosemite Valley and the Mariposa Grove were ceded to the State of California for the purpose of managing it as a public park; in 1890 a large area of Sierra watershed surrounding the valley was preserved as a national park; it was not until 1906 that the valley was receded by the State of California to the federal government, thereby establishing (with only a few subsequent modifications) the present-day Yosemite National Park. In addition to these fits and starts in the park's creation, the motivations behind Yosemite's initial preservation are not well documented. Unlike the several competing claims for priority in first proposing the preservation of Yellowstone as what was formally the first national park, there is very little known about the motivations underlying Raymond's proposal to Conness that the federal government cede Yosemite to California.

Some sense of these motivations, however, can be inferred from the response of the State of California to the federal government's grant. On September 28, 1864, roughly three months after President Lincoln signed the Yosemite bill into law, California Governor Frederick F. Low issued a

4 Clarence King and J. T. Gardner, *Map of a Portion of the Sierra Nevada*

proclamation accepting the grant on behalf of the state and announcing the board of Commissioners that he had appointed: Frederick Law Olmsted, Josiah Dwight Whitney, William Ashburner, I. W. Raymond, E. S. Holden, Alexander Deering, George Coulter, and Galen Clark. The identity of the commissioners was hardly a surprise. Whitney, Olmsted, Coulter, and Raymond had already been mentioned as prospective commissioners in the correspondence between Raymond and Senator Conness. And Olmsted's friend, Dr. Henry Bellows, had already written him in early August to congratulate him on being named to the commission. In a letter dated September 29, 1864, Low wrote Olmsted (who had come to California in 1863 to help revitalize the struggling Mariposa Mining Estate), telling him: "By today's mail I send you the Yosemite Commission."[12] Although Olmsted had only visited Yosemite Valley for the first time the previous month, his prior experience as architect-in-chief of Central Park and Secretary of the US Sanitary Commission made him an ideal choice for the commission. He quickly took charge, arranging for Clarence King and J. T. Gardner to survey Yosemite before the Sierra winter set in (see Figure 4), and advancing payment for the survey out of his own pocket. Thus it was that on August 8, 1865, at a meeting of the commission in the valley, Olmsted, survey in hand, presented to his fellow commissioners a draft report to the California legislature on the future administration of the park.

The first substantive statement on the philosophy and management of a national park, Olmsted's 1865 report does provide us with a clue to the motivations behind Yosemite's cession to the State of California. Although the suppression of his report by several of his fellow commissioners prevented it from exerting an extensive influence on the development of a coherent national park policy,[13] the report is indispensable for making sense of what the preservation of Yosemite might mean in the closing stages of the Civil War. Rediscovered by scholars only after the Second World War, Olmsted's report has led to widely divergent interpretations. Some see it as an early statement of environmental principles, while others see it as motivated by anti- or pre-environmentalist concerns.[14] I treat Olmsted's Yosemite report, on the other hand, as a complex expression of a cultural logic of recreation, a logic which relies upon structural parallels between the preservation of Yosemite and several of the related cultural practices in which the origins of American environmentalism are embedded. In addition I read the report as sketching out the configurations of human and natural agency within which these parallel practices are articulated. Locating the report in relation to a number of disparate discursive practices, I trace out in this chapter four ways in which Olmsted represents Yosemite's preservation in terms of a structure of aesthetic agency so systematic in late-nineteenth-century America as to appear to be natural. Placing the report in the setting of post-bellum reunification, I argue that Olmsted represents Yosemite's preservation as an aesthetic act which participates in the re-creation of American national identity after the Civil War. Next, I read the report in the context of Olmsted's landscape aesthetics, which sees artistic creation as relying upon the aesthetic agency of nature. I then place Olmsted's understanding of the social and psychological economy of recreation against the background of nineteenth-century neurological science, arguing that Olmsted sees recreation as re-creating the American worker by means of the same structure of agency at work in his landscape aesthetics. Returning to Olmsted's Yosemite report, I take up the way in which he tries to accommodate the fact that natural parks (whether Yosemite or Central Park) must provide a kind of recreation that is irreducibly private yet necessarily public at the same time. I conclude the chapter with a look at John Muir's role in advocating the creation of Yosemite National Park in 1890, focusing on his version of the logic of recreation in describing the creation and re-creation of the Yosemite landscape by means of glaciers and other natural agents.

RECREATING AMERICA

By all accounts Olmsted had no direct role in the sequence of events that culminated in the preservation of Yosemite Valley in 1864. Nonetheless, it is hard not to wonder whether the presence of the former architect-in-chief of Central Park in the foothills of Sierra Nevada did not somehow play a part in the thought processes of Raymond and those other California gentlemen "of fortune, taste, and refinement," who had proposed that Yosemite be made into a park. In any event Olmsted's presence in California at precisely that moment was fortunate. Not only did Governor Low benefit politically from Olmsted's membership on the Yosemite Commission, but Olmsted himself was presented with the opportunity to think through the question of creating national parks at a particularly significant moment in the nation's (and his own personal) history. Prior to taking over the management of the Mariposa Mining Company, he had spent two years as Secretary of the United States Sanitary Commission, a large-scale mobile relief unit for Union troops. Nor did this mark his initial encounter with the sectional divide between Northern and Southern states. Beginning in 1856 he had published a series of books on the culture and economy of the slave states, revised and republished in 1861 as a single volume entitled *The Cotton Kingdom.* Furthermore by the time he left the Sanitary Commission for

California in 1863 he had already begun to think about the role he might play in helping to unify the nation after the war.[15]

In this context it is interesting to note that Olmsted begins his report on the preservation of Yosemite by invoking the recently concluded war:

It is a fact of much significance with reference to the temper and spirit which ruled the loyal people of the United States during the war of the great rebellion, that a livelier susceptibility to the influence of art was apparent, and greater progress in the manifestations of artistic talent was made, than in any similar period before in the history of the country.[16]

By situating Yosemite in relation to the "livelier susceptibility to the influence of art" evident during the Civil War, Olmsted sets forth an account of national identity that envisions a symbiotic relation between America's political and artistic purposes – what he elsewhere calls, presumably with a nod to Emerson, his "Theory of Compensations in National Character" (*FLO* 1: 365). To elaborate the assertion that America underwent an artistic renaissance during the war, Olmsted recites a litany of nationalistic artistic accomplishments:

The great dome of the Capitol was wholly constructed during the war . . .; Crawford's great statue of Liberty was poised upon its summit in the year that President Lincoln proclaimed the emancipation of the slaves. Leutze's fresco of the peopling of the Pacific States, the finest work of the painter's art in the Capitol; the noble front of the Treasury building with its long colonnades of massive monoliths; the exquisite hall of the Academy of Arts; the great park of New York, and many other works of which the nation may be proud, were brought to completion during the same period. (*FLO* 5: 488)

Although all of these works had been undertaken in the East, Olmsted implies that during the war "a livelier susceptibility to the influence of art was apparent" in the West as well, citing both the construction of the California State Capitol and the creation of the California Art Union.

Olmsted's thinking about postbellum reunification participates in a discourse that dates back at least to President Lincoln's second annual report to Congress, which sets forth an argument for national unity on geographical grounds.[17] What distinguishes Olmsted's vision, however, is his conviction of the role that art could play in reuniting the nation. Calling attention to California's contributions to the wartime artistic renaissance, Olmsted sets forth an argument for national unity through art, offering a conceptual reorientation of national identity from the divisive North–South axis with which he and the nation had been preoccupied both prior to and during the Civil War to the East–West axis of post-war expansionism and manifest

5 Emmanuel Leutze, *Westward the Course of Empire Takes its Way*

destiny. In citing Leutze's *Westward the Course of Empire Takes its Way*, which depicts a tableau of Westward-bound settlers crossing the continental divide, Olmsted aligns himself with those artists who would use landscape painting to depict American national identity as oriented along an East–West rather than a North–South axis. Portraying the westward migration of the settlers as moving from right to left across the pictorial plane (see Figure 5), Leutze invokes an iconographical tradition evident in such paintings as Asher Durand's *Progress* or John Gast's later *American Progress*. Overlaying the pictorial space of the landscape painting with the cartographical space of the map, such works create an allegorical or iconographical image which conceptualizes the nation along an East–West axis. Combining the representational frameworks of the pictorial and the cartographic, Leutze underscores the allegorical or iconographic meaning of his painting in a way that not only obscures the North–South divisions of the Civil War, but also serves to naturalize the allegory by making it signify according to two different representational logics.[18]

In his Yosemite report, Olmsted uses verbal rather than visual rhetoric to help conceptualize the nation on an East–West axis. In so doing he participates in the postbellum cultural inclination to "turn away from the South and the trauma of the Civil War and toward the West and the expanding nation."[19] As the movement of the following passage indicates, Olmsted invokes both wartime representations of Yosemite and its subsequent preservation to reorient the national imagination.

It was during one of the darkest hours, before Sherman had begun the march upon Atlanta or Grant his terrible movement through the Wilderness, when the paintings of Bierstadt and the photographs of Watkins, both productions of the War time, had given to the people on the Atlantic some idea of the sublimity of the Yo Semite, and of the stateliness of the neighboring Sequoia grove, that consideration was first given to the danger that such scenes might become private property and through the false taste, the caprice or the requirements of some industrial speculation of their holders; their value to posterity be injured. To secure them against this danger Congress passed an act providing that the premises should be segregated from the general domain of the public lands, and devoted forever to popular resort and recreation. (*FLO* 5: 489)

Rhetorically this passage works to situate the preservation of Yosemite in the context of an ongoing nationalistic landscape tradition.[20] As the passage unfolds, its geographical orientation shifts from the North–South axis that structures Sherman's "march upon Atlanta" and Grant's "terrible movement through the Wilderness" to the East–West axis implicit in the exhibition of the sublime Yosemite landscapes of Bierstadt and Watkins (see Figures 6 and 7) "to the people on the Atlantic." Following Olmsted's earlier formulation of a wartime artistic renaissance, which links specific artistic accomplishments with particular wartime events, the passage leads us to expect a similar parallelism in emphasizing that "the paintings of Bierstadt and the photographs of Watkins" were exhibited back East "*during* one of the darkest hours" of the war (my italics). Instead, the artistic accomplishments of Bierstadt and Watkins function syntactically as appositive precursors of an artistic achievement of a different kind, the federal government's creation of Yosemite as a public park: "during one of the darkest hours . . . *when* the paintings of Bierstadt and the photographs of Watkins" were produced, *then* "Congress passed an act" preventing Yosemite from being appropriated as private property and preserving it as a public park, "devoted forever to popular resort and recreation." In shifting its imaginative orientation from the internal difference between North and South brought about by the war, however, this passage does not do away with sectional difference entirely, but reproduces it along a different axis, as the Congressional "segregation" of Yosemite from "the general domain of the public lands" reproduces in a positive way the Confederate "secession" from the Union by securing Yosemite from being appropriated by the Westward course of the American empire.[21]

6 Albert Bierstadt, *Looking Down Yosemite Valley, California*

7 Carleton Watkins, *River View – Down the Valley – Yo Semite*

The effect of this rhetorical inversion is not only to emphasize Bierstadt's and Watkins' representations of the Yosemite landscape but also to place its Congressional preservation in the context not only of landscape art but also of postbellum reunification. In associating the preservation of Yosemite with other wartime artworks, Olmsted means clearly to conceive of the preservation of Yosemite as an aesthetic act which simultaneously recognizes and constitutes Yosemite as art. In so doing, he provides the framework for a vision of postbellum national unity in which the preservation of Yosemite (and perhaps, as head of the Yosemite commission, he himself) would play an important part. Furthermore, by including Central Park in his list of wartime artistic achievements, he paves the way for thinking about the preservation of Yosemite as a particular type of art which (like Leutze's fresco or the landscapes of Bierstadt and Watkins) can help to reorient the nation's imagination of itself from the divisive North–South axis of the war to an East–West axis of post-war expansion and preservation. To create a public park in Yosemite would be to participate in recreating America, in part by recreating nature as a national landscape.

Inevitably Olmsted approaches the question of Yosemite's preservation from the perspective of landscape architecture. Although his professed reason for introducing "a short account of the leading qualities of [the park's] scenery" is that "few members of the Legislature can have yet visited the ground," not just any account of Yosemite's scenery will do (*FLO* 5: 490). In other words, it is important for Olmsted that the Legislature has the right (that is, his) account of the scenery as landscape. For insofar as he describes the withdrawal of Yosemite from the public domain as motivated by a concern that "*such scenes* might become private property," he is equally concerned to distinguish his representation of "the leading qualities of its *scenery*" not only from the landscapes of Bierstadt and Watkins but from whatever previous representations of Yosemite the legislature may have read or seen (emphasis added).

In light of his concern that the scenery of Yosemite be protected from private acquisition, it is interesting that Olmsted's description of the valley emphasizes not its uniqueness but the familiarity of nature's park-like design. "There is nothing strange or exotic in the character of the vegetation," he insists; "most of the trees and plants, especially those of the meadow and waterside, are closely allied to and are not readily distinguished from those most common in the landscapes of the Eastern States or the midland counties of England" (*FLO* 5: 490). A broad stream such "as Shakespeare delighted in" "meanders" through the "series of groves of magnificent trees, and meadows of the most varied, luxuriant and exquisite herbage," bringing "pleasing reminiscences to the traveller of the Avon or the Upper Thames" (*FLO* 5: 490). Throughout the year "the Yo Semite continues to receive frequent soft showers, and to be dressed throughout in living green"; late in the summer "a light, transparent haze generally pervades the atmosphere, giving an indescribable softness and exquisite dreamy charm to the scenery, like that produced by the Indian summer of the East" (*FLO* 5: 491). In comparing Yosemite Valley to the Avon or Upper Thames, and its climate to New England's Indian summer, Olmsted extends the imaginary East–West axis with which his report began back across the Atlantic Ocean to England. Conceiving of Yosemite aesthetically as a naturally created English park, Olmsted invokes the separation of America from England, the mythical and ideological precursor of the internal difference between Union and Confederacy produced by the Civil War. The consequences of this reorientation are seemingly contradictory: to preserve Yosemite from "the danger that such scenes might become private property" even while bringing the civilization of Europe or the Eastern seaboard to the Western wilderness by envisioning Yosemite in the image of Central Park.

Having described the valley's parklike features, however, Olmsted suggests that no verbal description of the particular features of the landscape can truly account for Yosemite's aesthetic effect on its visitors: "By no statement of the elements of the scenery can any idea of that scenery be given" (*FLO* 5: 493, 500). Nor can any visual representation do the scenery justice: "No photograph or series of photographs, no paintings ever prepare a visitor so that he is not taken by surprise" (*FLO* 5: 500). The claim that neither words nor pictures could describe the sublimity of Yosemite had by 1865 already become a cliché among the region's tourists.[22] But Olmsted's conviction that no representation can convey a true idea of Yosemite's scenery is based less on his sense of a crisis of representation than on his conviction that what distinguishes Yosemite from other spectacular landscapes is not any individual feature that can be captured in a frame, but the ensemble of what he elsewhere describes as its "landscape effect." Even if Yosemite's scenery could "be faithfully represented," he contends, "the visitor is affected not only by that upon which his eye is at any moment fixed, but by all that with which on every side it is associated, and of which it is seen only as an inherent part" (*FLO* 5: 500). In claiming that "for the same reason no description, no measurements, no comparisons are of much value," Olmsted further distinguishes himself from travel writers such as Samuel Richardson, Fitz-Hugh Ludlow, or Thomas Starr King, whose monumentalist descriptions of Yosemite's scenery are replete both with comparisons to familiar natural or cultural objects back East and with lists of measurements – whether of the width of the Merced river, the height of Yosemite's waterfalls, domes, and mountains, or the width, height, and circumference of the giant sequoias of the Mariposa Grove.[23]

For Olmsted the worthlessness of conventional representations of Yosemite's scenery stems from the fact that they fail to focus on what truly sets Yosemite apart: "The union of the deepest sublimity with the deepest beauty of nature, not in one feature or another, not in one part or scene or another, not in any landscape that can be framed by itself, but all around and wherever the visitor goes, constitutes the Yo Semite the greatest glory of nature" (*FLO* 5: 500). That is, neither Bierstadt's paintings nor Watkins' photographs can truly capture Yosemite's aesthetic qualities – only the representation of the valley through the means of landscape architecture can capture the valley's picturesque "union" of sublimity and beauty. In fact, Olmsted continues, the very attempt to call one's attention to the remarkable features of the landscape by "framing" them as artistic or cultural monuments works to detract from the scenery's effect on Yosemite's visitors: "fixing the mind on mere matters of wonder or curiosity prevents the true and far more extraordinary character of the scenery from being appreciated" (*FLO* 5: 500). This invidious distinction between "fixing the mind on mere matters of wonder" and appreciating the "true character of the scenery" derives from the account of landscape architecture that Olmsted had already been developing when he began his involvement with Central Park in 1857. Here, as elsewhere, Olmsted insists on understanding landscape architecture not simply as configuring nature but as representing it. Although careful throughout his career to distinguish landscape architecture from painting, his work as a landscape architect participates in the desire of mid-nineteenth-century aesthetic theory and practice to do away with the landscape's frame by concealing the signs of the artist's agency in creating his picture, thereby eliminating the separation between a work of art and its viewer. And as I argue in the next section, this landscape aesthetic also has affinities with the logic of photography, which requires the artist to relinquish his agency to nature in order to realize his artistic intention.

THE NATURE OF AESTHETIC AGENCY

For nearly a century after its invention, photography and its advocates were challenged to defend the new medium from the claim that it could never truly be a form of art. In an essay published in the March 1865 issue of the *Philadelphia Photographer*, less than six months before Olmsted would present his Yosemite report to his fellow commissioners, photographer John Moran (brother of landscape painter Thomas) takes up the question of "the relation of photography to the fine arts," contending that because photography "speaks the same language, and addresses itself to the same sentiments" as they do, it should be considered as one of the fine arts.[24] Like the painter, Moran contends, the photographer must "'know what is most beautiful'": "the value and importance of any work, whether canvas or negative," depends upon the artist's "power of seeing and deciding what shall be done." Because "any given scene offers so many different points of view," what "gives value and importance to the works of certain photographers over all others" is the ability to occupy more than one perceptual position at a time: "if there is not the perceiving mind to note and feel the relative degrees of importance in the various aspects which nature presents, nothing worthy the name of pictures can be produced." But no matter how refined the photographer's "art of seeing," photography itself "can never claim the homage of the higher forms of art." The photographer cannot exercise the same control over his creation as can the painter. Although like the painter the photographer must frame his picture, "in the actual production of the [photographic] work, the artist ceases, and the laws of nature take his place."[25]

Moran was by no means the first to notice this aesthetic logic of photography, which has regularly been distinguished from painting on the grounds that the mechanism of the camera requires that at the moment of exposure the artist must relinquish his agency to what Moran describes as "the laws of nature."[26] Nonetheless photography is not the only form of art in which the human agent relinquishes the task of reproduction to nature. Indeed I invoke Moran's formulation of the relation between natural and human agency in photography precisely for its pertinence to Olmsted's theory of landscape architecture, despite the fact that at first glance the differences between the two media might seem to outweigh their affinities. Where photography works in two dimensions, landscape architecture works in three. Where photography depends upon the mechanical reproduction of the camera, landscape architecture depends largely upon the organic reproduction of nature. And while the photographer recreates pictorially the image of whatever scene is in front of the camera at the time of exposure, the landscape architect recreates the landscape that is in front of him according to the pictures he has imagined of the scene. But despite these dissimilarities, photography and landscape architecture alike rely upon a similar structure of aesthetic agency: that in order to realize their intentions both the photographer and the landscape architect must relinquish their artistic control to the agency of nature, whether understood as the action of light on the photographic medium or as the action of light, soil, and water on the natural objects that make up the medium of the landscape architect.

Olmsted had singled out this structure of aesthetic agency in landscape architecture as early as 1852, at a time when he was planning on a career as a farmer: "What artist so noble as he who, with far-reaching conception of beauty and designing-power, sketches the outlines, writes the colors, and directs the shadows of a picture so great that Nature shall be employed upon it for generations, before the work he has arranged for her shall realize his intentions!"[27] For the landscape architect to realize his intentions he must, like the photographer, relinquish final control of his picture to nature: "our efforts should be to prepare a field for the operations of nature. We should depend on nature, not simply as some teach, [or] appear to do so, but actually trust nature only offering certain encouragements by means of ground work."[28] In calling attention to the logical affinities between Moran's and Olmsted's accounts of artistic agency, I do not mean to minimize the aesthetic affinities between landscape architecture and landscape painting. In fact it is equally significant that Olmsted's description of the landscape architect takes as its artistic model the painter – who "sketches the outlines, writes the colors, and directs the shadows of [his] picture." For despite Moran's employment of the conventional opposition between the assertion of artistic agency in painting and the elimination of such agency in photography, by mid-century the elimination of all signs of artistic agency was for the landscape painter an equally well-established goal.

Where photography requires the artist to relinquish his agency to nature for instrumental reasons, in order to bring the photograph into existence, painting aspires to the concealment of artistic agency in a formal, compositional, or technical sense. In mid-nineteenth-century America, Angela Miller explains, "the role of artistic means was to furnish a transparent expression of natural truth."[29] Thus, in his 1855 "Letters on Landscape Painting," Asher Durand characterizes truly great paintings as marked by "the concealment of pigments and not the parade of them."[30] Unsurprisingly he urges young painters to pay particular attention to "the study of the influence of atmosphere," which he describes as "an intangible agent, . . . that which above all other agencies, carries us into the picture, instead of allowing us to be detained in front of it."[31] In *The Art-Idea*, first published in 1864, James Jackson Jarves sets forth a similar aesthetic, finding the panoramic landscapes of Church and Bierstadt to be wanting in comparison with the landscapes of Inness precisely because they "always keep the spectator at a distance." The spectator, Jarves continues, "never can forget his point of view, and that he is looking at a painting. Nor is the painter himself ever out of mind. The evidences of scenic dexterity and signs of his labor-trail are too obvious for that."[32] The effect of "high art" like Inness', however, "is to sink the artist and spectator alike into the scene": "The spectator is no longer a looker-on, as in the other style, but an inhabitant of the landscape . . . He enjoys it with the right of ownership."[33]

Olmsted's theory of landscape architecture can be seen to combine the logic of photographic action set forth by Moran with the absorptive aesthetics of Durand and Jarves. One place we can see this fusion is in the "Greensward" plan with which Olmsted and his partner Calvert Vaux entered and won the 1858 design competition for Central Park, a plan in which Olmsted sets forth his first systematic exposition of a theory of landscape architecture. Defending the prominence that their plan gives to an artificial structure like the park's promenade, Olmsted likens the promenade's "position of relative importance" in a public park to that which "a mansion should occupy in a park prepared for private occupation." Like the spectator of a work of high art for Jarves, the visitor to Central Park "enjoys it with the right of ownership." Although, Olmsted continues, "the idea of the residence of the owner . . . finds no parallel in a public park," the promenade allows "the visitor, who, in the best sense is the true owner" of the park, to "concentrate on features of natural, in preference to artificial beauty." Artificial itself, the promenade works both ideologically to provide an illusion of ownership and aesthetically to conceal the artifice of the landscape architect: "The idea of the park itself should always be uppermost in the mind of the beholder."[34] Like painting, landscape architecture would conceal the signs of artistic agency in designing or laying out the composition or scene; like photography, it would do away with the artist's agency as a mediating technology or instrument.

Thus, although Olmsted sees both the landscape architect and the painter striving to draw viewers into their scenes by concealing their agency, he clearly distinguishes between the two forms of representation.[35] Unlike painting, Olmsted writes in an 1861 letter offering his resignation as Central Park's Superintendent,

The work of design necessarily supposes a gallery of mental pictures, and in all parts of the park I constantly have before me, more or less distinctly, more or less vaguely, a picture, which as Superintendent I am constantly laboring to realize.

The letter goes on to develop the distinctive characteristics of landscape design in what might best be described as Olmsted's portrait of the artist as a landscape architect.

I shall venture to assume to myself the title of artist and to add that no sculptor, painter or architect can have anything like the difficulty in sketching and conveying a knowledge of his design to those who employ him which must attend upon an artist employed for such a kind of designing as is required of me. The design must be almost exclusively in my imagination . . . Does the work which has thus far been done accomplish my design? No more than stretching the canvas and chalking a few outlines, realizes the painter's. Why, the work has been thus far wholly and entirely with dead, inert materials: my picture is all alive – its very essence is life, human and vegetable. The work which has been done has had no interest to me except as a basis, as a canvas, as a block.[36]

Olmsted distinguishes the art of landscape design from that of the "sculptor, painter or architect" because "his picture is all alive." Having seen the park constructed according to plan, Olmsted has no more accomplished his design than stretching the canvas and chalking a few outlines accomplishes the design of the painter. Central Park in 1861 interests Olmsted "as a basis, as a canvas, as a block." Unlike the architect, painter, or sculptor, however, Olmsted cannot accomplish his design himself but must relinquish control to nature, who "shall be employed upon it for generations, before the work he has arranged for her shall realize its intentions."

Even while thinking about landscape architecture on the model of painting – "The landscape is arranged to please the eye; it presents a picture more exquisitely pleasing to the mind through the sense of vision, than the most distinguished work of any master" – he is compelled to think about producing his landscapes not with paint, brush, and canvas but with rocks, shrubs, and trees.[37] Unlike a painter or a photographer, an "artist dealing with trees and plants," as he describes himself, must use the very natural objects he would represent as his artistic media. When painting a landscape an artist uses the materials of painting (pigments, brushes, canvas) to recreate a scene. Whether the scene is real or imagined, natural objects (like rocks, lakes, or trees) are among the features that landscape paintings represent. When Olmsted creates a landscape, however, or designs a park, natural features are his means as well as his objects of representation. Trees and plants, in representing trees and plants, are both real and imagined, both are and are not trees and plants.

This production of internal difference between nature and itself is what most clearly distinguishes landscape architecture from landscape painting.

8 John Bachmann, *Bird's Eye View of Central Park* (Lithograph, 1863)

Insofar as the landscape architect, like the landscape painter, aims to sink the artist and the spectator alike in the scene by concealing the signs of his agency in the park, he is concerned not with the concealment of pigments but with the concealment of plants and trees. Olmsted further develops this idea in a remarkable letter to Ignatz Pilat, the chief landscape gardener of Central Park, written en route to Mariposa in the autumn of 1863. In crossing the tropical landscape of the Isthmus of Panama, Olmsted writes, he had experienced the "complete satisfaction and delight of [his] love of nature"; how, he wonders, can he reproduce that emotion for a visitor to Central Park (*FLO* 5: 85)? In addressing the question of creating scenery that resembles that of the tropics, Olmsted's concern is not with imitating the formal or botanical features of tropical scenery but with reproducing the "moral" and "esthetic" "landscape effect" such scenery produced in him (*FLO* 5: 86). Considering what it would take to reproduce the effect of tropical scenery, he concludes that the impression of nature's extravagance received in the tropical forest derived from the way the identities of individual trees were obscured by the scene as a whole: "You know how we see a single tree – most frequently a Juniperus Virginiana – lost completely under the Ct-briar [sic]. Frequently – generally – the whole forest is lost in the same way here" (*FLO* 5: 88). And as he makes clear in likening this impression to the "landscape effect from the Clematis as we often see it showered over a Sumach" in Central Park, to reproduce the landscape effect of tropical scenery would be to erase the particularity of the natural objects he uses to make up his Central Park landscape (*FLO* 5: 88). To receive the landscape effect of tropical scenery from Clematis "showered over a Sumach" one must see neither Clematis nor tropical vines, but rather see Clematis as a representation of tropical foliage, to see it as both identical to and different from itself.

During his two years in California, Olmsted spent a good deal of time thinking about the structure of aesthetic agency in landscape architecture – partly because of his involvement with a number of landscape design projects in California (including Mountain View Cemetery in Oakland, the campus of the College of California in Berkeley, and an urban park for San Francisco), and partly because of his epistolary deliberations with Calvert Vaux over the nature and desirability of their continued partnership as landscape architects after Olmsted's impending return to New York.[38] In a passage written not long after arriving in Mariposa in 1863, Olmsted can be seen struggling to come to terms with the way in which landscape architecture requires the artist to conceal the signs of his agency as evidence of his exertion of agency on the landscape.

Landscape Architecture is the application or picturesque relation of various objects within a certain space, so that each may increase the effect of the whole as a landscape composition. It thus covers more than landscape gardening. It includes gardening and architecture and extends both arts, carrying them into the province of the landscape painter. In all landscape architecture there must not only be art, but art must be apparent. The art to conceal art is applicable to the manipulation of the materials, the method by which the grand result is obtained, but not to the result which should not be merely fictitious nature, but obviously a work of art – cultivated beauty.[39]

Although granting that landscape architecture "includes gardening and architecture," Olmsted maintains that it "extends both arts" into "the province of the landscape painter" because it requires the landscape architect to fashion the picturesque relation of various natural objects into a landscape composition.[40] Like the landscape photographer, the landscape architect must see nature from multiple perspectives at once; unlike landscape painting, however, "the grand result" of landscape architecture is both a landscape and a representation of a landscape. Consequently the landscape architect must, like the painter, apply "the art to conceal art" even while making sure that the art of landscape architecture is "apparent." That is, even while concealing the signs of his agency in "the manipulation of the materials" with which he constructs the landscape, the landscape architect must make evident his agency in composing the landscape. In describing the result of this double gesture not as "merely fictitious nature" but as "obviously a work of art," Olmsted means on the one hand to distinguish his practice of landscape architecture from the "fictitious nature" "of the great English landscape gardeners such as William Gilpin, Uvedale Price, Humphrey Repton, John Claudius Loudon, and their American disciple, Andrew Jackson Downing," while on the other hand distinguishing his practice from nature itself.[41] In other words, the "cultivated beauty" that constitutes "the grand result" of the landscape architect makes his landscape an obvious "work of art" rather than "fictitious nature" precisely because the "art to conceal art" has obfuscated the method by which nature has been made into art.

Olmsted's thinking about landscape architecture as an extension of landscape gardening and architecture into "the province of the landscape painter" can itself be seen as an extension of Immanuel Kant's thinking about landscape gardening and painting in a discussion of the division of the beautiful arts near the end of the *Critique of Judgment*'s "Analytic of the Sublime."[42] I introduce Kant here neither because his understanding of landscape gardening is identical to Olmsted's understanding of landscape architecture, nor because Olmsted is explicitly interested in the sublime (it's not an aesthetic concept he spends much time discussing, concerning himself more directly with the picturesque), but rather because many of the aesthetic issues with which Olmsted is concerned are precisely those which are at stake in the Kantian sublime. Indeed, in transforming conventional notions of landscape gardening into the new art of landscape architecture, Olmsted relies upon Kant's treatment of the relation between natural and artistic beauty in his analytic of the sublime. For Kant natural beauty is superior to artificial beauty because it arouses a more immediate, formal interest in the beholder (Kant 141). In explaining this claim, Kant furnishes as an example the "lover of the beautiful," who "regards the beautiful figure of a wild flower, a bird, an insect, etc., with admiration and love; who would not willingly miss it in nature although it may bring him some damage; who still less wants any advantage from it – *he* takes an immediate and also an intellectual interest in the beauty of nature" (Kant 141). Kant takes the source of this immediate interest to be the fact "that nature has produced" the beautiful forms, that they are not, as Olmsted might say, "merely ficti-tious nature": "if we secretly deceived this lover of the beautiful by planting in the ground artificial flowers . . . or by placing artificially carved birds on the boughs of trees, and he discovered the deceit, the immediate interest that he previously took in them would disappear at once" (Kant 141–142).

Kant concludes his discussion of the intellectual interest in the beautiful by noting that "the interest which we here take in beauty has only to do with the beauty of nature; it vanishes altogether as soon as we notice that we are deceived and that it is only art – vanishes so completely that taste can no longer find the thing beautiful or sight find it charming" (Kant 145). Like Olmsted's landscape effect, the beautiful "must be nature or be regarded as nature if we are to take an immediate interest in [it] as such, and still more is this the case if we can require that others should take an interest in it too" (Kant 145). Like the beautiful in nature, "Beautiful art is an art in so far as it seems like nature," as Kant titles section 45 of his discussion of beautiful art. "In a product of beautiful art, we must become conscious that it is art and not nature . . . Nature is beautiful because it looks like art, and art can only be called beautiful if we are conscious of it as art while yet it looks like nature . . . Hence the purposiveness in the product of beautiful art, although it is designed, must not seem to be designed, i.e., beautiful art must *look* like nature, although we are conscious of it as art" (Kant 149). As with any beautiful art, landscape architecture must also "look like nature, although we are conscious of it as art." The purposiveness of an Olmsted landscape must not seem designed, but must be concealed by "the art to conceal art." And as we have seen, the art to conceal art is dependent on the aesthetic agency of nature, which must re-create what the landscape architect has created in order to fulfill his artistic intentions. Like photography for Moran, the work of landscape architecture can only be completed when the artist ceases, and is replaced by the laws of nature.

THE RECREATION OF NATURE

Olmsted's concern with landscape architecture, in Yosemite or in Central Park, was always more than aesthetic. As he does throughout his career Olmsted understands aesthetic goals as inseparable from social and political aims. The purpose of creating a public park is to provide American citizens with opportunities for recreation, by which Olmsted specifically means opportunities for aesthetic encounters with scenes of natural beauty. In conceiving of Yosemite's preservation as an aesthetic act no different in kind from the creation of an urban park, he did not ignore the social and political consequences of these parks. Indeed, his report describes the benefits offered by Yosemite's preservation in terms of the social philosophy of recreation that lay at the heart of his professional involvement with landscape architecture. In so doing Olmsted makes both an aesthetic and a political point about Congress' motivation for ceding Yosemite to California. The report sets forth "two classes of considerations [that] may be assumed to have influenced the action of Congress." He dismisses as "less important" "the direct and obvious pecuniary advantage which comes to a commonwealth from the fact that it possesses objects which cannot be taken out of its domain that are attractive to travellers and the enjoyment of which is open to all" (*FLO* 5: 500–501). The "more important class of considerations" motivating "the action of Congress" is its obligation to provide the benefits of recreation to American citizens: "It is the main duty of government, if it is not the sole duty of government, to provide means of protection for all its citizens in the pursuit of happiness against the obstacles, otherwise insurmountable, which the selfishness of individuals or combinations of individuals is liable to interpose to that pursuit" (*FLO* 5: 501–502). Olmsted explicitly identifies the pursuit of happiness with the opportunity for recreation: "the occasional contemplation of natural scenes of an impressive character" (*FLO* 5: 502). This emphasis on the importance of recreation is by no means idiosyncratic, but draws on an influential post-bellum discourse on the role of recreation and play in American culture.[43]

One of the fullest expressions of Olmsted's social philosophy of recreation is set forth in the report for Prospect Park that he and Calvert Vaux presented to the Brooklyn Park Commission in January of 1866.[44] The first project undertaken after Olmsted's return to New York, Prospect Park and its accompanying report are consistent with the thinking about landscape architecture that Olmsted had been doing in California. According to this report, an urban park provides the community with real economic benefits – as certain "an increase of material wealth as good harvests or active commerce."[45] These benefits derive in part from Olmsted's fairly classical economic understanding of labor value, which is itself consistent with the nineteenth-century notion of "productive labor" in which labor produces capital or wealth:[46] "all wealth is the result of labor, and every man's individual wealth is, on the whole, increased by the labor of every other in the community, supposing it to be wisely and honestly applied" (*Landscape* 100). Because all labor involves "the expenditure of force," Olmsted continues, "it follows that, without recuperation and recreation of force, the power of each individual to labor wisely and honestly is soon lost, and that, without the recuperation of force, the power of each individual to add to the wealth of the community is, as a necessary consequence, also soon lost" (*Landscape* 100).

Olmsted's idea of recuperation and recreation of force is of a piece with the "true" or "rational recreation" advocated by (among other figures) the Reverend Jonathan Townley Crane, Stephen Crane's father and a Methodist minister. Such recreation, avers Bill Brown, "merely re-creates the individual for work: 'The aim is to renew, restore, create again . . . We rest, that we may be better prepared for work.'"[47] Recuperation and recreation participate in what Olmsted understands as a twofold economy – the fiscal economy of the community and the "physical economy" of the individual, described in the Yosemite report as "the action and reaction which constantly occur between bodily and mental conditions" (*FLO* 5: 503). Defining as expenditures of force "the slightest use of the will, of choice between two actions or two words, [or] the slightest exercise of skill of any kind" (*Landscape* 100), Olmsted conceives of force not in terms of physical exertion but in terms of purposeful action. Thus, to recuperate expended force one must refrain not from physical activity but from the expression of purpose. By redefining force as purpose Olmsted suggests that the only way for an individual to recuperate force is through non-purposeful activity, what the Prospect Park report refers to as "the unbending of the faculties which have been tasked" – an "unbending," he suggests, which is "impossible, except by the occupation of the imagination with objects and reflections of a quite different character from those which are associated with their bent condition" (*Landscape* 100–101).

In explaining how the preservation of nature can add to the wealth of the nation by allowing American citizens to "unbend" their faculties, Olmsted's Yosemite report provides a detailed account of the function of natural scenery in the psychological economy of recreation. This account begins with what he characterizes as the "scientific fact" "that the occasional contemplation of natural scenes of an impressive character, particularly if this contemplation occurs in connection with relief from ordinary cares, change of air and change of habits, is favorable to the health and vigor of men and especially to the health and vigor of their intellect beyond any conditions which can be offered them" (*FLO* 5: 502). Olmsted does not cite a source for this "scientific fact," but his explanation of the consequences that befall those denied opportunities to contemplate impressive natural scenes clearly derives from the emerging discourse of neurology: "The want of such occasional recreation often results in a class of disorders the characteristic quality of which is mental disability, sometimes taking the severe forms of softening of the brain, paralysis, palsy, monomania, or insanity, but more frequently of mental and nervous excitability, moroseness, melancholy or irascibility, incapacitating the subject for the proper exercise of the intellectual and moral forces" (*FLO* 5: 502).[48]

Although this diagnosis of the dangers of lack of recreation may seem hyperbolic today, it is not out of line with the received wisdom of mid-nineteenth-century neurological science. Neurology did not reach its popular zenith until the last quarter of the century, but "had its beginnings as a specialty in the United States at the time of the Civil War," in the work of Silas Weir Mitchell and William Alexander Hammond, "the fathers of American neurology."[49] Olmsted's involvement with mid-century medical science, both as a patient and as an agent of the medical profession, was (it would be fair to say) "overdetermined." His own lifelong health problems were exacerbated by the war. By the end of August 1862 "he was jaundiced (possibly from hepatitis), had developed a severe skin disorder which itched incessantly, and was on the verge of nervous collapse" (*FLO* 4: 33). At the same time his position as Secretary of the US Sanitary Commission provided him with both the responsibility of administering what was essentially a collection of mobile military hospitals and the opportunity of working with physicians like Mitchell and Hammond.[50] Regardless of the precise extent of his involvement with the emerging scientific discourse of neurology, however, what is distinctive about Olmsted's insistence on the therapeutic value of natural scenery is his translation of conventional physiological arguments about the benefits of recreation into psychological and finally aesthetic terms.[51] Olmsted ascribes these physiological and psychological benefits of natural scenery to its aesthetic qualities: "If we analyze the operation of scenes of beauty upon the mind, and consider the intimate relation of the mind upon the nervous system and the whole physical economy, the action and reaction which constantly occur between bodily and mental conditions, the reinvigoration which results from such scenes is readily comprehended" (*FLO* 5: 503).

In Olmsted's philosophy of recreation the demands of the marketplace in mid-nineteenth-century America produce precisely the kind of mental exertion for which "the reinvigoration of those parts which are stirred into conscious activity by natural scenery is more effective . . . than that of any other" (*FLO* 5: 503). His account of the physical and psychological stresses of urban commercialism participates in the diagnosis of "American nervousness" offered by Hammond, Mitchell, and especially George Miller Beard, whose analysis of neurasthenia made him one of the most popular (as well as most controversial) of late-nineteenth-century neurologists.[52] Indeed in the following passage from his Yosemite report, Olmsted anticipates one of the central features of Beard's etiology of American nervousness, the "habit of forethought":[53]

The severe and excessive exercise of the mind which leads to the greatest fatigue and is the most wearing upon the whole constitution is almost entirely caused by application to the removal of something to be apprehended in the future, or to interests beyond those of the moment, or of the individual; to the laying up of wealth, to the preparation of something, to accomplishing something in the mind of another, and especially to small and petty details which are uninteresting in themselves and which engage the attention at all only because of the bearing they have on some general end of more importance which is seen ahead. (*FLO* 5: 503–504)

In claiming that this passage anticipates what would become a neurological truism, I am interested not in making a case for Olmsted's historical priority but in calling attention to the way in which his Yosemite report dramatizes an aesthetic structure of natural agency that recurs in a number of diverse and seemingly unrelated cultural discourses.[54] Indeed the sanative influence of nature functions as an axiom of antebellum romanticism, epitomized by Emerson's claim in *Nature* that "To the body and mind which have been cramped by noxious work or company, nature is medicinal and restores their tone. The tradesman, the attorney comes out of the din and craft of the street, and sees the sky and the woods, and is a man again."[55] But where for Emerson the "medicinal" quality of nature is largely spiritual, moral, and metaphorical, for Olmsted it is clearly physiological, scientific, and quite literal.[56] In a paper presented in 1870 to the American Social

Science Association, for example, he quotes the following testimony from an older physician about the health benefits of Central Park: "'Where I formerly ordered patients of a certain class to give up their business altogether and go out of town, I now often advise simply moderation, and prescribe a ride in the Park before going to their offices, and again a drive with their families before dinner. By simply adopting this course as a habit, men who have been breaking down frequently recover tone rapidly, and are able to retain an active and controlling influence in an important business, from which they would have otherwise been forced to retire.'"[57]

As this anonymous physician's prescriptions attest, both Olmsted's parks and his discursive practices provide sites for the medicalization of the antebellum axiom of the sanative influence of natural scenery. Where occupying the mind on some future purpose produces mental fatigue and nervous exhaustion, the Yosemite report explains, "in the interest which natural scenery inspires, there is the strongest contrast to this. It is for itself and at the moment it is enjoyed. The attention is aroused and the mind occupied without purpose, without a continuation of the common process of relating the present action, thought or perception to some future end" (*FLO* 5: 504). The effacement of purpose in the appreciation of natural scenery is not unrelated to the effacement of aesthetic agency in the creation of Yosemite as a park. Although Olmsted's point about the recuperative powers of natural scenery is broadly applicable to a variety of landscapes, his assertion at the beginning of the report that Yosemite's scenery is best appreciated as a whole, not by "fixing" the mind on one spectacular feature or another as in a frame, underscores that the Yosemite landscape is of a type particularly suited for therapeutic recreation. In ascribing the therapeutic value of natural scenery to its ability to occupy the mind without purpose, Olmsted invokes the Kantian definition of the feeling of aesthetic beauty as disinterested even while appropriating this disinterestedness for social or therapeutic purposes. In so doing he participates in the broader logic of aesthetic agency at work in photography and landscape architecture. Only by relinquishing purpose, by discontinuing "the common process of relating the present action, thought or perception to some future end," can individuals realize their intention of recuperating expended force, of unbending their faculties. Similarly, in prescribing the appreciation of natural scenery as a cure for nervous exhaustion, either Olmsted or his physician informant must relinquish control to nature. In the actual production of a cure, as of a photograph, one might say, the physician ceases and the laws of nature take his place.

The idea that a physician could heal his patient by relinquishing control to nature constitutes what Oliver Wendell Holmes, Sr. (who published three important articles on photography in the *Atlantic Monthly* in 1859, 1861, and 1863[58]) christened the "nature-trusting heresy" in 1860.[59] In trusting many diseases to the "healing power of nature," Holmes and other mid-nineteenth-century American physicians were responding to the active intervention of the bold or heroic therapies that constituted the normative practice of American physicians in the first decades of the nineteenth century.[60] The most influential advocate of heroic medicine was Benjamin Rush, who "accorded bloodletting and purgative mercurials like calomel the dominant positions in his armamentarium, suggesting that 'when the physician step[s] into the sick room, nature should be politely asked to step out.'"[61] Reacting against the abuses of heroic therapeutic practice, doctors like Jacob Bigelow argued that the medical profession "must come to recognize both the role of nature in healing disease and the limits of medical art." For Bigelow "the physician is but the minister and servant of nature," who can "do little more than follow in the train of disease, and endeavor to aid nature in her salutary intentions, or remove obstacles out of her path."[62] Other physicians concurred. Elisha Bartlett argued that "the courses of many diseases could not be altered favorably by the intervention of medical art; the physician should trust the 'recuperative energies of the system' to provide a cure in such cases."[63] Similarly Holmes criticized the practice of homeopathy as a delusion, contending that 90 percent of all homeopathic patients "would recover, sooner or later, with more or less difficulty, provided nothing were done to interfere seriously with the efforts of nature."[64] For these physicians as for others, the art of medicine, like the art of photography or landscape architecture, can only realize its intentions when the artist relinquishes his control to the laws of nature. Not unlike Central Park or Yosemite, the mid-nineteenth-century medical body provides a discursive site on which aesthetic agency can be simultaneously created, elided, and recreated by the therapeutics of nature.[65]

USE, RESORT, AND THE LOGIC OF RECREATION

According to Alfred Runte, "the tension between preservation and use," which informs "the most enduring – and most intense – " debate "affecting America's national parks," has been manifest in regard to Yosemite since the valley's cession to California in 1864. But it is worth noting, however, that "preservation" figures only incidentally in the Congressional Act of

1864, appearing just twice, both times in connection with the stipulation that income from leases be expended "in preservation, improvement, and protection of the property, or the roads leading thereto." The key phrase in the act, repeated nearly verbatim in the 1872 act to create Yellowstone National Park, is "that the premises shall be held for public use, resort, and recreation; and shall be inalienable for all time." The tension between preservation and use, while central to environmental history, is not at the core of Olmsted's concerns in the 1865 report. More central to his perspective as a landscape architect is the tension between "public use" and the irreducibly private experience at the heart of individual recreation, a tension which he addresses in considering how best to design and manage the Yosemite grant for "public use, resort, and recreation."

The first design problem facing Olmsted derives from the psychological economy of recreation. In terms of individual parkgoers, the park must provide an opportunity for a private aesthetic experienced within a space of public exchange. For Olmsted the recreational benefits offered by a park operate according to a logic of aesthetic agency which simultaneously produces and conceals difference through the network of social and psychological exchanges that constitutes the capitalist marketplace.[66] Thus, in the Prospect Park report he explains that the challenge of designing an urban park is to devise a way to provide it with two incompatible qualities: "scenery offering the most agreeable contrast to that of the rest of the town; and opportunity for people to come together for the single purpose of enjoyment, unembarrassed by the limitations with which they are surrounded at home, or in the pursuit of their daily avocations" (*Landscape* 101). In designing a park that allows for irreducibly private aesthetic experiences to take place within a system of social circulation and exchange, Olmsted finds himself faced with a number of problems, not the least of which is that "scenery which would afford the most marked contrast with the streets of a town, would be of a kind characterized in nature by the absence, or, at least, the marked subordination of human influences, [while] in a park, the largest provision is required for the human presence" (*Landscape* 101). As a landscape architect, Olmsted operates according to competing imperatives: not only must he create scenery in which the signs of human agency (including his own) are concealed by the signs of natural agency, but he must at the same time provide for the accommodation of humans in the park, potentially reintroducing signs of the very agency he must try to conceal.[67]

In devising a strategy for managing the Yosemite grant, Olmsted sees the state of California faced with a similar dual obligation for the preservation and use of natural scenery. Accordingly his Yosemite report suggests that "the main duty with which the Commissioners should be charged should be to give every advantage practicable to the mass of the people to benefit by that which is peculiar to this ground and which has caused Congress to treat it differently from other parts of the public domain" (*FLO* 5: 506). Because "this peculiarity consists wholly in its natural scenery," Olmsted contends, "The first point to be kept in mind then is the preservation and maintenance as exactly as is possible of the natural scenery" (*FLO* 5: 506). Although Runte and others take such points of emphasis as evidence of Olmsted's uncompromising environmentalism, Olmsted himself consistently refuses to separate aesthetic preservation from social use. Olmsted's interest is not in the environment or the ecosystem or the biotic community, concerns which were not available to him in the same way they are available to ecologists or environmentalists or park managers today. As a landscape artist, Olmsted is interested in a structure of aesthetic agency in which natural objects are simultaneously themselves, elements of a scenic landscape, and the media through which scenic landscapes are represented. Even when he provides examples of how "without care many of the species of plants now flourishing [in Yosemite and Mariposa] will be lost and many interesting objects be defaced or obscured if not destroyed," his concern is not with the ecological impact but with the aesthetic effect such destruction would have on the scenery: "not only have trees been cut, hacked, barked and fired in prominent positions, but rocks in the midst of the most picturesque natural scenery have been broken, painted, and discolored, by fires built against them" (*FLO* 5: 506–507). As a social reformer, Olmsted argues that the value of preservation must be measured in terms of the wants of future generations; he computes the value of preservation according to a calculus of use, "because the millions who are hereafter to benefit by the Act have the largest interest in it, and the largest interest should be first and most strenuously guarded" (*FLO* 5: 508).

Indeed, simply reserving scenic lands like Yosemite "from monopoly by individuals" is not all that is required of the government, but these lands must be "laid open to the use of the body of the people" (*FLO* 5: 505). For Olmsted the separation of the park from public use is associated not with preservation but with the danger that the park will become private property: "Thus without means are taken by the government to withhold them from the grasp of individuals, all places favorable in scenery to the recreation of the mind and body will be closed against the great body of the people" (*FLO* 5: 505). If the body of the people, like people's bodies, is to benefit from the preservation of Yosemite's scenery, the park must be made accessible to the public; it must be both set aside from and incorporated into a national network of circulation and exchange. Olmsted thus conceptualizes Yosemite, and indeed national parks in general, as works of landscape architecture in which the act of creating the park conceals the agency of the government in creating or designing the park as well as simultaneously requiring that the agency of nature prevail if it is to be maintained as a park. To make this happen the park must be designed as a place free from the networks of circulation and exchange that are part and parcel of the westward expansion of nineteenth-century industrial capital, at the same time that it be more extensively linked to those very networks.[68]

Because in 1865, Olmsted argues, only the rich can afford to make the journey to Yosemite, "the first necessity is a road from the termination of the present roads leading towards the district" (*FLO* 5: 509). Similarly the valley itself should be provided with a system of traffic circulation. "Within the Yosemite the Commissioners propose to cause to be constructed a double trail, which, on the completion of our approach road, may be easily made suitable for the passage of a single vehicle, and which shall enable visitors to make a complete circuit of all the broader parts of the valley and to cross the meadows at certain points, reaching all the finer points of view to which it can be carried without great expense" (*FLO* 5: 509).[69] As in Central or Prospect Park, Olmsted designs Yosemite's roads to prescribe a particular sequence of scenes and events for its visitors. Although the appreciation of Yosemite's scenery allows the mind to be occupied without purpose, Olmsted designs the roads and trails that take the visitors through that scenery with very specific scenic purposes in mind. "When carriages are introduced" into Yosemite, he proposes, "they shall be driven for the most part up one side and down the other of the valley, suitable resting places and turnouts for passing being provided at frequent intervals. The object of this arrangement is to reduce the necessity for artificial construction within the narrowest practicable limits, destroying as it must the natural conditions of the ground and presenting an unpleasant object to the eye in the midst of the scenery" (*FLO* 5: 509).[70] In designing a circuit through the park, Olmsted would both make Yosemite accessible and preserve "the natural conditions of the ground." But designing a circuit of roads and trails that will not destroy "the natural conditions of the ground" does not mean preserving the valley in its natural state. Nor does it mean eradicating its natural state. Rather it means reproducing the valley as nature by simultaneously creating and effacing the difference between natural and aesthetic agency. Preservation, as Derrida says of deconstruction, "must neither reframe nor dream of the pure and simple absence of the frame."[71] Although Yosemite must look like art, it must not look designed, which paradoxically only happens by creating networks of trails and roads, by simultaneously setting it aside and enmeshing it in the networks of markets, travel, media, and communication. Inscribing a boundary between artifice and nature, the Olmsted circuit simultaneously creates Yosemite as a series of aesthetic experiences, conceals the artistic agency that constitutes Yosemite as a park, and recreates Yosemite as nature for others to use again.

YOSEMITE'S ART OF NATURE

In his Yosemite report Olmsted is careful to emphasize the need to link the valley to the networks of communication and transportation that enable tourists to circulate through and within the park. The 1864 Congressional Grant, however, while anticipating such cultural and technological links, does not concern itself with linking the valley to the biological and ecological systems of circulation of which it is a part. In order to rectify this failing, John Muir, *Century Magazine* editor Robert Underwood Johnson, and representatives of the Southern Pacific Railroad, among others, helped support a proposal in 1890 to create a forest reserve from the mountainous watershed surrounding the valley. Muir, who had first come to Yosemite in 1868, was an important advocate of this bill, lobbying Johnson during an 1889 Sierra camping trip and writing two articles for *Century* urging the creation of the park. On October 1, 1890, the bill was ultimately signed into law, formally creating Yosemite National Park.[72]

While Muir's 1868 arrival in Yosemite was in many respects the product of a series of historical and biographical accidents, it does not seem accidental that a young man with his intellectual and personal background would find himself compelled by a landscape that appeared to be designed by the aesthetic agency of nature. Throughout his extensive writings, Muir is frequently concerned with understanding and explaining the actions of nature. In explaining the relation between human and natural agency, he often employs a logic of aesthetic agency in which human agency gets relinquished to nature. For example, in "Twenty Hill Hollow," an essay first published in the 1869 *Overland Monthly* and reprinted in 1916 as the final chapter of his autobiographical *A Thousand-Mile Walk to the Gulf,* Muir ends with the following Emersonian account of the experience of being in the Hollow:

It may be asked, What have mountains fifty or a hundred miles away to do with Twenty Hill Hollow? To lovers of the wild, these mountains are not a hundred miles away. Their spiritual power and the goodness of the sky make them near, as a circle of friends. They rise as a portion of the hilled walls of the Hollow. You cannot feel yourself out of doors; plain, sky, and mountains ray beauty which you feel. You bathe in these spirit-beams, turning round and round, as if warming at a camp-fire. Presently you lose consciousness of your own separate existence: you blend with the landscape, and become part and parcel of nature.[73]

Muir's self-conscious allusion in the final sentence to the "transparent eye-ball" passage in Emerson's *Nature* is part of a persistent Emersonian strain in his life and writings. For Muir, this relinquishment of human agency or identity to nature often takes the form of a pantheism similar to that expressed by Ishmael in *Moby Dick*. But unlike Ishmael, Muir also sees such moments as working instrumentally, much like the way in which aesthetic experience functions in Olmsted's philosophy of recreation.

The instrumentality of such pantheistic moments is evident in "The Glacier Meadows," a chapter from *The Mountains of California* (1894) in which Muir clearly reveals this double stance towards relinquishing one's agency to nature. He first provides the following description of wading through a typical Sierra glacier meadow:

With inexpressible delight you wade out into the grassy sun-lake, feeling yourself contained in one of Nature's most sacred chambers, withdrawn from the sterner influences of the mountains, secure from all intrusion, secure from yourself, free in the universal beauty. And notwithstanding the scene is so impressively spiritual, and you seem dissolved in it, yet everything about you is beating with warm, terrestrial, human love and life delightfully substantial and familiar. The resiny pines are types of health and steadfastness; the robins feeding on the sod belong to the same species you have known since childhood; and surely these daisies, larkspurs, and goldenrods are the very friend-flowers of the old home garden. Bees hum as in a harvest noon, butterflies waver above the flowers, and like them you lave in the vital sunshine, too richly and homogenously joy-filled to be capable of partial thought. You are all eye, sifted through and through with light and beauty. Sauntering along the brook that meanders silently through the meadow from the east, special flowers call you back to discriminating consciousness.[74]

Describing in loving detail a paradigmatic moment of pantheistic one-ness with nature, Muir refers implicitly in this passage both to Emerson's "Nature" ("types of health and steadfastness" and "all eye, sifted through and through with light and beauty") and to Thoreau's "Walking" (with the word "sauntering"). Indeed such descriptions of the relinquishment of agency or identity to nature places him squarely in an Emersonian–American tradition with roots in the romanticism of Wordsworth or Goethe.

But not unlike Olmsted's understanding of the recuperative value of aesthetic experience, Muir goes on in this passage to emphasize that these moments of relinquishment of individual purpose, in which one is incapable of "partial thought," have instrumental value once one is called back "to discriminating consciousness":

The influences of pure nature seem to be so little known as yet, that it is generally supposed that complete pleasure of this kind, permeating one's very flesh and bones, unfits the student for scientific pursuits in which cool judgment and observation are required. But the effect is just the opposite. Instead of producing a dissipated condition, the mind is fertilized and stimulated and developed like sun-fed plants.[75]

In *Mountains of California* Muir carefully punctuates what is for the most part a natural history of the Sierra Nevada (the book's chapters move ecologically from "The Sierra Nevada," "The Glaciers," "The Snow," "The Passes," "The Glacier Lakes," "The Glacier Meadows," and "The Forests" to "Sierra Thunder-Storms," "In the Sierra Foot-Hills," and "The Bee-Pastures) with brief autobiographical interludes of his own personal experiences of oneness with nature. His point throughout the book, as in this passage from "The Glacier Meadows," is that such epiphanic experiences are not dissipating but rather make one's mind more suited for such purposeful activities as natural history or scientific observation.

The assertion that relinquishing one's agency to nature helps suit the mind for scientific "judgment and observation" is in large part meant as a defense of Muir's own scientific practices. In the early 1870s Muir had put forth the hypothesis that Yosemite was created by the action of glaciers. His theory of glacial creation challenged the accepted scientific theory that Yosemite had been created by the violent and catastrophic subsidence of the valley floor, published initially in 1865 by Josiah Dwight Whitney, first director of the California Geological Survey, and supported subsequently by Clarence King in his autobiographical adventure narrative, *Mountaineering in the Sierra Nevada*.[76] The difference of opinion between Muir and Whitney has most often been portrayed as a contest between amateur and professional science, with Muir playing David to Whitney's Goliath.[77] But what is more interesting for our purposes is the way in which Muir consistently describes Yosemite's creation by glacial action in aesthetic terms.

Muir's theory of Yosemite's glacial creation is fully laid out in a series of articles published in *The Overland Monthly* in 1874–1875.[78] The articles begin with the formation of the Sierra Nevada itself, which Muir describes as a "work of art": "instead of being a huge wrinkle of the earth's crust without any determinate structure, is built up of regularly formed stones like a work of art" (*Sierra* 5). In describing the Yosemite region he makes a point to refer to it as a "glacial" or "glaciated landscape," which, he explains, "is unrivaled in general effect, combining as it does so many elements of sublimity" (*Sierra* 12). For Muir it is important that glaciers recreate Yosemite specifically as a "landscape," thus underscoring that the natural agency of glacial action is aesthetic. It is also significant that Muir does not see Yosemite valley as the product of exceptional or mysterious forces, but as the result of the regular and continuous processes of nature. Beginning with the nearly invisible and immeasurable agency of snowflakes, nature forms glaciers which recreate the landscape of the Sierra Nevada into valley formations which Muir names "yosemites." One such yosemite is Hetch Hetchy Valley, to which he devotes several pages in the second of his 1890 *Century* articles.

Interestingly Muir describes the formation of these yosemite valleys as acts not so much of glacial creation as of re-creation. "Glaciers do not so much mold and shape," he writes, "as disinter forms already conceived and ripe" (*Sierra* 16). After disinterring these forms, glaciers have not actually created them, but have "only developed the predestined forms of mountain beauty which were ready and waiting to receive the baptism of light" (*Sierra* 16). Just as the act of preserving Yosemite as a park involves both the recognition and constitution of it as art, so the act of glacial creation both reveals and constitutes the Sierra Nevada's "forms of mountain beauty." Although glacial action works to reveal nature's prior agency in creating these "predestined forms," it does not start with a blank slate but must first destroy the forms into which nature had previously created the landscape.

The ice-sheet of the glacial period, like an immense sponge, wiped the Sierra bare of all pre-glacial surface inscriptions, and wrote its own history upon the ample page . . . Glacial history upon the summit of the Sierra page is clear, and the farther we descend, the more we find its inscriptions crossed and recrossed with the records of other agents. (*Sierra* 52)

As he does elsewhere in referring to Mount Ritter as a "text-book" (*Sierra* 75), Muir characteristically describes the mountains as manuscripts upon which Nature has written the history of glacial action. Consequently the process of creating Yosemite through glacial action is invariably a process of re-creation:

When Nature lifted the ice-sheet from the mountains she may well be said not to have turned a new leaf, but to have made a new one of the old. Throughout the unnumbered seasons of the glacial epoch the range lay buried, crushed, and sunless. In the stupendous denudation to which it was subjected, all its pre-glacial features disappeared. Plants, animals, and landscapes were wiped from its flanks like drawings from a blackboard, and the vast page left smooth and clean, to be re-pictured with young life and the varied and beautiful inscriptions of water, snow, and the atmosphere. (*Sierra* 62)

As Muir's discussion of post-glacial denudation emphasizes, the cycle of creation, destruction, and re-creation must be understood as ongoing and continual, aided by a variety of natural agents, including rain, snow, and periodic avalanches. In his argument against Whitney's catastrophic account of Yosemite's creation, Muir must be careful not to characterize the glacial re-creation of the landscape as exceptional or catastrophic. Indeed the final sentence of the final essay of the *Overland Monthly* series concludes with the two points that the glacial landscapes of the Sierra were not created, but recreated, and that the process was "universal," not exceptional: "In all this sublime fulfillment, there was no upbuilding, but a universal razing and dismantling, and of this every mountain and valley is the record and monument" (*Sierra* 100).

Muir sees the Yosemite landscape as "the record and monument" of the aesthetic agency of nature. Muir's interest is not, as with Olmsted, in the artistic creation of the landscape by the relinquishment of human agency to nature but in the geological or ecological creation of the landscape by means of the aesthetic agency of glaciation. Insofar as Muir is interested in the relinquishment of human agency to nature, his interest is not primarily psychological or epistemological. More central to Muir is the fact that nature is always in a process of metamorphosis or change; the logic of recreation operates not only in terms of making Yosemite into a park but in creating and recreating the Yosemite landscape prior to or independent of any human artistic or aesthetic intervention.[79] In advocating the 1890 establishment of Yosemite National Park in the mountains surrounding the valley, Muir himself acts as an agent in the ongoing process of natural creation, in which the landscape is destroyed and recreated by the glacial agency of nature. For Muir nature is the artist that has created Yosemite; preserving it as a park only recreates it through relinquishing human agency to nature. The 1890 creation of Yosemite National Park, by preserving the watersheds that nourish and replenish the falls and rivers of the valley, also recreates the valley by preserving it together with the glacial pathways that had earlier created it.[80]

Muir's interest in Yosemite's creation by the glacial agency of nature reveals an almost Chomskian notion of the "deep structure" of mountain production, of the production of "yosemites." That is, Muir is interested in the underlying geological rules by which these yosemites are produced, evident in his use of the name "yosemite" for a whole type or class of valleys, of whose deep structure he is interested in making sense. In taking up the question of the design and management of the Yosemite grant as a public park, Olmsted, too, sees Yosemite as a technology for reproducing nature as landscape. His interest, however, is in the deep structure of picturesque landscapes. For him, the generative rules or principles are those of landscape aesthetics, which not only generate landscapes but also generate a particular response or landscape effect in people who view them.

The differences between Olmsted's aesthetic and Muir's more ecological accounts of Yosemite could easily lend themselves to narratives of teleological development of something like an environmentalist ethic, understood variously as "preservationism," "land ethic," "biocentrism," "deep ecology," and so forth. While such narratives are tempting, they depend upon a strict logical opposition between natural and human agency that is not upheld by the cultural logic that we have been tracing across a number of disparate nineteenth-century discourses. What is more telling is that, despite their different accounts of natural agency, both Olmsted and Muir understand Yosemite's preservation in terms of a similar logic of recreation. Neither man sees the effacement of human agency by nature as a goal that can ever be definitively or decisively achieved, but as an ongoing process which reconfigures itself according to the cultural logics of different times or places. For Muir this means that Yosemite, like all nature, is continually undergoing the mutually constitutive processes of destruction and creation. For Olmsted it means that the relinquishment of human agency involved in the preservation of Yosemite must work in concert with the assertion of human agency both at the individual and at the national level. The creation of Yosemite as a public park has played itself out according to a logic of recreation in which the relation between natural and aesthetic agency is fluid and the two terms often interchangeable. Partly because of the features of the Yosemite landscape itself, which looked in 1864 as if it had been created precisely in accord with the deep structure of nineteenth-century landscape aesthetics, and partly because of the historical circumstances which brought both Olmsted and Muir to the Sierra Nevada in the 1860s, Yosemite National Park emerged in the late nineteenth century as a technology for reproducing nature as landscape through the elision of human agency by the aesthetic agency of nature. If it has come down to us as such today, it is in certain respects because the very idea of environmentalism became thinkable in nineteenth-century America only in terms of a logic similar to that exemplified in Olmsted's report. Indeed from its very inception environmental preservation has operated according to a structure of aesthetic agency that works by setting aside tracts of land in which human purpose must be relinquished to the laws of nature in order to realize the purpose of setting aside these tracts of land. And not only does this double act of ascribing agency to nature at the same time that this ascription is effaced constitute what environmentalism meant in nineteenth-century America, but something not very different from this nature of aesthetic agency can be seen to constitute what environmentalism and the national parks mean for us today.[81]

2

Representing Yellowstone: art, science, and fidelity to nature

HISTORICAL DISCOVERY AND THE ILLUSION OF PRIMITIVE AMERICA

In Yellowstone's Norris Geyser Basin several summers ago, I was struck with the idea that to experience Yellowstone was to experience the moment of wonder at the heart of historical discovery.[1] My observation was prompted by a remark from an elderly man to his wife, overheard on the Porcelain Basin interpretive trail: "Imagine what it would have been like to have been the first person to see this, to have come across these geysers and hot springs without knowing they were here." What was striking about the man's fascination with the scene of discovery wasn't that I hadn't heard anything like it before, but rather that I had been hearing such exclamations of wonder ever since my arrival in the park – about geysers, hot springs, mud pots, and other thermal features; about the spectacular scenery of Yellowstone's Grand Canyon or Yellowstone Lake; about the park's buffalo, moose, elk, bear, and other wildlife. Known from its inception as "nature's wonderland," Yellowstone is "culture's wonderland" as well. This sense of historical discovery as wonder so frequently articulated by visitors is supported by the park's impressive interpretive program, one of the principal strategies of which consists of foregrounding the history of Yellowstone's discovery through an aggregation of verbal and visual texts (pamphlets, signs, nomenclature, markers, trails, and exhibits) that inscribe the park's cultural history both on the land and into the parkgoer's experience. Consequently it is not uncommon to hear parkgoers talking of Langford, Hayden, Jackson, or Moran, as well as of the Nez Perce or Shoshone Indians, Colter, Bridger, and (frequently, if often erroneously) Lewis and Clark.

But if the Yellowstone experience is about the wonder of historical discovery, it is also about the wonder of scientific discovery – not only because many of the discoveries that took place in the region were scientific in nature, but because the geothermal forces that continue to shape the park's natural landscape make it inevitable that new scientific discoveries will continue to occur. As rangers repeatedly remind park visitors, hot springs and other geothermal features are dynamic; Minerva's Terrace at Mammoth Hot Spings, for example, is not the same feature it was when William Henry Jackson photographed Thomas Moran standing on the edge of one of its pools (see Figure 9). Similarly, every eruption of a geyser produces an experience of scientific discovery, even for the casual observer, by revealing a phenomenon (*this* particular eruption) that has never been seen before. Viewing the eruption of a geyser active when Yellowstone was first discovered also lets the park's visitors reenact the process of historical discovery by reproducing an experience that connects them with a long line of prior "discoverers," extending back to the earliest explorations of the region.

Of course, viewing a long-active geyser connects the contemporary visitor with the experience of early tourists as well, an experience whose rhythm is delightfully captured in Owen Wister's 1936 reminiscence for *Harper's Monthly* of his youthful trips through Yellowstone.[2] Wister first visited Yellowstone in 1887 and then again in 1896. In addition to informing his *Harper's* piece, these trips provided the germ for his melodramatic 1928 Yellowstone story, "Bad Medicine," to which I will return at the conclusion of this chapter.[3] In the *Harper's* essay, which is much more whimsical in tone, Wister describes a young bell-hop at the Upper Geyser Basin hotel, the predecessor of today's Old Faithful Inn:

We would be sitting tilted back, reading our mail, the tourists would have ceased talking and be lounging drowsily, the boy would be at the door, motionless as a set steel trap. Suddenly the trap would spring, the boy would catapult into the door, and in his piping treble scream out:

> "Beehive's a-goin' off!"

at which every tourist instantly started from his chair, and a leaping crowd gushed out of the hotel and sprinted down over the formation to catch the Beehive at it. Beehive finally quiescent, they returned slowly, sank into chairs and exhausted silence; you could have heard a mosquito. But the steel trap was again set, sprang soon, and again the silence was pierced:

> "There goes Old Faithful!"

Up and out they flew once more, watched Old Faithful, and came back to their chairs and to silence more exhausted.

Was the boy exhausted? Never. It might be the Castle, it might be the Grotto – whatever it might be, that pre-Ritz-Carlton bell-hop routed those torpid tourists from their repose to set them trooping across the formation to gape at some geyser in action, and again seek their chairs, feebler each time. Has he in mature years ever known more joy? I doubt it.[4]

9 William Henry Jackson, *Mammoth Hot Springs*

Wister's light-hearted sketch reproduces the wonder of the moment of discovery still at the heart of the Yellowstone tourist's experience. Stopping just short of likening the behavior of the tourists to the action of the geysers, Wister provokes his readers to discover these connections themselves, just as the bell-hop's proclamations prompt the hotel's tourists to see the geysers for themselves. Like the geysers, the tourists at the hotel spend most of their time at rest, "lounging drowsily" in their chairs. When a geyser erupts so does the bell-hop, screaming out in his "piping treble," "'Beehive's a-goin' off!'" This linguistic eruption prompts the eruption of the tourists, who "gushed out of the hotel" like Beehive's superheated waters. When Beehive's waters subside and the geyser becomes "quiescent," the tourists do, too, "[sinking] into chairs and exhausted silence," until a geyser's (and the bell-hop's) next eruption rouses them again.

Wister's excitable bell-hop anticipates an intriguing present-day phenomenon, the presence of the tribe of "geyser gazers" that one often encounters in the Upper Geyser Basin of the Firehole River or at other thermally active areas in the park. Although the Upper Basin is home to Old Faithful, the regularly erupting patriarch of Yellowstone's geysers is of little interest to members of the geyser tribe. Equipped with notebooks and lap-tops, cameras and camcorders, PDAs, cell phones, handheld GPS systems, and walkie-talkies; wearing hats, long-sleeved clothing, and layers of heavy-duty sun-screen; carrying food, drinks, diapers, and toys for their infants and children – geyser gazers come to the Upper Basin with the hope of chronicling the eruptions of lesser-known and less-regular geysers. Recording time, duration, and frequency of both the eruptions themselves and a variety of pre- and inter-eruption phenomena, the park's geyser gazers seek to uncover such hidden secrets of Yellowstone's geothermal mysteries as underground connections between particular geysers, previously unnoticed eruption periodicity, or unrecognized patterns or pre-eruption behavior. Not unlike pilgrims returning to a shrine, these devotees return time and again to pay homage to the park's geysers. Each visit, each moment spent waiting for the next geyser to erupt, testifies to a faith in the regularity of nature's processes, a belief in the fidelity of nature attested to by its inscription in the very name of Yellowstone's most famous geyser. At the same time, this devotional fidelity inspires the representational fidelity to nature evident in the geyser gazers' almost cult-like obsession with the accuracy and completeness of their information. The park's geyser gazers participate in a logic underlying Yellowstone's reproduction of the moment of historical or scientific discovery, in which the faithful preservation of Yellowstone's natural environment (particularly but not exclusively its geothermal features) makes possible the faithful reproduction of its historical environment (particularly but not exclusively the moment of scientific discovery).

This conjunction of natural preservation and historical reproduction officially became part of Park Service management policy in 1963, when Secretary of Interior Stewart Udall received a report from his Advisory Board on Wildlife Management, a five-person committee chaired by A. Starker Leopold, son of the famed conservationist Aldo Leopold. Recognized as a landmark in the history of National Park policy, the Leopold Committee's report fundamentally redefines Yellowstone's management objectives from protecting the park's "geothermal curiosities" to the more ecologically sensitive goal of preserving the park's ecosystem as a whole – a redefinition which has culminated in the currently held management paradigm of the Greater Yellowstone Ecosystem, an area that includes more than 18 million acres of public and private lands in Wyoming, Montana, and Idaho.[5] Adopted as official policy within the year, the report recommends that "the biotic associations within each park be maintained, or where necessary recreated, as nearly as possible in the condition that prevailed when the area was first visited by the white man. A national park should represent a vignette of primitive America."[6] Even if this "goal cannot be fully achieved," the report continues, "it can be approached. A reasonable illusion of primitive America could be recreated, using the utmost in skill, judgment, and ecologic sensitivity."[7]

In the previous chapter, I argued that the creation, elision, and recreation of the distinction between aesthetic and natural agency constitute something similar to what we mean by environmentalism or preservationism today. A similar logic is at work in the Leopold report's articulation of the relation between natural and human agency in the act of park management. Seeking to preserve or recreate the biotic associations that obtained when Europeans first encountered Yellowstone, the committee would simultaneously produce and conceal signs of human agency in the park. Even while recommending that the Park Service employ "the utmost in skill, judgment, and ecological sensitivity" to recreate "a reasonable illusion of primitive America," the report insists that "observable artificiality in any form must be minimized and obscured in every possible way."[8] Although recognizing that the reproduction of nature would require active management rather than passive protection, the committee advises that the methods used by the Park Service should have as their "objective . . . to manage 'invisibly' – that is, to conceal the signs of management."[9]

Managing the park's ecosystem as an "illusion" or "vignette of primitive America," the Leopold Committee would simultaneously preserve or recreate the biotic associations that existed before the first white men arrived in the area, and restage their disappearance by reproducing for the park-goer the scene of discovery in which those "primitive" associations were changed forever. Defining preservation in terms of representational fidelity to nature, the Leopold report conceives of nature as art, following the classical philosophical opposition (formulated most powerfully in Kant's third critique) between aesthetics and use. Striving to provide an ecological ground or philosophical foundation upon which the management of national parks can be securely based, a barrier or limit or boundary beyond which park management cannot or should not go, the Leopold report is in effect setting off nature from use, defining nature as that which is prior to, or independent of, any particular human purpose, thus making nature (or at least national parks) structurally identical to art. In singling out the biotic associations that prevailed when the area was first visited by the white man, however, the Leopold report announces both an originary condition and an act of transgression that must be compensated for – introducing "illusion" and "re-creation" as necessary to the continued survival of those natural conditions which existed prior to the arrival of the white man. This uneasy alliance between natural preservation and historical reproduction hinges upon two not entirely compatible notions of what it means to establish and manage a national park. The report articulates a double logic of representational fidelity to nature in which national parks are described alternately as accurate and truthful ecological representations of biotic associations and then as theatrical reproductions of a culturally significant moment of historical discovery, a moment that entails the loss of the very same biotic associations that the creation of the park would aim to preserve. In this chapter I look at a crucial moment in the cultural construction of "nature" as simultaneously the prior condition of representation and as its consequence, that is as a reproduction. In so doing I aim to demonstrate how the preservation of Yellowstone provided an important cultural site not only for the emergence of environmentalism in America, but more interestingly for the articulation of a logic of representational fidelity to nature that underwrites the significance of national parks for America's cultural identity.

FIDELITY TO NATURE

Representational fidelity to nature is what has always been at issue in Yellowstone – whether nature is conceived of as art, as "biotic associations," or as "ecosystemic processes." In its most basic form the question of representational fidelity has been associated with Yellowstone ever since John Colter, "the area's white discoverer," first explored the region in 1807.[10]

From the earliest rumors of mud volcanoes, boiling rivers, hot spouting geysers, and petrified forests, the fidelity of both word-of-mouth and written representations of Yellowstone has been subject to doubt and disbelief. Even as late as 1870, when David Folsom and Charles Cook offered a collaborative diary of their 1869 expedition to the *New York Tribune*, *Harper's*, and *Scribner's*, the publications "refused the manuscript because 'they had a reputation that they could not risk with such unreliable material.'"[11] A year later, however, when Nathaniel Pitt Langford sought to publish an account of the Washburn Expedition of 1870, *Scribner's* gladly obliged – at least partly because Langford's report was legitimated by the accompanying military expedition led by Lieutenant Gustavus C. Doane.

But *Scribner's* was also interested in publishing this account because Langford furnished the magazine with eyewitness sketches, which would be transformed into the first published illustrations of some of Yellowstone's wonders.[12] For the editors of *Scribner's*, representational fidelity derives both from institutional validation and from the valorization of the visual over the verbal. An editorial in the magazine's first issue explains its use of graphic illustrations as verification of the fidelity of its stories: "The feature of illustrations has been adopted to meet a thoroughly pronounced popular demand for the pictorial representation of life and truth, and in the well-assured belief that there is no person, young or old, literate or illiterate, to whom it will be unwelcome."[13] Despite *Scribner's* commitments to "the pictorial representation of life and truth," the obvious inaccuracies and exaggerations of the Langford article's illustrations were clearly outweighed by the "thoroughly pronounced popular demand" for illustrations. The article's illustrations were printed from woodcuts made from the black-and-white watercolor sketches that Thomas Moran, who would not even see the Yellowstone region until the following summer, had produced from drawings and descriptions brought back by the Washburn expedition (one of these woodcuts is shown here as Figure 10). In an era before widespread photographic reproduction, *plein air* watercolors sketched in the field played an important and culturally well-defined role in the visual reporting of natural and historical events, a role dependent on the eyewitness experience of the watercolorist. In the case of these Yellowstone illustrations, although an additional intermediary was inserted, the eyewitness chain was still taken to be preserved, regardless of the mimetic fidelity of the resulting illustrations.

Indeed it was partly the inaccuracies of the verbal, visual, and cartographic representations produced by the Washburn and other early explorations that prompted Congress to finance Hayden's request to lead his

THE GREAT CANON OF THE YELLOWSTONE.

10 Thomas Moran, *The Great Canon of the Yellowstone, Scribner's Monthly,* May 1871

US Geological Survey of the Territories on an expedition to Yellowstone the following summer. Along with the concurrent but independent military reconnaisance mission led by Captains John Barlow and David Heap, Hayden's 1871 expedition is credited with bringing back "incontrovertible evidence of the existence and nature of those thermal features that had been so long rumored to exist upon the Yellowstone Plateau. In the mass of field notes, sketches, photographs, and specimens they brought back was material for two official reports and the beginning of an accurate map."[14] It was not mapping, however, but illustration that typically constituted the primary visual focus of Hayden's early surveys. Among the instructions Hayden received for his first federally funded survey in 1867, for example, was a request for the presentation of "'graphic illustrations' of striking and beautiful landscapes for inclusion in the annual reports of the General Land Office, which was official sponsor of the survey."[15] And in the formal letter of instructions for 1870, the year prior to his first survey of Yellowstone, Hayden was "required to secure as full material as possible for the illustration of [his] final report, such as sketches, photographs, & c," a requirement that helps to account for the fact that "nearly a sixth of the [1870] force was . . . visual artists."[16] Like *Scribner's*, the Hayden survey was dedicated to supplying the "thoroughly pronounced popular demand for the pictorial representation of life and truth," particularly insofar as such representations could aid in the development of the Western territories. As early as 1862 Hayden had begun to articulate the role of his survey in the nation's westward expansion, proposing to "lay before the public such full, accurate, and reliable information . . . as will bring from the older states the capital, skill, and enterprise necessary to develop the great natural resources of the country."[17]

Hayden's 1862 proposal for a geological survey nicely schematizes the competing ideologies of representation entailed in his scientific project. On the face of it the aim of the survey is to convey to the public "full, accurate, and reliable information" about the nation's Western territories. Nature provides the prior condition for the survey's mimetic aim: to bring back to the East faithful scientific and cartographic representations of the natural conditions that awaited him (and ultimately the nation) in the West. In so doing, however, the survey reproduces nature as "natural resources," the development of which constitutes nature not only as the survey's prior condition but also as its practical consequence. Following a kind of symbolic economy of venture capitalism, what Bruno Latour characterizes as science's "cycle of accumulation," the survey's representations will help to attract "the capital, skill, and enterprise necessary to develop the great natural resources" of the West according to the prior model offered by the "older states" back

East.[18] Even in the midst of the Civil War, at a time when the nation was preoccupied with the relation between Northern and Southern states, Hayden remained focused on the appropriation of Western resources by Eastern, and also European, capital.[19]

Competing commitments to representational fidelity also inform Yellowstone's establishment as a national park in 1872, when fidelity to nature was repeatedly invoked both to justify the truth or accuracy of particular representations of the Yellowstone landscape and to articulate the need for preserving it. This dual logic of fidelity to nature is captured visually in Thomas Moran's seven by twelve foot painting of *The Grand Canyon of the Yellowstone* (see Figure 11), which was "the first American landscape painting by an American artist to be bought by the United States government."[20] In purchasing Moran's painting for the Capitol in the spring of 1872, shortly after President Grant had signed the legislation establishing Yellowstone as a national park, Congress sought to commemorate its preservation of Yellowstone as an important legislative episode in the nation's history, with Moran's painting as a monumental illustration of Congress' legislative text. Moran also used his painting to illustrate and commemorate the preservation of Yellowstone; dominated by the spectacular scenery of Yellowstone's Grand Canyon, the painting provided the nation with geologically and topographically accurate representations of the canyon's natural features. But in portraying as its central historical action an encounter between an unidentified Indian and members of the Hayden survey with which Moran travelled to Yellowstone in the summer of 1871, the painting also thematizes the moment of discovery that the Leopold committee would alternately reproduce and conceal. Not unlike the Leopold report, Moran's painting seeks to reproduce nature faithfully by representing the Grand Canyon of the Yellowstone as a "vignette of primitive America," at the moment of its "official" scientific discovery by the members of Ferdinand V. Hayden's US Geological Survey of the Territories. Placing members of Hayden's survey at the paradigmatic moment of discovery, Moran illustrates and helps formalize Hayden's originary role both in Yellowstone's discovery and in its preservation.

If we pause to consider the identity of the figures Moran places in the landscape, however, we can see that the painting reproduces more than a simple moment of historical discovery. Joni Kinsey has argued that Hayden himself is the figure overlooking the canyon with the unidentified Indian (despite the fact that both figures have their backs to the viewer; see Figure 12). She speculates that the two men in the left foreground – one standing by the horses and the other seated, looking at a notebook, sketch pad, or some maps (see Figure 13) – are Moran and William Henry Jackson,

11 Thomas Moran, *The Grand Canyon of the Yellowstone*

12 Moran, *Grand Canyon of the Yellowstone* (detail)

13 Moran, *Grand Canyon of the Yellowstone* (detail)

the survey's photographer.[21] Although the implications of this identification are intriguing, Moran's letters indicate that he meant the figures in the left foreground to be Hayden and Stevenson; his failure to identify the figures overlooking the canyon could suggest that they are meant to remain unidentified.[22] If this identification is correct, the painting can be seen to represent not only a particular historical encounter between the Hayden survey and the Yellowstone wilderness, but also a more complicated, if also generalized, moment of mythical discovery – encompassing on the one hand the cultural encounter of European Americans with both untouched nature and untouched Native American culture, and on the other hand the encounter of both nature and Native Americans with the cultural practices and technologies of representation that made up nineteenth-century American science.[23] This moment of mythical discovery is accentuated by the fact that while the survey member at the center of the painting looks and gestures towards the wonder that is Yellowstone's Grand Canyon, the Indian looks back over his shoulder to marvel at the survey members in the left foreground. Not only is this juxtaposition of historical landscapes with real or mythical cultural encounters a recurrent characteristic of Moran's Western landscapes, but it is also of a piece with the moment of historical and scientific discovery still reproduced in Yellowstone today.

In suggesting these affinities between the reproductive logics of the Leopold Committee's report and Moran's *Grand Canyon*, I do not mean to posit an identity between two historically disparate understandings of environmentalism (or the preservation of nature). Describing the management goals of the Park Service in terms of ecosystems and biotic associations, the Leopold report relies upon ecological concepts, indeed on scientific paradigms, that did not exist as such when Yellowstone became a national park. Nor do I mean to suggest that Yellowstone's preservation should not, therefore, be seen as an early instance of environmentalism in action. Environmentalism in 1872 was an emergent discursive formation constituted at least in part by an internally contradictory notion of fidelity to nature. These inconsistencies do not make the preservation of Yellowstone any less environmentalist than do the internal inconsistencies of the Leopold report. In taking up the competing logics of fidelity to nature which circulated through the verbal and visual representations surrounding both Hayden's survey and Yellowstone's preservation, I argue that in 1872 these competing logics enabled the notion of fidelity to nature to hold together a number of contradictory interests, much as the Park Service's policy of preserving or recreating biotic associations did in 1963, or the current acceptance of the management paradigm of the greater Yellowstone ecosystem does today.

The remainder of the chapter is divided into four sections, each of which looks at one aspect of these competing notions of representational fidelity. First, I look at the competing logics of fidelity to nature which run through Hayden's scientific discourse, after which I take up the alliance of scientific and photographic models of representation, focusing on Jackson's photographs for the Hayden survey. The next section traces these models of representation in relation to Moran's *Grand Canyon of the Yellowstone*, which is itself informed by a Ruskinian sensibility that helps to make sense of the broader cultural discourse about the preservation of nature in America. The chapter concludes with a coda: a brief look at Owen Wister's "Bad Medicine," a story that ties together the notions of representation, loss, and fidelity to nature which inform the rest of the chapter.

THE SCIENTIFIC PROGRESS OF AMERICA

In addition to official government reports, Hayden wrote three articles on the 1871 survey for readers of the *American Journal of Science*. In the last of these he characterizes the establishment of Yellowstone National Park as "an event which marks an era in the scientific progress of the country . . . This noble deed may be regarded as a tribute from our legislators to science, and the gratitude of the nation, and men of science in all parts of the world, is due them for this munificent donation."[24] Hayden's depiction of the preservation of Yellowstone as "a tribute from our legislators to science" can be explained at least partly by the federal government's burgeoning support for "the launching of modern American science," and partly by his need to accommodate the journal's science-minded audience.[25] And in urging the gratitude both of the nation and of scientists worldwide, Hayden is not only expressing his own gratitude for the steadily increasing Congressional funding of his survey, but also lobbying for continued increases. His claim that the preservation of Yellowstone "marks an era in the scientific progress of the country" is more enigmatic, suggesting on the one hand the progress of science, and on the other hand, the progress of America itself. Alone, neither of these explanations can fully account for Hayden's meaning. Taken in light of the dual commitment to nature and to nationalism that marked his survey from its inception, however, Hayden would seem to be saying that the preservation of Yellowstone marks an era in the progress both of American science and of American expansion according to scientific principles.[26]

The first of these claims, that the preservation of Yellowstone marks an era in the progress of American science, was elaborated in 1874 by Theodore Comstock in a two-part article in the *American Naturalist*.[27] For Comstock, Yellowstone's scientific value derives both from its efficient use of natural resources and from its reproduction of a vignette of primitive America as a laboratory for the scientist, evident in his argument for preserving and protecting the park's geothermal formations. Describing the geological lessons that scientists can learn in the park, Comstock repeatedly describes the goal of Yellowstone's preservation in terms of the reproduction of the moment of scientific discovery. The park's geothermal features having been "preserved by act of Congress," he writes,

the earnest student of nature will always find an abundance of fresh matter for research in nearly every department of science. Here he will find ready to his hands a laboratory of physics in which he may observe on a large scale the action of the various forces of attraction and repulsion . . . He will find the laws of crystallization exemplified in forms novel and instructive, and will doubtless witness many new and varied phenomena of heat, light and electricity . . . Speaking from a geological standpoint, I can, from my own experience, promise the enthusiastic student of our earth's history a view at once so complete and so overwhelming as to enchain his whole attention.[28]

Curiously, Comstock also sees the preservation of Yellowstone as beneficial to microscopy, writing that "there is one young but active science – microscopy, – which has as yet scarcely entered this field, but which, I firmly believe, will discover within the limits of the Park most valuable treasures."[29] In some senses Comstock considers all science as microscopy; whether physics, chemistry, or geology, science is invariably characterized in terms of visual observation. The preservation of Yellowstone allows for the continual reproduction of the moment of scientific discovery, a microscopic moment characterized by the scientist's reproduction of nature into the "most valuable" visual "treasures."[30]

In the *American Journal of Science*, Hayden, too, describes scientific knowledge as invariably taking the form of the discovery of visual treasures. Like the preliminary reports from which they are taken, these articles are constructed in the form of narratives of discovery. At the same time that he strives to represent nature faithfully, Hayden reproduces nature as the object of scientific discovery. This dual gesture can be seen in the following passage narrating the survey's discovery of what is today known as the Mammoth Hot Springs.

After ascending the hill among the pines, about three-fourths of a mile from the river bottom, we came suddenly upon one of the most remarkable exhibitions of the hot spring deposits that we have seen in this land of wonders. In the distance it looks like a vast glacier of snow and ice, and on that account we have named it the White Mountain . . . But let us pass along the west side of this beautiful structure, and examine it in detail. We find, first, a broad flat terrace, on which are plainly visible the remains of once active springs . . . A little farther up we come to a series of basin-like pools, varying in diameter from 4 to 8 feet, with water from one to four feet deep, having semi-circular rims most beautifully scolloped . . . These continue for about fifty yards, gradually ascending, when we come to an abrupt declivity of about one hundred and fifty feet . . . As the water flows from the basin down the declivity from one of the beautiful pools to the other, it loses a portion of its heat, and one may find a bathing pool with any desired temperature.[31]

The scientific fidelity of this passage derives both from its accurate description of what Hayden's party found and from its re-creation of the experience of scientific discovery. Like Comstock, Hayden characteristically depicts the moment of scientific discovery in visual terms. Hayden structures his description as a narrative of possession, employing what Michel de Certeau describes as utterative markers and modalities of the narrator's presence ("we came suddenly upon," "we find," "we come to") in order to verify his own role as discoverer.[32] But Hayden also employs such markers to inscribe the reader within the survey's exploration ("In the distance it looks like," "let us pass along . . . and examine," "one may find"). Like a national park, scientific knowledge does not belong only to its discoverer.

Paradoxically, however, Hayden's commitment to competing notions of representational fidelity seems most explicit in those cases when he insists, as he does about White Mountain, that the picture presented "to the eye . . . transcends any description in words"; or when he says, as he does of the various hot springs basins, that "the exquisite beauty of the coloring and the variety of forms baffles any attempt to portray them whether with pen or pencil."[33] Hayden's expression of his own inability to describe the visual appearance of a natural phenomenon, characteristic of the rhetoric of the sublime, depends upon the sense that his language is unfaithful to its object, that his discourse lacks the fidelity to nature that constitutes the regulatory principle of nineteenth-century scientific representation. But interestingly Hayden is also concerned with the fidelity of his verbal representations in reproducing the excitement of the moment of discovery produced by the eruptions of some of the geysers in the Upper Geyser Basin. After describing the eruption of one geyser, for example, he writes that he can "compare the noise and excitement which it produced only to that of a charge in battle"; and after describing the eruption of Old Faithful, he apologizes that "words can convey but an inadequate conception of the intense excitement which the scene produces upon the mind."[34] A spiritual precursor to today's geyser gazers, Hayden describes the details of the eruption as accurately and fully as he can, providing numerical information as well as verbal descriptions. But it is not the eruptions themselves that he feels unable to convey but rather the sensations of excitement they produce upon the mind. Although the experience produced by the moment of scientific discovery cannot be adequately represented in words, preserving Yellowstone as a faithful representation of nature makes possible the intersubjective reproduction of the inexpressibility of the moment of scientific discovery. In other words, while Hayden may fail to capture the excitement of scientific discovery, the preservation of Yellowstone lets others share the experience not only of discovery but of its inexpressibility as well.[35]

Hayden's concern with scientific fidelity did not originate in the *Journal of American Science* articles, but had already become an explicit preoc-cupation by the time he was writing the preliminary report for his 1870 survey, prior to his first Yellowstone survey. Indeed, in the official letters transmitting both his 1870 and 1871 preliminary reports to the Secretary of Interior, fidelity to nature appears as both a scientific and a spiritual goal. In these letters he repeatedly describes the work of the survey in quasi-religious terms, acknowledging "the great fidelity of all [his] assistants to the interests of the survey." In the letter transmitting the report for 1870, he writes that Jim Stevenson rendered "the same faithful and indispensable services that have characterized his labors in previous expeditions"; Cyrus Thomas' re-port "will furnish ample proof of his constant fidelity to his duties"; "Mr. [Henry] Elliott, the artist, worked with untiring zeal"; Jackson "performed his duties throughout with a true enthusiasm for his art"; and the report of John Beaman, the meteorologist, "will show his zeal in the work."[36] In the following year's letter of transmission, Hayden similarly reports that: Stevenson "labored with his usual efficiency and fidelity throughout the entire trip"; "Elliott labored with his usual zeal and efficiency"; "Jackson performed his duties with great zeal"; Dr. C. S. Turnbull performed his medical duties with "great fidelity"; Campbell Carrington performed his zoological duties "with great zeal and efficiency"; and Anton Schonborn, although dying shortly after the survey's completion, took topographical notes "with zeal and ability."[37]

In praising the fidelity of his men both to the survey and to their duties, Hayden invariably describes the survey's work in the discourse of religion.

But it becomes clear in the 1870 letter of transmission that the fidelity of the members of his surveying corps stands for fidelity of another kind. Although Hayden models the survey on a religious community, the faith he expects from his men is not a faith in God or in religious values but a faith in the role of science in bringing about his vision of American progress.

My explorations of the country west of the Mississippi began in the spring of 1853, prior to the organization of Kansas and Nebraska as territories, and I have watched the growth of this portion of the West year by year, from the first rude cabin of the squatter to the beautiful villages and cities which we now see scattered so thickly over that country. We have beheld, within the past fifteen years, a rapidity of growth and development in the Northwest which is without a parallel in the history of the globe. Never has my faith in the grand future that awaits the entire West been so strong as it is at the present time, and it is my earnest desire to devote the remainder of the working days of my life to the development of its scientific and material interests, until I shall see every Territory, which is now organized, a State in the Union. Out of the portions of the continent which lie to the northward and southward of the great central mass, other Territories will, in the mean time, be carved, until we shall embrace within our limits the entire country from the Arctic Circle to the Isthmus of Darien.[38]

As he did in describing the survey's scientific discoveries, Hayden depicts the history of the nation's growth in visual terms: "I have *watched* the growth of this portion of the West"; "We have *beheld* . . . a rapidity of growth and development in the Northwest" (emphasis added). As in the articles for the *American Journal of Science*, Hayden's discourse is marked with the modalities of the narrator's presence, offering an eyewitness testimony to (as well as participating in) America's westward expansion. The nature of this participation is twofold: Hayden both provides the information needed by those who would develop the Western territories and testifies to the fidelity of this development through the act of witnessing. Though couched in terms of faith and devotion, his commitment to the cause of national expansion is not to any particular set of spiritual purposes or values but to the "scientific and material interests" of the nation. Thus, the spiritual fidelity of his survey is underwritten by an ideological fidelity to nature in which the eyewitness observer of American progress finds the nation's natural boundaries to consist in no less than the limits of the continent itself.

Hayden's dual notion of "the scientific progress of our country" is by no means an idiosyncratic one. A similar duality can be seen in John Gast's *American Progress* (Figure 14), a painting commissioned and designed by George A. Crofutt to promote his own travel guide to the West. Completed

14 John Gast, *American Progress*, oil on canvas, 1872

in the same year that Yellowstone was preserved, the painting employs the same iconographical convention of depicting westward movement from right to left that is employed in Emmanuel Leutze's *Westward the Course of Empire* (see Figure 5), Fanny Palmer's *Across the Continent* (Figure 15), or Albert Bierstadt's *Emigrants Crossing the Plains* (Figure 16).[39] Just as Gast employs both cartographic and perspectival conventions to organize his pictorial space, so he combines historical with allegorical representation. The painting's historical subject is the westward movement of American civilization. On foot, horseback, covered wagon, stage-coach, railroad, and ship, the American people are shown moving inexorably across Gast's canvas, dislodging buffalo and Indians in their wake. The painting's central allegorical figure – described by Crofutt as a "beautiful and charming female . . . floating westward through the air, bearing on her forehead the 'Star of Empire,'" – could easily be taken as a symbol of Hayden's dual notion of the "scientific progress of our country." "In her right hand," Crofutt explains, "she carries a book – common school – the emblem of education and the testimonial to our national enlightenment, while with the left hand she unfolds and stretches the slender wires of the telegraph, that are to

15 Fanny Palmer, *Across the Continent*

16 Albert Bierstadt, *Emigrants Crossing the Plains*, oil on canvas

flash intelligence throughout the land."[40] For Gast as for Hayden, faith in American progress and the progress of science form two parts of the same cultural picture.

To single out Hayden's fidelity to the scientific progress of America is not to deny his commitment to representational fidelity. This dual fidelity can, however, be difficult to maintain, as when he writes in the 1870 letter of transmission about his relation with the railroads and other corporate interests:

Scientific men who are truly devoted to their calling cannot be speculators or ardently given to pecuniary gains. Citizens of the country and great corporations must ever be largely the recipients of the material benefits of these labors. Generosity on the part of such corporations toward men who are devoted to the advancement of knowledge or the good of the world, may be regarded as the index of their tone or character. I am glad to say that, with comparatively few exceptions, I have received from the railroad men of the West every mark of appreciation I could desire. In former reports I have frequently mentioned the cordial sympathy of the citizens of the Territories in my labors. I am obliged to speak the truth as I read it in the great book of nature, whether it is in accordance with the preconceived notions of the inhabitants of a district or not, and I cannot depart from this inexorable law for fear or favor. It is my earnest wish at all times to report that which will be most pleasing to the people of the West, providing there is any foundation for it in nature. When I cannot do so, I shall wait for time to place me right in their estimation.[41]

Hayden's description of science as the "calling" to which he is "devoted," a calling that obligates him "to speak the truth as [he reads] it in the great book of Nature," participates in the Victorian substitution of scientific for religious authority. The religious language of the passage's final sentence, with its implications of an almost cosmic time-frame for measuring human patience, also reinforces the discourse of Hayden's scientific capitalism, which is essentially a science of appropriating and incorporating the "natural resources" of the West into the network of military, railroads, corporations, and politics that already exists in the "older states." But insofar as Hayden's devotion to the survey is a substitution of science for religion it is a substitution that works not because science is somehow purer or more logically coherent than religion but because science is able to ally itself with other discursive practices and formations in ways that religion no longer can. This quasi-religious devotion to science is inseparable from a nationalistic devotion to American expansionism, indeed to the growth of capital itself.

Furthermore, this devotion to science entails a devotion not only to the practice of science or scientific method but to nature itself. In thinking about his survey Hayden consistently maintains two accounts of scientific fidelity, evident in his "earnest wish at all times to report that which will be most pleasing to the people of the West, providing there is any foundation for it in nature." On the one hand he holds that fidelity to nature is the "foundation" of his survey's work, and that his goal as scientist is to "speak the truth as [he reads] it in the great book of Nature." Like "biotic associations" for the Leopold report, the book of nature functions for Hayden as a prior constraint, a limit or ground which the scientist cannot transgress. But simultaneously the almost religious devotion of his "earnest wish at all times to report that which will be most pleasing to the people of the West" suggests that he considers his work as a scientist to be subordinate to his faith in America's westward development. Hayden's faith in the scientific progress of America simultaneously precedes his work as a scientist (it is what motivates him to read the book of nature in the first place) and stands as its goal (it is the ultimate outcome of his scientific work).

In underscoring Hayden's commitment both to westward expansion and to the reproduction of the moment of scientific discovery, I do not mean to dismiss the postbellum notion of scientific fidelity of representation but to reconfigure it. With Latour and others, I would argue that the authority of modern science derives neither from its objectivity, neutrality, or rigorous methodology, nor from its independence of social, economic, and political interests, but rather from its ability to marshal these competing interests through the creation of what Latour calls "fragile networks," in which mathematical, linguistic, and pictorial inscriptions work to hold together an often diverse and heterogeneous network of actors and actants – people, nature, laboratories, instrumentation, professional organizations, and other discursive and institutional practices. Hayden's twofold notion of representational fidelity to nature, like the survey itself, operates as a discursive technology for producing a heterogeneous and polysemous network of visual, verbal, and mathematical inscriptions – not only in government reports but in popular and scientific publications. In making this claim I do not mean to question the validity of the scientific discourse produced by Hayden's survey; indeed I am not interested in judging the validity of Hayden's scientific work at all. What I am interested in is the way in which Hayden stages the moment of discovery according to a logic of fidelity to nature in which the scientist must accurately and exactly represent nature at the same time that he must reproduce nature according to a set of prior commitments, interests, and practices. In other words Hayden stages knowledge or representation according to a narrative of visual discovery in which the scientist comes upon something that has never been come upon before. Not unlike the Leopold Committee's desire to recreate the biotic associations that existed when the first white man arrived on the scene, Hayden's conviction that Yellowstone marks an era in the scientific progress of America depends upon the idea that nature must be preserved so that the moment of scientific discovery can be reenacted, so new discoveries can continue to be made. For Hayden the Congressional preservation of Yellowstone reproduces the possibility not only of America but of science itself.

STEREOSCOPE AND ARCHIVE

Before Yellowstone was preserved as a park, it was represented in photographs. If Yellowstone's preservation as a park can be said to mark the reproduction of the possibility of science, then its photographic representation could be said to mark its preservation as superfluous for science. Curiously Hayden almost says as much in the letter of transmission reporting on the next summer's survey, when he cites James Dwight Dana's praise of William Henry Jackson's photographic work for the 1872 season. Dana, the long-time editor of the *American Journal of Science*, had reviewed Jackson's photographs in the journal's January 1873 issue, noting:

Next to a personal visit to this land of geysers, hot springs, fountains of boiling mud, waterfalls, lakes, and majestic mountains, is a morning spent over these photographs. They would do credit to the best photographic laboratory, and, considering the difficulties inherent in a long and arduous journey, they are really admirable. The Yellowstone series well illustrates the advantage of photography over any hand drawings in bringing out details of structure, especially where the artist is guided by the geologist in selecting the best points of view.[42]

One implication of Dana's reasoning is to imagine that, insofar as science is primarily visual, the photographic reproduction of the park's natural features creates the possibility of doing away with the need to preserve Yellowstone. In praising the superiority of Jackson's "geyser views" to "any hand drawings," for example, Dana not only remarks the views "of basins and cones in which the varied tracery of the surface may be studied with much of the satisfaction to be had from actual examination," but also notes that "such views give an opportunity for the geologist to compare beds of chemical deposition with our ordinary limestone."[43] Like visitors to Don

Delillo's "Most-Photographed Barn in America," scientists (or tourists) might no longer need to see Yellowstone at all; in many cases the photographs themselves would suffice.[44]

But even in the world of *White Noise*, it is important that the most-photographed barn exists, no matter whether anybody sees it. Dana's notice of Jackson's photographs reminds us not only of the fact that photographs can often stand in for the objects they represent but also of the powerful nineteenth-century alliance between scientific and photographic logics of representational fidelity to nature. The force of this alliance can be seen in a single issue of the 1872 volume of Dana's *Journal*, in two different notices in the "Scientific Intelligence" section, the first of which concerns the "Application of Photography to Illustrations of Natural History" in Alexander Agassiz's *Bulletin of the Museum of Comparative Zoology*. After describing "two excellent samples of what can be done toward securing most accurate and permanent plates by some of the new photographic methods," the notice concludes: "There can be no doubt but that these and similar processes are destined to create an entire revolution in the illustration of works on Natural History, where absolute accuracy and *fidelity to nature* are of paramount importance."[45] Like Jackson's photographs of Yellowstone, Agassiz's *Bulletin* uses photographs to preserve "specimens" for scientific illustration and examination. And like Jackson's Yellowstone series, these photographs both represent and stand in place of nature.

This alliance between scientific and photographic logics of representational fidelity to nature reappears on the following page in a notice of some works of "stellar photography," in which Benjamin Gould had used the spectroscopic inventions of Lewis Rutherfurd to "obtain photographs of the principal constellations in the southern heavens." The notice cites a letter from Benjamin Peirce (head of the Coast Survey and father of philosopher Charles Sanders) to Josiah Quincy, in which Peirce maintains:

The photographs afford just as good an opportunity for new and original investigation of the relative position of the near stars, as would be derived from the stars themselves as seen through the most powerful telescopes. They are indisputable facts, unbiased by personal defects of observation, and which convey to all future times the actual places of the stars when the photographs were taken.[46]

Although "unbiased by personal defects," these photographs were clearly marred by technological ones. Nonetheless, Peirce's conviction that photographs are as useful for astronomy as observations made through even the most powerful telescopes literalizes Dana's hyperbolic praise of Jackson's photographs. Peirce's belief that photographs are "indisputable facts, unbiased by personal defects of observation," underlies an affiliation between photographic and scientific models of representation that marks the practice of astronomy to this day. Interestingly, this representational model implies an incipient preservationist ethic, in which photographs can preserve an image for "all future times," much as the Congressional establishment of Yellowstone as a park preserves its natural wonders for future generations.

The imagination of a representational ideal in which a reproduction can be so faithful to nature that it can stand in place of nature is not limited to photography and science.[47] In the same letter of transmission that quotes Dana's notice of Jackson's photographs, for example, Hayden also reports that James T. Gardner, "so long favorably known as the chief topographer of the geological survey of the fortieth parallel, under the direction of Mr. Clarence King, has become associated with [Hayden] as chief of the topographical staff." Hayden goes on to cite Gardner's account of the geological purpose of topographical maps:

For making maps suited to geological purposes it is necessary to carry over the country a systematic trigonometric and topographical survey, checked by astronomical observations. The maps must represent the features of the country accurately, and in bold relief; or, in other words, they must be a picture of the earth's surface as one would see it looking down from above.[48]

This rather remarkable equation of a map whose features are "accurately" represented "in bold relief" with a "picture of the earth's surface as one would see it looking down from above" assumes a photographic ideal for topographical maps virtually identical to that espoused by Dana and Pierce in regard to photographs of geology or natural history or astronomy – an ideal in which representational fidelity to nature is identified with seeing nature for oneself, but seeing it without the perspectival constraints of point of view. Gardner's equation is further remarkable not only because he seems untroubled by the fact that a map is mediated by a historically specific complex of representational conventions (including those entailed in "a systematic trigonometric and topographical survey, checked by astronomical observations"), but also because he does not acknowledge that these cartographic conventions represent space very differently from the way it is depicted in a perspectively organized "picture" of any kind. Unlike photography or painting, topographical cartography cannot properly be described as producing a picture at all.

Nor, according to Jonathan Crary, can the stereoscope, which he characterizes as, next to photography, "the most significant form of visual imagery in the nineteenth century." Although Crary points out that "conceptually, structurally, and, initially, historically," the stereoscope was developed independent of photography, he also notes that by the time of the Civil War the stereoscope "defined a principal mode of consuming photographically produced images."[49] Indeed stereoscope cards were by far the most widely circulated form of Jackson's photographs not only from the Yellowstone surveys but from his other survey-work as well.[50] Nonetheless the structural independence of the stereoscopic image from the photograph is evident in the discontinuity between their representational logics. Photography uses the monocular conventions of classical perspective to represent three-dimensional objects in a single, two-dimensional image, which claims accurately to reproduce the object or photographed "view."[51] The stereoscope, on the other hand, uses the conventions of binocular vision to produce the effect of three-dimensional vision from two-dimensional images. Unlike painting, photography, or cartography, Crary argues, the stereoscope brought about a "radical repositioning of the observer's relation to visual representation," in which the observer is no longer separate from the representation because the representation is situated not in relation to external space but in relation to the embodied observer.[52] Rosalind Krauss describes this radical repositioning as banishing the observer's "own surrounds": "The apparatus of the stereoscope mechanically focuses all attention on the matter at hand . . .[;] the refocusing of attention can occur only within the spectator's channel of vision constructed by the optical machine."[53]

Although, like Gardner's maps or Jackson's photographs, the stereoscope aims both to represent nature accurately and to reproduce the experience of seeing an object for oneself, there is no single stereoscopic image equivalent to a map or a photograph. Relying on the "binocular disparity" of the human body, the stereoscope presents the observer not with one image or two but with an experience of disparity between two different images: "there never really is a stereoscopic image[;] . . . it is a conjuration, an effect of the observer's experience of the differential between two other images."[54] But even this experience of disparity does not exist as such; the optical disparity between the two images is experienced instead as a feeling of three-dimensionality. Thus the stereoscope successively produces and eliminates the difference between two optical images. This in turn produces an "effect" or "experience" of three-dimensionality that elides the difference between the two representational images by eliding the images themselves. But as anyone who has looked through a stereoscope knows, the elimination of two-dimensionality by nineteenth-century technology is by no means complete, especially in regard to the appearance of figures

17 William Henry Jackson, *View of Terrace Hot Springs*

or natural objects. One effect of figures in a stereograph, as well as of foreground trees, rocks, or other natural specimens, is to accentuate the three-dimensional effect by producing an experience of depth. But in the process of producing this experience, which Krauss describes as a kind of "stereoscopic tunnel," such figures look something like two-dimensional cardboard figures, with the effect being a series of two-dimensional planes receding in three-dimensional space.[55]

This effect is especially evident in Jackson's stereographs for the 1871 survey, where he uses human figures not only to provide scale for his photographs of hot springs and geysers, but also to help produce the effect of three-dimensionality (see, for example, Figure 17). The figure who appears most frequently in the 1871 stereos (as in all of Jackson's photographic formats) is Thomas Moran, who regularly accompanied Jackson in his photographic excursions, helping him to select sites and to compose his views. Insofar as Jackson (like Moran) is concerned with the significance of representing figures in landscapes, it is likely that Moran's appearance as a figure in Jackson's landscapes is significant for reasons other than the fact that he

18 William Henry Jackson, *Crater of the Castle Geyser*

was there. Peter Hales notes that, unlike Jackson's photographs from the previous year, which emphasized the heroism of the survey by including its members in numerous views, the pictures from 1871 minimize the survey's heroism. Instead of groups of figures, Jackson's 1871 pictures focus on single figures like Moran, thus emphasizing the moment of discovery as a form of individual artistic appropriation.[56]

But even more suggestive for our purposes are Jackson's stereos of Yellowstone's geothermal "curiosities" (see Figure 18). Accurately record-ing "specimens" of unusual natural objects, these stereos not only create for the viewer the "effect" of three-dimensionality but also reproduce the experience of being a scientist. That is, if the stereos with Moran as a figure reproduce for the viewer the effect of artistic appropriation, the stereos of geothermal features reproduce the experience of scientific appropriation. Like Hayden's science or Gould's spectrographs or Gardner's maps, these stereos operate according to a twofold logic of fidelity to nature, providing an accurate record or representation of the object photographed as well as an accurate reproduction of the experience or feeling of scientific discovery. Unlike scientific, photographic, or cartographic representation, however, the stereoscope is distinguished by its ability to use the illusion of three-dimensionality to reproduce faithfully the scene being photographed. The stereoscope claims fidelity to nature both in the relation of each of the two photographic images to nature and in the relation of these visual representations to the experience of being there and viewing the scene. But the stereoscope produces this experience at the expense of the fidelity of the individual photographs. When the viewer sees a stereoscopic image, the images on the card no longer appear faithful either to the viewer's experience or to the objects the images represent. And while this characteristic of the stereoscopic experience is true of stereoscopes generally, it is particularly interesting in regard to Yellowstone, where the preoccupation with scientific discovery and fidelity to nature suit it especially to the effects of steroscopic photography. Although stereoscopic images of Yosemite circulated as extensively as those of Yellowstone, the resemblance between the scenery of Yosemite Valley and the conventions of picturesque landscape painting suited it more for two-dimensional representations. And as I will argue in the next chapter, the immensity of the Grand Canyon worked to frustrate the stereoscopic effects sought both by photographers and by stereoscopic viewers.

Indeed, Alan Trachtenberg has cautioned against reading survey photographs as landscapes, arguing that the aesthetic purposes of landscape art are incompatible with the documentary purposes of survey photographers. "Landscape," he contends, "distracts attention from the survey itself."[57] Rosalind Krauss describes these documentary purposes as operating according to the multiple logics of the Foucauldian "archive," which Foucault himself describes first as "the law of what can be said, the system that governs the appearance of statements as unique events."[58] Jackson's photographs for the survey certainly appear to be governed by such a law or system, cataloguing fairly exhaustively the region surveyed in a particular season. In Jackson's photographic archive not only do we get an accumulation of shots of principal features (waterfalls, lakes, hot springs, geysers, canyons, mountain peaks, and so forth), but we also get pictures of particular views and approaches to areas, often taken with very little variation in the view (for example, Yellowstone River leading to the Upper or Lower Falls, or the Falls and the Canyon from Artist's or Inspiration Point, from above or below the Falls), as well as pictures documenting historical events (records of camps, of the first boat on Yellowstone Lake, of bridges, even of slaughtered animals and fish). As Foucault insists, "the archive is also that which determines that all these things said do not accumulate endlessly in an amorphous mass, nor are they inscribed in an unbroken linearity, nor do they disappear at the mercy of chance external accidents; but they are grouped together in distinct figures, composed together in accordance with specific regularities."⁵⁹

But to acknowledge the archival purposes of Jackson's survey photographs is not to dismiss their aesthetic ones; Jackson's intentions partake of aesthetic as well as archival goals. In a certain sense the archival nature of Jackson's photographs can be seen to compensate for what painting can do but photography cannot. That is, where (as I shall argue in the next section) Moran works in a medium that allows him to create a composite painting that incorporates many aspects of the survey in a single picture, Jackson must compile an archive if he is to reproduce the heterogeneous network of discursive practices that make up the survey. But this archive is not identical with the totality of Jackson's photographs and stereos. As Foucault insists, the archive determines not only what counts as significant but also how different elements of the archive relate to one another. In representing the survey, Jackson has two photographic strategies available for reproducing the experience of the Hayden survey. He can make a stereoscopic image, which although limited to a single view, offers the spectator the effect or illusion of being a member of the survey. Alternatively he can compile an archive or catalogue in which the assemblage of views strives for an exhaustive record, in which each photograph of a single element is distinct but gains a certain meaning from being one of a catalogue, archive, or system. And despite the fact that stereos make up part of this archive, the law of the archive relegates the stereos to a marginal, second-class status. Not only does the descriptive catalogue (which Jackson compiled to accompany Hayden's survey reports) number the stereos independently of the glass-plate photographs (which are also numbered independently according to the size of the plate), but the catalogue also relegates the stereos, unlike the glass-plates, to an appendix without note or comment. Although the archive represents a fidelity to the aims of the survey as well as a fidelity of each individual photograph to the object it represents, the compilation effect achieved by Jackson's photographic archive of the Hayden survey works to represent the survey not by addition or accretion but (like the stereoscope) by subtraction or erasure. Thus the relation of the stereoscopic image to the viewer's stereoscopic experience parallels the relation between individual photographs and the archive, in which the archive, like the stereoscope, exists both as a result of and at the expense of the individual photographs of which it is comprised.

Yet it is not only individual photographs at whose expense the stereoscope and the archive exist. For as Roland Barthes reminds us in his discussion of the *punctum* and the *studium* in *Camera Lucida*, photography itself is always about loss.[60] Barthes variously describes a photograph's *studium* as its formal, mimetic, mechanical reproduction of a scene; its participation in a system of structural or semiotic coding; its inclusion in a certain type or group of similar kinds of photographs (for example, landscapes or portraits). He describes the *punctum* more mysteriously as a "wound" or "prick" produced by the photograph in its viewer, a feeling that comes from some detail added to the picture. For Barthes the *punctum* works according to the Derridean logic of the supplement, in that it is both added to the picture and already there – though, unlike the *studium*, it appears in the picture by accident, as a result of the contingent nature of photography. In addition, he comes to realize, photography entails another *punctum* that is about time, about the fact that the photograph of an object announces the object's death. In this way, the photograph announces both the past and the future; it tells the beholder that the photographed object has been and will be no more. From this perspective the archival nature of Jackson's photography already assumes the destruction of the landscape that the federal government will preserve as a national park. The act of preservation, like the act of photography, assumes the death or destruction of the photographed landscape, the fact that it has always already been transformed into something else.

FIDELITY TO PICTORIAL NATURE

If thinking about Jackson's photographic archive strictly in terms of nineteenth-century landscape aesthetics would distort or obscure Jackson's documentary purposes, the same could hardly be said for Moran's monumental *Grand Canyon of the Yellowstone*. The landscape aesthetic of John Ruskin was central to Moran's conception of himself as an artist. Because Moran was so strongly influenced by and indebted to Ruskin, it is unsurprising that initial reviews of the painting were consistently couched in terms of a Ruskinian distinction between scientific or topographical truth and artistic merit.[61] This distinction has a long pedigree in the history of art, manifesting itself in the nineteenth century as (among other things) the debate between art as expression and art as mimesis.[62] Despite Ruskin's refusal to accept a strict opposition between realism and idealism, these concepts structure the postbellum American rhetoric of art and nature evident in the popular and critical reception of Moran's painting.[63] For Moran, however, realism and idealism function not as logically distinct aesthetic categories but as inseparable yet discontinuous elements which structure the scientific and the artistic discourse on nature in America, both of which define the preservation of Yellowstone as an act of fidelity not only to nature but to the highest American cultural and political ideals.

Like Ruskin and his reviewers, Moran, too, begins with the distinction between topographical truth and artistic merit. In the same letter in which he had asked for a photograph on which Hayden's figure could be modelled, he enthusiastically describes the progress and aims of his painting in explicitly Ruskinian terms:

> The picture is now more than half finished & I feel confident that it will produce a most decided sensation in Art circles. By all artists it has heretofore been decried next to impossible to make good pictures of strange & wonderful scenes in Nature, & that the most that could be done with such material was to give topographical or geologic characteristics. But I have always held that the grandest or most beautiful, or wonderful in Nature would, in capable hands, make the grandest, most beautiful, or wonderful pictures; & that the business of a great painter, should be the representation of great scenes in Nature. All the above characteristics attach to the Yellowstone region; & if I fail to prove this, I fail to prove myself worthy the name of painter. I cast all my claims to being an Artist into this one picture of the *Great Cañon* & am willing to abide by the judgment upon it. All my friends in this region declare that it is already a great success. But I cannot feel confident about it, until *you* have seen it. In fact I cannot finish it until you have seen it, as your deep knowledge of Nature & her workings would make your judgment on the truth of the picture of far greater value to me than that of any other man in the country. Your knowledge of cause & effect in Nature, would point out to me many facts connected with the place that I may have overlooked.[64]

In distinguishing between "topographical" and "geological" features on the one hand, and "the representation of great scenes in Nature" on the other, Moran characterizes his work-in-progress in terms that sound very much like those in which it was eventually reviewed. But where reviews of the painting would contrast its topographical accuracy with its artistic accomplishment, Moran is unable (and unwilling) to separate the two. Thus although he distinguishes between painting "topographical or geologic characteristics" and making "good pictures," his assertion that "the grandest or most beautiful, or wonderful in Nature would, in capable hands, make the grandest, most beautiful, or wonderful pictures" does not eschew topographical accuracy but demands it. Moran seeks Hayden's "judgment on the truth of the picture" precisely because his "knowledge of cause & effect in Nature, would point out . . . many facts connected with the place that [Moran] may have overlooked." This represents not empty flattery of someone from whom he is seeking a favor, but Moran's conviction that the greatness of a work of art is measured by its fidelity to nature.

Six years later, Moran would more fully work out his ideas of fidelity to nature in a "conversation" published in George Sheldon's *American Painters.* Defending the painter Turner from those who criticized his pictures as if they were mere "transcriptions of Nature," Moran explains that although "literally speaking, [Turner's] landscapes are false[,] they contain his impressions of Nature, and so many natural characteristics as were necessary adequately to convey that impression to others." Turner, Moran continues, "generalizes Nature always; . . . he sacrificed the literal truth of the parts to the higher truth of the whole. And he was right. Art is not nature; an aggregation of ten thousand facts may add nothing to a picture, but be rather the destruction of it. The literal truth counts for nothing; it is within the grasp of anyone who has had an ordinary art-education. The mere restatement of an external scene is never a work of art, is never a picture."[65]

Moran's defense of Turner is derived from Ruskin's own – particularly his dismissal of a merely literal or topographic art.[66] But at the same time that such statements as "topography in art is valueless" would support Turner's conviction that "Art is not Nature," Moran is careful simultaneously to insist on the literal truths of his *Grand Canyon* painting. Indeed Moran's request for Hayden's scientific judgment resulted in the extremely un-Turner-like consequence that "The rocks in the foreground are so carefully drawn that a geologist could determine their precise nature." Similarly, Moran is proud to be able to say that the painting is "so correct . . . that every member of the [Hayden] expedition . . . declared, when he saw the painting, that he knew the exact spot which had been reproduced."[67] Although, like Turner, Moran's goal is to "preserve and convey" to his viewers the "true impression" of a scene in nature, his fidelity to "pictorial Nature" carries with it a commitment to topographical accuracy. Unlike those who reviewed the *Grand Canyon of the Yellowstone* in terms of a strict opposition between topographical fidelity to nature and fidelity to the higher aims of art, Moran's notion of fidelity to pictorial nature resists this strict dichotomy between realism and idealism at the same time that it declares his allegiance to a Ruskinian aesthetic.

Moran's notion of pictorial fidelity derives in large part from the chapter on Turnerian topography in the fourth volume of *Modern Painters.* This chapter offers an account of truth to nature in which the artist begins neither with a literalistic copy nor with an imagined idea but with the impression made upon him by a particular scene. Ruskin cautions that the "poetical art" of Turnerian topography does not allow an artist to paint what he doesn't see:

If, therefore, when we go to a place, we see nothing else than is there, we are to paint nothing else, and to remain pure topographical or historical landscape painters. If, going to the place, we see something quite different from what is there, then we are to paint that – nay, we *must* paint that, whether we will or not; it being, for us, the only reality we can get at.[68]

Once an artist sets out to paint a simple topographical painting, Ruskin writes,

then not a line is to be altered, not a stick nor stone removed, not a color deepened, not a form improved; the picture is to be, as far as possible, the reflection of the place in a mirror; . . . so that it may be for ever afterwards in the power of all men to lean on his work with absolute trust, and to say: "So it was: – on such a day of June or July of such a year, such a place looked like this; these weeds were growing there, so tall and no taller; these stones were lying there, so many and no more; that tower so rose against the sky, and that shadow so slept upon the street."[69]

While in simple topography the artist begins with the documentary imitation of the facts of a particular scene on a particular day, in Turnerian topography "the artist who has real invention sets to work in a totally different way. First, he receives a true impression from the place itself, and takes care to keep hold of that as his chief good . . . ; and then he sets himself as far as possible to reproduce that impression on the mind of the spectator of his picture."[70] Where simple topography concerns itself with imitating an exterior landscape, Turnerian topography concerns itself with reproducing the impressions made upon the internal landscape of the artist.

Although in his discussion of "Ideas of Truth" elsewhere in *Modern Painters*,[71] Ruskin describes faithful imitation of the facts of nature as logically necessary and temporally prior to the reproduction of the moment of artistic perception, his discussion of Turnerian topography endeavors to classify the two forms of topographical truth as fundamentally, categorically distinct:

Any topographical delineation of the facts, therefore, must be wholly incapable of arousing in the mind of the beholder those sensations which would be caused by the facts themselves, seen in their natural relations to others. And the aim of the great inventive landscape painter must be to give the far higher and deeper truth of mental vision, rather than that of the physical facts, and to reach a representation which, though it may be totally useless to engineers, geographers, and, when tried by rule and measure, totally unlike the place, shall yet be capable of producing on the far-away beholder's mind precisely the impression which the reality would have produced.[72]

Such inconsistencies in Ruskin's text are often explained by describing Ruskin's aesthetic theories either as contradictory or, more charitably, as evolving over the course of the five volumes of *Modern Painters*. By understanding his thinking as inconsistent, these explanations miss the point: that Ruskin's attempt to distinguish the higher truth of Turnerian topography from the factual imitation of simple topography works to resist any meaningful categorical distinction between the two forms of topographical truth. In both the first and the fourth volumes, Ruskin is consistent in describing the aim of simple topography as placing the spectator where the painter himself stood in relation to the scene depicted in the painting. Similarly he is consistent in describing the result of this "conveyance" as reproducing not the ideas or emotions that the scene impressed upon the artist, but only the scene itself. But in insisting that both kinds of artists paint only what they see, he effectively refuses the categorical difference between the two kinds of topographical truth by implying that all true art both preserves the appearance of a particular natural scene at a particular historical moment and reproduces the impression that scene made upon the artist. That is, rather than being inconsistent, Ruskin is in fact remarkably consistent in his attempt to find a way to reconcile or at least hold in some uneasy alliance or relation, two contradictory notions of fidelity to nature.[73]

Thus, although Ruskin would at times confine simple topography to the realm of imitation, his description of the effects of topographical art on the spectator is of a piece with the dual logics not only of photographic and scientific fidelity to nature but also of the pictorial fidelity of Moran's *Grand Canyon of the Yellowstone*. Like photographs of Yellowstone's geothermal features, or Hayden's scientific descriptions, Moran's painting faithfully preserves a scene in nature at the same time that it reproduces for future generations "with absolute trust" the experience of having been there himself. And as an example of Turnerian topography, Moran's painting "brings before the public the true character of the region," by preserving and conveying to its spectators the "true impression" of "the gorgeous display of color that impressed itself upon" him.[74]

While Moran's insistence on the importance of color clearly allies him with Turner, color is also crucial in distinguishing his representations from those of Jackson and others, as Hayden himself maintains in the preface to an expensive and elaborate annotated 1876 edition of Moran chromolithographs of the Yellowstone region. Hayden notes in the preface that Yellowstone's "exquisite scenery" "has become tolerably well known to the public by photographs, and by illustrations in magazines and books." Nonetheless, he writes, these representations "were all wanting in one particular, which no woodcut, engraving, or photograph can supply": color. While all landscapes "must necessarily lose the greater part of their charm when deprived of color," Hayden contends, a black-and-white illustration of Yellowstone's scenery "is like *Hamlet* with the part of Hamlet omitted." "To a person who has not visited the Yellowstone and the territory adjacent to it," Hayden explains, "even the most vivid description is utterly insufficient to give an accurate idea of it, unless accompanied by colored illustrations." Paradoxically, however, both Moran's chromolithographs and Hayden's prose appear untruthful without "strong faith" from the reader. "So strange, indeed, are the freaks of color which nature indulges in habitually in this wonderful country," Hayden warns, "that it will no doubt require strong faith on the part of the reader in the truthfulness of both artist and writer to enable him unhesitatingly to accept the statements made in the present volume by the pen as well as by the brush."[75]

In the preliminary report for 1871 Hayden had recorded that Moran, too, had worried that even painting would be unable to represent faithfully the colors of Yellowstone's Grand Canyon: "Mr. Thomas Moran, a celebrated artist, and noted for his skill as a colorist, exclaimed, with a sort of regretful enthusiasm that these beautiful tints [of the Grand Canyon] were beyond the reach of human art . . . Mr. Moran is now engaged in transferring this remarkable picture to canvas, and by means of a skillful use of colors something like a conception of its beauty may be conveyed."[76] Moran's exclamation of "regretful enthusiasm" is not debilitating, however, but empowering. He responds to the sense that the colors of the Grand Canyon are beyond the reach of human art by determining to transfer "this remarkable picture to canvas, and by means of a skillful use of colors" to convey "something like a conception of its beauty." Like Hayden's inability to describe in words the excitement conveyed by the eruption of Old Faithful, Moran's "regretful enthusiasm that these beautiful tints were beyond the reach of human art" constitutes part of the impression produced upon him by the colors of Yellowstone's Grand Canyon. Moran's success at conveying this "regretful enthusiasm" can be inferred from William Blackmore's remark upon first seeing the canyon with Hayden's second survey of Yellowstone in 1872 that the "coloring" was "indescribable – Moran[']s picture in this respect perfectly faithful."[77] For Blackmore, as for Moran, fidelity to the coloring of the canyon means faithfully conveying the impression of its "indescribability." And paradoxically to be faithful to the impression of indescribability is to fail to be faithful to its coloring.

As Ruskin's notion of an artist's true impression of a place implies, however, the fidelity of Moran's *Grand Canyon* in conveying his impression of the scene could never have been produced by the "mere piece of scenery which can be included within the limits of the picture. It depends on the temper into which the mind has been brought, both by all the landscape round, and by what has been seen previously in the course of the day; so that no particular spot upon which the painter's glance may at any moment fall, is then to him what, if seen by itself, it will be to the spectator far away."[78] Ruskin's sense that the true impression of a landscape cannot be produced merely by the particular details of its scenery is similar to Olmsted's contention that no verbal description or visual representation of the particular features of the Yosemite landscape can truly account for its aesthetic effect. But where Olmsted understands the experience of natural beauty in a public park to consist in having one's mind occupied without purpose, for Ruskin the goal of experiencing a representation of the landscape is to receive an impression similar to that of the artist. In other words, where Olmsted would elide both the specificity of the scene and the purposefulness of both artist and spectator, Ruskin would have the artist seek to preserve, or represent faithfully, the impression created on him by the landscape and to reproduce that impression in the viewer. To define Turnerian topography as historical topography passed through the temper of the artist's mind is thus also to describe the aesthetic paradigm Moran worked under in commemorating both the Hayden survey's "official" historical discovery of Yellowstone and the more mythical encounter between European and Native Americans in the Western wilderness. In seeking to reproduce the impression the canyon's scenery produced upon him, Moran's *Grand Canyon* incorporates a variety of scenic elements and figures – the Grand Tetons, geysers, the unidentified Indian, a wounded deer, and a bear – that have as much to do with his desire "to bring before the public the character of that region" as with his desire to represent exactly what he saw when he first encountered the canyon. The composite nature of his painting allows Moran to represent elements that reflected not only the temper of his mind on that day but also the temper of the survey more generally. In so doing he does not simply reproduce what a spectator of his painting would have seen "if he had come to the reality through the steps which Nature has appointed to be the preparation for it, instead of seeing it isolated on an exhibition wall." Rather he attempts to reproduce the impression that Yellowstone's Grand Canyon made upon him as a member of the first "official" government survey of the Yellowstone region, an impression that included his "regretful enthusiasm" that the canyon's colors were "beyond the reach of human art."

If we examine the compositional strategy of Moran's painting, however, we can see that his "regretful enthusiasm" extends beyond the inability to represent the canyon's colors. Rather than depicting the canyon as seen from a single point of view, Moran incorporates a number of scenic elements both from his own sketches and from different Jackson photographs of the region. For example, the view of the canyon that dominates the painting derives from a photograph that Jackson took while his camera faced away from the falls at which the viewer of the painting directly looks.[79] But Moran's painting represents a compilation of representational conventions as well. Moran incorporates Jackson's photographs partly to attempt in a single canvas something like the comprehensiveness of the survey experience that Jackson strived for in his photographic archive. But where the goal of the archive is accretive and cumulative, the goal of Moran's painting, similar to Jackson's stereoscopic images, is to capture in a single (albeit quite large) image a true impression of his experience of Yellowstone's Grand Canyon. Simultaneously conveying his impression of the natural scene and compensating for the limitations of human art, Moran incorporates elements of a number of the representational conventions employed by various members of the Hayden Survey. To understand his painting as scientifically accurate or faithful in its representations is to understand Moran's awareness of the way fidelity to nature is constituted differently by different forms or technologies of pictorial or graphic representation. In the *Grand Canyon of the Yellowstone*, representational fidelity is constituted both as resemblance to nature and as conformity to prior conventions. That is, its resemblance to nature is constituted by and through its resemblance to a variety of conventional representational techniques.

The least unexpected of these techniques is the conventional tripartite Claudean organization of the space of the canvas into foreground, middle ground, and background. The extended rock-ledge in the lower left corner of the painting provides the traditional point of view for the painting's spectator. But it also serves as the spectator's entrance both to the stage on which Hayden and Stevenson enact the survey's business and to the vantage point at the edge of the canyon on which the unidentified survey member and the mythical Indian are perched. Although much of what this survey member gestures towards is visible to a spectator of the painting, at least some portion of it is blocked by the trees that frame the painting on the

19 Thomas Moran, *Grand Canyon of the Yellowstone* (detail)

left. Nonetheless, the walls of the canyon function as a traditional middle ground. The painting's vanishing point is shrouded in the mist that rises from the falls, where the "V"-shape of the canyon walls extends almost indefinitely into the depths of the picture (see Figure 19).

But Moran challenges mid-nineteenth-century landscape conventions as much as he follows them. Practically the largest object in the picture-space is in the lower-right-hand corner – a huge rock formation jutting out from next to a gothic-looking, ghostly dead tree (see Figure 11). The effect of this formation mimics the effect sought in stereographs, where near objects are used not to frame the picture in the conventional sense but rather to produce the stereoscopic illusion of three-dimensionality in which depth is provided from multiple focal points. This is also true of the tree, whose three left-hand branches protrude towards the viewer, the lower one disappearing off the bottom right corner of the picture into the abyss of the canyon that divides the rock platform of the left foreground from the rocks on the right. Similarly the painting alludes to the stereo-effect in the progression of tree groupings that proceeds from the lower-right-hand corner diagonally into the center of the picture to the edge of the canyon. Depth is provided not only by the central vanishing point in the mist above the falls, but also by the fact that the composite perspective of the painting creates several focal points. The act of moving from one focal point to another employs the representational technology of landscape painting to imitate the kind of depth or perspective effect sought in a good stereographic image.

Conceptually, the painting can be seen to incorporate an archival effect as well. "The canvas is a virtual panorama, encompassing a much wider view of the scene than would be possible even with a camera's wide-angle lens or the natural peripheral vision of an individual standing at the site."[80] This panoramic quality contains a cartographic impulse, in which objects like the geyser-basin in the distance are placed roughly where they would be located if they could be seen from the point from which the scene was painted. Although the composite nature of Moran's painting makes problematic the location of such a point on a map, the three geyser plumes on the left horizon rising parallel to the central vanishing point of the falls suggest the possibility of yet other vanishing points as well. In other words, if the painting has multiple vanishing points it must also have multiple station points for the artist or viewer. This effect of multiple vanishing points is repeated by the three Tetons depicted next to but far beyond the geysers. The Tetons serve to suggest even further vanishing points, which not only imply the existence of further scenes, but map these scenes in terms of an archive of pictures or views like this one.

To describe Moran's painting as incorporating a cartographic effect, however, is not to imply that the painting visually resembles a map. Thus, although the space of the canvas is structured with a number of strong verticals (the pine trees on the left, the trees and rocks on the right, the trees throughout the canyon, the falls, and the basalt cliffs on the right), the sky and the horizon are the only strong horizontals. And any suggestion of a map-like or grid-like structure gives way to the brightly colored walls of the "V"-shaped canyon. In calling attention to the cartographic effect of Moran's painting, I mean to indicate its commitment to the scientific, photographic, and cartographic logics of fidelity to nature that inform Hayden's surveys. That is to say, in seeking out Hayden's scientific judgment in respect to his painting, Moran is not simply asking Hayden to affirm the topographical accuracy of his depiction of geological details, but asking him to affirm the fidelity of Moran's painting to Hayden's scientific understanding of the origins and character of Yellowstone's remarkable geothermal features.

Following the predominant geological paradigms of the late nineteenth century, Hayden understands Yellowstone as fundamentally a dying landscape, its geysers and hot springs the geothermal remnants of "the vast crater of an ancient volcano," "the scene of as great volcanic activity as that of any portion of the globe."[81] Hayden explains that "the hot springs and geysers of this region, at the present time, are nothing more than the closing stages of that wonderful period of volcanic action that began in Tertiary times. In other words, they are the escape pipes or vents for those internal forces which once were so active, but are now continually dying out."[82] These geysers and hot springs, Hayden explains, "have continued to decline down to the present time, and will do so in the future, until they cease entirely . . . We may therefore conclude that the present system of hot springs and geysers is only a feebler manifestation of those remarkable internal forces of the earth, which were so wonderfully intensified during the periods of volcanic activity, that they really present for our study a miniature form of *volcanism*."[83] If, as Roland Barthes came to realize, the photograph of an object announces the object's death, then we might want to say that the *punctum* of Yellowstone's geysers is that they announce the loss of that "wonderful period of volcanic action that began in Tertiary times," the absence of "the scene of as great volcanic activity as that of any portion of the globe." And in their uniqueness, the geysers mark the loss of each particular eruption as well.

In a report for the Committee on Public Lands regarding the bill to set aside Yellowstone as a national park, Hayden reiterates the fact that the hot springs and geysers "represent the last stages – the vents or escape pipes – of these remarkable volcanic manifestations of the internal forces." Although they are dying out, that is all the more reason that they should be preserved. Because they are "adorned with decorations more beautiful than human art ever conceived, and which have required thousands of years for the cunning hand of nature to form," it is incumbent upon the United States government to preserve them for future generations.[84] Indeed in some real sense their imminent disappearance (in geological time) becomes not only the reason that Yellowstone's geothermal features should be preserved but the very experience that their preservation aims to reproduce. Because he ascribes the coloration of the canyon to the chemical composition of the volcanic deposits out of and through which the canyon is carved, Hayden also emphasizes that the colors that Moran thinks of as beyond the reach of human art are themselves remnants or traces of the region's volcanism, the record of a more glorious and powerful geological past, "which have required thousands of years for the cunning hand of nature to form." Thus

in urging the preservation of Yellowstone as a national park, Hayden urges
the preservation of geothermal phenomena that are always dying out, that
are in many ways already lost. And in conveying the impression produced
upon him by the glorious colors of Yellowstone's Grand Canyon, Moran
means not only to convey his regretful enthusiasm about the limitations of
human art but also to reproduce his sense that, like the hand of the painter,
the "cunning hand of nature" announces the loss or death of that which it
would represent.

"BAD MEDICINE"

The nexus of Yellowstone, loss, and fidelity to nature is also central to
Owen Wister's melodramatic short story, "Bad Medicine."[85] Published in
1928, "Bad Medicine" represents the park as a "vignette of primitive America," reproducing the wonder at the moment of discovery embodied in
the preservation of Yellowstone in 1872. Told in the first person, the story
concerns a hunting trip undertaken by the narrator, his friend George
Tews, their reluctant Shoshone guide Sun Road, and his son Little Chief
Hare. Opening with the narrator's arrival at Fort Washakie to meet up with
George, take on supplies, and hire a guide, the narrative moves inexorably
towards Yellowstone National Park. The "Bad Medicine" of the title refers
both to photography and to the Yellowstone region's geothermal features.
The story plays upon two common nineteenth-century cultural conceptions of Native American superstitions: that "taking a person's likeness"
stole away "some part of his strength or spirit";[86] and that "the geysers
and the smells and the rumblings" of Yellowstone "had terrorized all red
men until the white man came and confronted the infernal powers without
harm."[87] When the narrator first sees Sun Road and Little Chief Hare at
Fort Washakie, he seeks to "catch" their "wildness" with his "kodak," but
before he can press the shutter they "had vanished noiseless in their moc-
casins among the trees."[88] After overcoming both his fear of the narrator's
kodak, and his hesitation at the prospect of going into the Yellowstone
region, Sun Road agrees that he and his son will accompany the hunters.

The story focuses on the way in which Sun Road, who as a boy had spent
five years learning the culture and the language of the white man in Carlisle,
begins to reconsider his superstitions about both cameras and geysers. When
Sun Road sings "a ballad of war, of the victory of the Shoshones over the
Blackfeet in Warm Springs Cave," George explains that "at some time or
other, the cave had been an active geyser; geysers were 'bad medicine.'"[89]
After the narrator responds that "the cave had not proved bad medicine

for the Shoshones," and that it would be better for Sun Road "to begin dropping some of those ideas he had brought along," he discovers a sign the next morning that Sun Road may be doing just that: "while George was posing for a picture of him throwing the diamond hitch, Sun Road, instead of holding aloof from all such operations as 'bad medicine,' came up and watched intently."[90] When the party arrives at Warm Springs Cave, Sun Road again watches the narrator take a picture of George in front of the cave, then accompanies the two white men inside. Running his hand through the tepid water, the narrator dislodges "what was left of a piece of human jaw," remarking to Sun Road: "'Bad medicine for Blackfeet.'"[91] When Sun Road responds, "'Heap bad medicine for Blackfeet,'" the narrator is overjoyed that Sun Road might be "subjecting" his superstitions "to some dawning criticism": "He was already almost as curious as he was suspicious about kodaks. Bad Medicine! What a good word!"[92] But where Sun Road might be willing to reconsider his superstitions for himself, he draws a "very singular" line "between himself and Little Chief Hare," even though, the narrator points out, Sun Road wished that, like himself, his son would "go to Carlisle, to be made like the white man."[93]

As the party enters Yellowstone, Sun Road persists in what the narrator describes as his "double state of mind."[94] When "cameras were pointed at our Indians" at the Thumb of Yellowstone Lake, the narrator records, "Sun Road flung a blanket over Little Chief Hare, and I requested that we be let alone."[95] Yet Sun Road also "began gradually to investigate the paint pots heaving up continuously their viscous discharges," even going so far as to allow Little Chief Hare to cook some of his freshly caught trout in the boiling water of one of the hot springs.[96] As the party follows the road from one tourist attraction to another, however, Sun Road shies from the kodaks, making himself "inconspicuous among the pack horses, while George Tews took his place" in the lead: "The figure of George in his cowboy dress evoked sufficient excitement and admiration when stages drove by," the narrator notes, "and I imagine that his likeness may be seen today in many American homes."[97]

Once the party reaches Inspiration Point at Yellowstone's Grand Canyon, however, Sun Road's fate as an object of photography is sealed. While Sun Road "stood far out at the end of the point gazing at the falls, and the majestic world of crag and tawny citadel and saffron minaret into which their waters descended," the narrator noticed a lovely "young lady watching Sun Road more than she watched the view."[98] Identifying the Native American figure with the Canyon, the young lady exclaims: "'How handsome, how superb! He is a part of all this. How I should like to see him in Indian dress! I shouldn't think of taking his picture without his permission, and I would never find the courage to ask him.'"[99] But when the young lady subsequently encounters Sun Road in native dress at Mammoth Hot Springs, she finds the courage, prompting him to assent: "'I like you to do what you wish.'"[100] Placing himself "where the light favored . . . as he was asked," Sun Road "stiffened, straight, facing the instrument, controlled from head to foot. At the click of the machine," the narrator writes, "I saw his taut muscles respond as if a galvanic current had struck them."[101] While Sun Road persists in protecting Little Chief Hare from the camera, "after that final breaking down of his opposition at the Mammoth Springs, he ceased to hide himself from the general curiosity; nor was it long – not two days – before the notice he attracted began to give him pleasure, and to be courted . . . Before we had reached the Norris Basin, the sight of each approaching party no longer aroused aversion, but expectancy, in Sun Road: always in the lead, he seemed to sit a little more erect, to become a little more a prince of the wilderness; and it was now his likeness, not George's, that travelers carried away upon their films."[102]

As Barthes notes in *Camera Lucida*, "once I feel myself observed by the lens, everything changes: I constitute myself in the process of 'posing,' I instantaneously make another body for myself, I transform myself in advance into an image. This transformation is an active one: I feel that the Photograph creates my body or mortifies it, according to its caprice."[103] At first the "caprice" of being photographed "creates" Sun Road's body. Transforming himself into an image enables Sun Road to "sit a little more erect," to acquire an increased sense of himself as "a prince of the wilderness." It seems also to bring about what Barthes describes (following the logic of Lacan's "mirror stage") as "the advent of myself as other: a cunning dissociation of consciousness from identity."[104] But if Sun Road had begun to give up some of his superstitions about photography, the narrator seemed to be acquiring them for himself, fearing that "in truth" the photographic likenesses of Sun Road "had drained out of him a portion of himself, something that he had been was gone, as if he had lost his spiritual virginity."[105] For as Barthes explains about having his portrait taken, "the Photograph (the one I *intend*) represents that very subtle moment when, to tell the truth, I am neither subject nor object but a subject who feels he is becoming an object: I then experience a micro-version of death (of parenthesis): I am truly becoming a specter."[106] Despite the fear that Sun Road "had lost his spiritual virginity," however, the narrator recognized that "something of the untainted Sun Road persisted," so that when the "official photographer" at the Upper Geyser Basin seeks to take the party's picture, Sun Road again refuses to "expose [Little Chief Hare] to the eye of civilization," refuses to let him recognize himself as other, to let him experience the "dissociation of consciousness from identity" that Sun Road himself experienced both at the white man's school in Carlisle and in front of the tourists' cameras in Yellowstone."[107]

"Bad Medicine" reaches its end in the twilight at Old Faithful, where the official photographer seeks to take a portrait of Sun Road's "figure alone, without the rest of us, for his collection on sale."[108] Choosing Old Faithful "'as an appropriate background for your Indian chief,'" the photographer sets up his apparatus for a flash picture, while Sun Road dons his "war crest" of "eagle feathers," completing his own transformation into "part of all this," into the image of "a prince of the wilderness," the image that the young lady had longed for at Inspiration Point.[109] As Old Faithful prepares to erupt, "Sun Road waited, absorbed, rigid; a figure, even in this dusk, wholly different from the city-bred shapes which had lined themselves to look on from behind."[110] This time, however, the caprice of the photograph does not create Sun Road's body but "mortifies" it, as the narrator recounts:

I saw the column of Old Faithful shoot up, and a blinding flare follow like a stroke of lightning. Like lightning, it left me for a moment sightless; the whole scene vanished in an obscurity through which the roar of the geyser resounded. Then I began to see again. The figure of Sun Road was no longer there. The camera stood where it had been. I looked at that, and at Old Faithful, now at the climax of its fury. Then I grew aware of a confusion beyond the camera, and shouts were raised, and I saw the man running from his camera, and I began to run. When I had got over the bridge and again to the level of the formation, I saw a group shouting more desperately, and wildly waving arms. Next, beyond this, I discovered Sun Road as I came among them. Then I began to shout. The Indian heeded neither voices nor gestures. With his head thrown back as if in defiance, his eyes were fixed upon the geyser; and nothing else in the world existed for him. As he watched this portent, for which he had been so utterly unprepared, and whose arrival from the depths below had apparently been attended by lightning from above, if he was aware of us at all, it is likely that he thought our terror was on our own account, and not for him. He stood on the hollow crust from which visitors were warned away. The column of water sank to half height, because its force was spent; but Sun Road must have taken this as a threat of some kind, as if the shaft was about to step down from its pedestal, and come in search of him; for he made an abrupt and backward start. At this, a rending crack went across the crust where he had sprung, and the whole surface gave way. The tall figure sank with it, stretching his arms to Little Chief Hare, and clouds of steam burst from the cavern into which he had gone, and everything was hidden from our sight.[111]

Sun Road, Wister might seem to suggest, was right. Photography and gey-sers were indeed "bad medicine." But as a fairly accomplished photographer himself, Wister (like his narrator) might just as readily assent to Barthes' reminder that photography is always about the *punctum* of loss. Indeed Sun Road's official portrait produces a *punctum* of another sort – not in the viewer but in the photograph's subject-become-object. Or more precisely the portrait's subject-become-object produces this *punctum* in nature itself, as the "rending crack went across the crust where [Sun Road] had sprung, and the whole surface gave way."

Reading Wister's story in light of Barthes' analysis of the *punctum* and the *studium* suggests that, just as the act of photographing Yellowstone announces the death or destruction of the photographed landscape, so the act of preservation, as an act of representation, acknowledges both that Yellowstone was a certain way at a particular time and that it will not be the same way again. And just as the preservation of the Yellowstone landscape announces the loss of that landscape, so the photographic reproduction of Sun Road announces his loss as well. In the Native American encounter with Western technologies of representation, the preservation of the im-age of the Native American is simultaneously the acknowledgment of the Native American's loss. Similarly the preservation of Yellowstone as a faith-ful representation of nature is simultaneously the announcement of the destruction or disappearance of the Native Americans who inhabited the land previously. The preservation of Yellowstone entails not, as the young lady of "Bad Medicine" thinks, Sun Road as "part of all this," but rather Sun Road's absence or death, his disappearance from "all this." Or more precisely the preservation of Yellowstone *is* the preservation of Sun Road as "part of all this," but as his death emblemizes, to be part of Yellowstone is to be dead, gone, absent – swallowed up by the landscape both in the sense that he is part of it, that is, not alien to it, and in the sense that, like the landscape, he, too, embodies the dying out of a prior historical forma-tion. As Hayden's account of Yellowstone's geological history attests, loss did not come to Yellowstone as a consequence of its discovery by European Americans; loss is what they found waiting for them in the Yellowstone landscape.

If loss is that which European Americans encountered in the moment of historical discovery that I have been arguing is paradigmatic of the experience of Yellowstone National Park, then how are we to make sense of the conjunction of representational fidelity and the desire to preserve this moment of loss? In a discussion of the Lacanian symptom, Slavoj Zizek points the way to an illuminating gloss on what we might characterize as the "ideological fantasy" entailed in Yellowstone's preservation as a national park. Arguing that the "repressed content" of the Lacanian symptom returns "from the future and not from the past," Zizek explains:

The past exists as it is included, as it enters (into) the synchronous net of the signifier – that is, as it is symbolized in the texture of the historical memory – and that is why we are all the time "rewriting history," retroactively giving the elements their symbolic weight by including them in new textures – it is this elaboration which decides retroactively what they "will have been."[112]

Although the preservation of Yellowstone was (and still is) figured accord-ing to a twofold logic of representational fidelity to nature, in which nature is conceived of both as historically prior to and as a consequence of the act of representation, what counts as a faithful representation is variable both through time and across different discursive domains. Because in Yellow-stone nature is always already transformed into something else, any single manifestation of representational fidelity (whether preservation, science, or photography) must reproduce the past at the same time that it announces the future. Hayden's scientific representation of Yellowstone's geology both records the glorious volcanic past and announces that it will be no more. Similarly, Jackson's photographic archive both records the history of the Yellowstone survey's discoveries and tells the beholder that the Yellowstone landscape will never be seen as it was when it was first photographed. The moment of historical, scientific, or aesthetic discovery that the preservation of Yellowstone seeks to reproduce is inevitably experienced as a moment of loss, as symptomatic of a collective national trauma, the meaning of which is "not discovered, excavated from the hidden depths of the past, but constructed retroactively."[113]

It is precisely this process of retroactively rewriting history that is at work in the Leopold report – and that still obtains as a goal of National Park management policy at the end of the twentieth century. In attempting both to reproduce the biotic associations that existed before Yellowstone was discovered by white men, and to restage the moment when these biotic associations were lost forever, the Leopold report can be seen to reenact what, following Zizek, we might want to describe as the basic paradox of the American national subject, in which

the subject is confronted with a scene from the past that he wants to change, to meddle with, to intervene in; he takes a journey into the past, intervenes in the scene, and it is not that he "cannot change anything" – quite the contrary, only through his intervention does the scene from the past *become what it always was*: his intervention was from the beginning comprised, included. The initial "illusion" of the subject consists in simply forgetting to include in the scene his own act – that is, to overlook how "it counts, it is counted, and the one who counts is already included in the account."[114]

The scene that the Leopold report seeks to change is the moment of Yellowstone's first discovery by white men. The intervention that the Leopold Committee seeks to bring about is the recreation of the biotic associations that prevailed at the moment of Yellowstone's discovery, even while operating under the illusion that its own intervention in the scene doesn't count. To reproduce the moment of historical discovery in Yellowstone, however, is not to confront a national trauma that the parkgoing subject is powerless to change, but rather to recognize that it is only through the subject's intervention that Yellowstone can become what it always was. The reproduction of the moment of discovery does not mark the disappearance of the biotic associations that prevailed when the first white men arrived in the area, but the recognition that it is only through the repeated interventions of the parkgoing subject that Yellowstone becomes what it always was – America's first national park.

3

Recognizing the Grand Canyon: naming, sublimity, and the limits of mediation

In 1869 – one year before the Washburn Expedition discovered the geysers of Yellowstone and two years before the Hayden Expedition officially surveyed them – Major John Wesley Powell and his crew became the first known humans (European, American, Native American, or otherwise) to navigate the Colorado River through the entire Grand Canyon.[1] Where the Washburn and Hayden Expeditions astounded Americans back East with spectacular verbal descriptions and pictorial illustrations of Yellowstone's rumored, but hitherto undiscovered, geysers, Powell and his men accomplished something more mythical: they filled in "the last white space on the map" by successfully exploring "the last great unmapped and unknown part of the continental United States."[2] In 1872, the year after Hayden's first government-sponsored expedition, Congress made Yellowstone the world's first national park. But it wasn't until 1919, fifty years after Powell's first exploration, that Congress made Grand Canyon a national park. It is true that parts of what is now Grand Canyon National Park were set aside as a national forest as early as 1893; that a game preserve was established in the area in 1906; and that the Grand Canyon was proclaimed a national monument by President Theodore Roosevelt in 1908. Nonetheless, there is still reason to wonder why it took so long for Congress to make the Grand Canyon a national park.[3]

Clearly, it was not for lack of the idea. Indeed, in 1874 when Congress purchased *The Chasm of the Colorado*, Thomas Moran's second "big picture," to hang as a pendant to 1872's *Grand Canyon of the Yellowstone*, it would have seemed inevitable to many Congressmen that the Grand Canyon itself would soon join Yellowstone as a pendant park.[4] Nor was Congressional failure to make Grand Canyon a national park due to lack of trying. Three proposals to establish Grand Canyon National Park were brought to Congress by Indiana Senator Benjamin Harrison between 1882 and 1886. In 1910 and 1911, with the support of President Taft, California Senator Frank P. Flint introduced two more bills to create Grand Canyon National Park. Finally, a year after the establishment of the National Park Service in 1916, bills were introduced in both the House and Senate to create a national park at Grand Canyon. On February 26, 1919, President Woodrow Wilson signed the Senate bill into law. Why did it take so long for Grand Canyon to become a national park?

The delay is often explained in terms of competing political and economic interests or by noting that physical inaccessibility protected the region from social, economic, and technological development, thus precluding the need for preservation. Not only did the river and inner gorge present significant obstacles to human exploration, but the entire region was remote and relatively hard to get to in the 1870s. Where Yellowstone was just off of the proposed northern branch of Jay Cooke's Northern Pacific Railroad, and within 100 miles of the burgeoning frontier town of Bozeman, in the Montana territory, neither the south nor the north rim of the Grand Canyon was nearly so accessible. As persuasive as these explanations are, they leave out another important element of the story: that the landscape of the Grand Canyon is cognitively as well as physically inaccessible. In pointing this out, I do not mean to suggest that the reason it took fifty years to make the Grand Canyon a national park was because it was difficult to comprehend. Nor do I mean to claim that the establishment of Grand Canyon National Park in 1919 succeeded in making the Grand Canyon landscape easier to understand. Rather I mean that from its exploration by Powell to this very day, the Grand Canyon has been characterized as cognitively inaccessible – and that the preservation of this inaccessibility is critical to the establishment and continued attraction of Grand Canyon National Park.[5]

One consequence of this cognitive inaccessibility involves the possibility of recognition: can you recognize something if it has not already been cognized? In the history of the canyon the question of recognition functions on a number of different levels. In perhaps the most rudimentary sense, the problem of recognizing the Grand Canyon concerns the fact that, as Stephen Pyne notes, when you approach the rim the landscape provides virtually no indications that the canyon is there.

It is possible to pass within a score of miles, or sometimes of meters, from that rim and never see the gorge, and more than one traveler has done just that. There is no measured transition: the plateau instantly ends; the canyon instantly begins . . . No impression of the place is more constantly invoked than the abruptness of its vision, a perspective almost wholly formed upon first view.[6]

But Pyne also notes that even when seen, the canyon is not immediately recognized. In 1540, when an exploring party led by García López de Cárdenas, the first European explorers to encounter the canyon, arrived at the South Rim, Pyne writes, they were conceptually unequipped to comprehend what they were seeing: "the Spanish had little context for the revelation of the Canyon."[7] Nor were they alone in this. Although the canyon was "among the earliest of North America's natural wonders to be visited," it "was among the last of these wonders to be assimilated, much less celebrated."[8] Early explorers were unable to recognize either the geographical extent of the canyon or the extent of its future appeal as a tourist destination. Indeed as late as 1857–1858, when Lieutenant Joseph Ives navigated the canyon up-river from its mouth to discover the limits of the Colorado's navigability, he was unable to imagine that anybody else could be interested in the Grand Canyon. Having reached what he determined to be its navigable limits, Ives concluded:

The region last explored is, of course, altogether valueless. It can be approached only from the south, and after entering it there is nothing to do but to leave. Ours has been the first, and will doubtless be the last, party of whites to visit this profitless locality. It seems intended by nature that the Colorado river, along the greater portion of its lonely and majestic way, shall be forever unvisited and undisturbed.[9]

I cite Ives here not to lampoon him for failing to foresee that the Grand Canyon would some day become the most visited of America's national parks, but to note that the unavailability of the trope of the canyon's cognitive inaccessibility (as well as the area's physical inaccessibility) made it impossible for Ives to have conceived what would make the Grand Canyon arguably the most famous natural feature of the United States.

The logic of recognition informing the idea of the Grand Canyon's cognitive inaccessibility has its origins in the aesthetic of the Kantian sublime, an aesthetic that has structured (and in some senses, I would argue, continues to structure) the almost innumerable representations of the Grand Canyon landscape in the American cultural imagination. The multiple representations that arise out of the early years of the Grand Canyon's exploration work both to dramatize the difficulty of human thought or action to comprehend the canyon or to celebrate the appropriation of the canyon by its early explorers. Where the cultural discourse surrounding the preservation of Yosemite repeatedly elided and reproduced the signs of human agency in the representation of the park, and where a twofold logic of fidelity to nature constituted the goal of representation in the formation of Yellowstone National Park, the incomprehensibility of the canyon gives rise not to a paucity of representation but to a proliferation of attempts, by a variety of conceptual and technological media, to make sense of it. In this chapter I trace out the articulation of a cultural logic of re-cognition in which the canyon is constituted as cognitively inaccessible. I undertake what might be called a genealogy of recognition – looking at the proliferation of attempts within different technological media and conceptual frameworks to recognize the Grand Canyon. In characterizing the Grand Canyon as cognitively inaccessible, I do not mean to suggest that the canyon is in some metaphysical sense impossible to cognize or comprehend. Rather I mean to suggest that part of what it means to comprehend the canyon is to experience the sense that it somehow eludes or even transcends comprehension, that it must be re-cognized in order to be cognized at all. Strictly speaking, then, the canyon is cognitively accessible – albeit according to a different cultural logic than Yosemite or Yellowstone. But like the sublime, which manifests itself in relation to the Grand Canyon according to a logic of recognition, this experience of the Canyon's incomprehensibility seems almost inevitably to be followed by a proliferation of attempts at re-cognition.

These attempts to mediate or represent the Canyon's cognitive inaccessibility should not be seen as immediate or intuitive responses to the canyon's sublimity; rather they need to be understood according to the cultural logic of recognition articulated most prominently by Powell and Clarence Dutton, who worked under Powell's geological and geographical survey of the Grand Canyon region. Powell and Dutton were instrumental in articulating a logic of recognition in which it is necessary repeatedly to cognize or re-cognize the Grand Canyon. Although this multiplication of diverse perspectives occurs in part because no single cognition or cognitive frame is able to capture or fully comprehend the canyon, the sense of the canyon's cognitive inaccessibility is not overcome by this plurality of perceptual frames but rather is dramatized by them. I begin my discussion with Powell himself, whose multiple representations of his explorations of the Grand Canyon region both underscore the inability of human thought or action to comprehend the canyon and celebrate his own achievement in going where no (white) man had gone before.[10] I then turn to the verbal and visual technologies of representation at work in Clarence Dutton's *Tertiary History of the Grand Canon District*, not only his scientific and aesthetic prose descriptions, but also the landscape illustrations of Thomas Moran, the photographs of Jack Hillers, and the panoramic illustrations that William Henry Holmes created for the *Tertiary History* and its accompanying *Atlas*. The chapter concludes with a discussion of three cinematic attempts to "remediate" the canyon as a way to consider some of the different ways in which a logic of recognition still persists today: the 1911–1913 attempts by the Kolb Brothers to use early motion picture technology to capture the experience of running the Colorado River through the Grand Canyon; the 1984 IMAX film that greets tourists at the gateway to Grand Canyon National Park; and Lawrence Kasdan's 1991 film *Grand Canyon*.

THE NECESSITY OF NAMING

One of the fruits of Powell's heroic achievement was the right to name what he and his men discovered, an Adamic act that in itself would respond to the canyon's cognitive inaccessibility by appropriating and thereby making accessible the canyon's sublime features. Powell's naming practices participate in the structure of recognition I have been describing. His initial response to the canyon is in many respects the standard response of an explorer in making what he has explored recognizable – to name the features of the explored territory and to bring back verbal descriptions, maps, and illustrations of them so that these features can be recognized by others who follow, whether explorers, capitalists, scientists, artists, or tourists. Of the variety of representations brought back by Powell, naming is in some senses the fundamental form of representation through which people are enabled to recognize the landscape and its features. Indeed subsequent scientific or cultural cognition of the region is dependent upon the recognition of its features made possible by Powell's naming. Naming is essential to the process of recognition that follows his exploration, whether that recognition occurs back East in the centers of capital and calculation or in the field in return trips by subsequent scientific or other explorations. But naming also works to enable a broader cultural recognition, in which illustrations and other representations permit the Grand Canyon to circulate within the discursive practices of knowledge production in postbellum American culture.

Although at first glance the naming practices that Powell describes seem random and haphazard, he clearly gave a good deal of thought to the question of naming. Every time he and his men name a natural feature, Powell furnishes a reason for the name they choose. Indeed, in a journal entry from June 21, Powell provides some insight into how thoughtfully they considered the question of naming:

At night we camp at the mouth of a small creek, which affords us a good supper of trout. In camp, to-night, we discuss the propriety of several different names for this cañon. At the falls, encountered at noon, its characteristics change suddenly. Above, it is very narrow, and the walls are almost vertical; below, the cañon is much wider, and more flaring; and, high up on the sides, crags, pinnacles, and towers are seen. A number of wild, narrow side cañons enter, and the walls are much broken. After many suggestions, our choice rests between two names, Whirlpool Cañon and Craggy Cañon, neither of which is strictly appropriate for both parts of it; but we leave the discussion at this point, with the understanding that it is best, before finally deciding on a name, to wait until we see what the cañon is below.[11]

Powell and his men see themselves operating according to a logic of naming under which their object was to provide a name appropriate to what the 1895 version of this passage calls the "character" of the canyon being named.[12] Because the canyon in which they are camped does not seem to have a unified character, Powell and his men are stymied. They decide to wait until they can get to know its character more fully, which they do by the next day when they "decide to call the canyon above, Whirlpool Cañon."[13]

In the philosophy of language the descriptivist account of naming holds that a name refers to the object it identifies because of some cluster of descriptive attributes possessed by this object, what John Searle has called its "identifying description."[14] Like the above passage on the "propriety of naming," most of the instances of naming recorded by Powell can be seen to operate according to this descriptivist account, in which names are chosen because of "some uniquely identifying marks, some unique properties satisfied by the referent and known or believed to be true of that referent by the speaker."[15] Thus, features like Red Canyon, Gray Canyon, Rainbow Park, and Vermilion Cliffs are named for their coloration.[16] Still other features are named for their shape or size – for example, Split Mountain Canyon, Trin-Alcove Bend, or Narrow Canyon.[17] Some names are given on account of resemblance: Horseshoe Canyon looks like a horseshoe; "Bowknot Bend" is named for the "figure 8" shape of the course of the river bed through what the men call "Labyrinth Canyon"; and "tower cliffs" lead them to name an expansion of the river "Tower Park."[18] An interesting instance of these descriptivist namings by resemblance occurs when the sight of "a butte in the form of a fallen cross" prompts the men "to note its position on [their] map and name it 'The Butte of the Cross.'" What makes this name interesting is that even though Powell and his men later discover that the "butte with its wonderful form, is indeed two buttes, one so standing in front of the other that from [their] last point of view it gave the appearance of a cross," the "butte" is still so-named in the illustration of it in both the

20 John Wesley Powell, *Butte of the Cross*

1875 and 1895 editions of Powell's narrative of the exploration.[19] The Butte of the Cross may not describe a feature of the landscape but it does provide an apt name for one of Powell's illustrations (Figure 20).[20]

Descriptivism manifests itself in other forms as well, such as those places named not for how they appear but for their natural inhabitants. Kingfisher Creek, Park, and Canyon are so named because Powell and his men saw kingfishers playing there.[21] Swallow Canyon is so named because "a vast number of swallows have built their adobe houses on the face of the cliffs, on either side of the river" – this despite the fact that earlier in the voyage Beehive Point was also named for swallows which, flitting around the cliffs, "look like swarms of bees, giving to the whole the appearance of a colossal beehive of the old-time form."[22] Other places are named for their natural attributes. Gypsum Canyon is named for the "great quantities of gypsum [that] are found at the bottom of the gorge"; Glen Canyon for the "oak glens" that grow along the curves of the canyon's various "brooklets."[23] Marble Canyon is named for what Powell mistakenly thinks is a "great bed of Marble a thousand feet in thickness" through which the river passes just before entering the main canyon.[24] Still other places are named for river-related attributes: Triplet Falls for a group of three falls the men pass; Rippling Brook for "the music of falling waters" the men hear "away up the cañon"; Stillwater Canyon for the deep waters at the junction of the Grand and Green Rivers; and Cataract Canyon for the abruptness of a series of "difficult rapids and falls."[25] Despite their different derivations, all of these names are given according to the necessity of descriptivist principles. They all describe an attribute or cluster of attributes of the natural object being named – even in those cases (like Marble Canyon or the Butte of the Holy Cross) when the objects turn out not to possess the attributes which are ascribed to them.

Unlike these clearly descriptive acts of naming, there are a number of instances in which names are given to commemorate some historical person or event that Powell and his crew wish to associate with a particular place. These names operate according to what is known as the antidescriptivist account of naming, in which a name is said to refer to the object it identifies not because of any necessary cluster of internal or intrinsic attributes the object possesses but because of what Saul Kripke characterizes as a "primal" or "initial baptism" that links the name both to the object it identifies and to other words and names through a series of external communicative links.[26] In these cases the act of naming can be seen to function as initiating a chain of communicative links by which a particular emotional reaction or historical event can be passed on to posterity. Thus we find a particularly difficult stretch of the river below Triplet Falls that is named by Powell Hell's Half-Mile.[27] Entering "the mouth of a stream" in which "the water is exceedingly muddy, and has an unpleasant odor," one of the men, "much disgusted," exclaims that the stream is "'a dirty devil,' and by this name the river is to be known hereafter."[28] And discovering a "little affluent" that is "clear" and "beautiful," the men "conclude to name it 'Bright Angel'" in contradistinction to the one they had just named "in honor of the great chief of the 'Bad Angels.'"[29] Among those names which commemorate either events that occurred on the expedition or men whom Powell and his crew chose to honor, Ashley Falls is named for an inscription Powell's men found on a rock.[30] The Cliff of the Harp is named for the fact that the men could see the constellation Lyra from their camp at that spot; Disaster Falls is named for a place where both Ashley's party and one of Powell's boats were wrecked; Echo Rock is named for a location near where Powell's men hear their voices echoed repeatedly; Music Temple is similarly named for its echoing of one of the men's nighttime songs.[31] Mount Hawkins is so named because Hawkins, one of Powell's crew, shot "a fine, fat deer" there; Sumner's Ampitheater is named for another of Powell's men, although it's never made clear why; and Vasey's Paradise, named "in honor of the botanist who traveled with [the men] the previous year," is described as a wall with "fountains bursting from the rock, high overhead," where "the rocks below the fountain are covered with mosses, and ferns, and many beautiful flowering plants."[32]

Despite the fact that these latter two groups of names derive from subjective emotional responses or historical accidents, it might be possible for a descriptivist like Searle to argue that in these latter acts of naming Powell can still be seen to be operating according to the linguistic necessity of descriptivist principles. Hell's Half-Mile and Dirty Devil River, for example, do refer to certain attributes of the Colorado and its tributaries, as does, in a different way, Bright Angel. Kripke, on the other hand, would counter that even in those cases where Powell explicitly chooses his names according to a descriptivist logic, the antidescriptivist account would still hold – that names refer to the objects they identify because of an "initial 'baptism,'" in which "the object may be named by ostension, or the reference of the name may be fixed by a description."[33] Indeed in some cases, Kripke contends, reference is fixed precisely because of some descriptive attribute or feature. But it is not description that guarantees the recognition of a connection between a name and its object but rather the establishment of a "chain of communication" in which "the name is passed on from link to link."[34] Even in those cases, Kripke argues, where "a referent is determined by a description, by some uniquely identifying property, what the property is doing in many cases of designation is not giving a synonym, giving something for which the name is an abbreviation; it is, rather, fixing a reference. It fixes the reference by some contingent marks of the object. The name denoting that object is then used to refer to that object, even in referring to counterfactual situations where the object doesn't have the properties in question."[35] One such example can be found in the misnamed Butte of the Holy Cross. The counterfactual situation is similarly exemplified in the case of Marble Canyon, a name that still holds today, even though the interpretive materials put out by the National Park Service insist on reminding us that Powell and his men were mistaken in thinking that the walls of the canyon were composed of marble.

Granted then that Powell's naming practices can be seen to operate according to both descriptivist and antidescriptivist accounts of reference, but that even his descriptivist practices can be explained by Kripke's antidescriptivist theory, how does this help to illuminate the question of the Grand Canyon's cognitive inaccessibility? One way to get at this question is through Powell's preface to the 1895 popular edition. In this preface Powell acknowledges the competing purposes of his multiple explorations of the Grand Canyon, as well as of his multiple accounts of these explorations. Thus in explaining how the 1895 edition came into being, Powell distinguishes between recording the scientific results of the exploration and writing a historical account of it. "The exploration," he contends, "was not made for adventure, but purely for scientific purposes, geographic and geologic"; Powell insists that he had "no intention of writing an account of it, but only of recording the scientific results."[36] Although ostensibly interested only in describing the scientific results of his exploration, he nonetheless acceded when "in 1874 the editors of Scribner's Monthly requested [him] to publish a popular account of the Colorado exploration in that journal."[37] Powell reiterates this distinction between science and adventure in recounting his presentation of "an account of the progress of the geographic and geologic work" of his survey to a House Appropriations Committee in that same year, 1874. When asked by the chairman of that committee why "no history of the original exploration of the canyons had been published," Powell again replied that he "had no interest in that work as an adventure, but was interested only in the scientific results."[38] When the chairman "insisted that the history of the exploration should be published by the government, and that [Powell] must understand that [his] scientific work would be continued by additional appropriations only upon [his] promise that [he] would publish an acount of the exploration," he "made the promise, and the task was immediately undertaken" – the result of which was the 1875 Smithsonian edition, which Powell supplemented in the 1895 popular edition both with additional illustrations and with "several new chapters descriptive of the region and of the people who inhabit it."[39]

Although Powell's 1895 preface does not reconcile his descriptivist and antidescriptivist naming practices, it does offer a gloss on these practices. To consider Powell's exploration a scientific expedition would be to underscore the descriptivist character of his naming practices, in which natural objects or features derive their names by necessity from the scientific purposes of geographic or geological description. To consider his exploration an adventure, however, would be to underscore the antidescriptivist character of his naming practices, in which natural objects or features derive their names accidentally from their "primary baptism" by the first men to have successfully navigated the Colorado through the length of the Grand Canyon, and in which these names continue to refer to the objects or features they denote not through their descriptive character but through the communicative links established by the publication both of Powell's scientific results and of his historical narratives. Indeed insofar as his 1874 testimony before a House Appropriations Committee made continued appropriations for his scientific work contingent upon his publication of a historical account of his exploration as an adventure, one might be tempted to conclude that, despite Powell's insistence that his work was essentially scientific (and thus descriptivist) in nature, the continuation of the scientific purposes of Powell's exploration (like the descriptivist motivations for his naming practices) were historically contingent on the antidescriptivist purposes of his exploration as an adventure.

But I want to resist the temptation of concluding with a straightforward account of the triumph of historical narrative over scientific description or of antidescriptivism over descriptivism. Neither descriptivism nor antidescriptivism can succeed in accounting fully for what is at stake in Powell's naming practices. Both accounts of naming conceal something more fundamental – what Slavoj Zizek characterizes as "the radical contingency of naming, the fact that naming itself retroactively constitutes its reference."[40] Zizek argues that in attempting to provide a conclusive account of the way in which names refer to the objects or features they denote, both descriptivism and antidescriptivism create a myth of the (absent) father who guarantees the necessity of that which is radically contingent: whether descriptive attributes or the primal baptism of naming. In relying upon the authorizing role of the discourse of science, then, Powell's descriptivist practices of naming would conceal or ignore the arbitrariness of the scientific appropriation of nature. In commemorating the exploration of the Colorado as an adventure, an act of historical discovery, Powell's more antidescriptivist practices of naming would conceal or ignore the historical contingency of the American appropriation of the Western territories. In regard to Powell's practice of naming, Zizek's insistence on the radical contingency of naming lets us see that in either account some kind of "necessity" is being claimed for Powell's names, thus making things which are in themselves logically or historically contingent (his naming, his exploration, the possession of the canyon by the United States government, or the canyon's features themselves) seem as if they had a necessary role within the authorizing discourse of the ideological network of postbellum America – indeed, as if that ideological network were itself necessary. For Zizek, "Naming is necessary, but it is, so to speak, necessary afterwards, retroactively, once we are already 'in it.'"[41]

The retroactive necessity of naming ("once we are already 'in it'") is made practically manifest in Powell's discussion of the Canyon of Desolation. On July 8, after passing through "a region of the wildest desolation," Powell notes: "We are minded to call this the Cañon of Desolation."[42] Three days later, having spent some time surveying the area and repairing some broken equipment, Powell writes: "Just here we emerge from the Cañon of Desolation, as we have named it, into a more open country, which extends for a distance of nearly a mile, when we enter another cañon, cut through gray sandstone."[43] Powell's matter-of-fact interjection of the phrase "as we have named it," just after noting the men's emergence from the Canyon of Desolation, reveals the way in which here, as throughout the text, the narrative works to reify, objectify, or validate the naming of a natural feature. Here, Powell calls attention to the fact that this is only the Canyon of Desolation because "we have named it" that. Elsewhere he doesn't. He just uses the name as if this is what the canyon or river or point was always called, what it was already called both when they arrived and when they left. What is interesting, however, and what gets omitted throughout Powell's narrative, is the fact that when they entered the Canyon of Desolation they did not recognize it as the Canyon of Desolation; indeed it wasn't the Canyon of Desolation at all. Only after they named it could they recognize it as the Canyon of Desolation. Did they, then, pass through the Canyon of Desolation? This question is not answered – or rather the assumed answer is, yes, of course they did. But it is interesting to note that the act of exploration and discovery, the act of passing through the Colorado's canyon, is simultaneously the act of transforming natural entities from unnamed and unknown entitities into individualized, named, mapped and surveyed features. The act of naming effects a kind of magical transformation, the magic of individuation: we enter an unnamed canyon, we come out of the Canyon of Desolation. Although serving the ostensible function of making the canyons of the Colorado recognizable and therefore more cognitively and physically accessible, Powell's repeated acts of naming end up reenacting in dramatic fashion the cognitive inaccessibility at the heart of US culture's fascination with the Grand Canyon. Following Zizek's lead, however, I would aver that Powell's attempt to give his names a kind of necessity, to make it seem as if his naming came from the object rather than being imposed upon it, conceals but does not obviate the radical contingency not only of naming but of the appropriation of the Grand Canyon that Powell's naming enables.

THE INDIAN FASHION OF NAMING

But does this have to be the case? Is there another practice of naming that Powell could have employed that might have enabled a different kind of relationship to the land – a practice that acknowledges or embraces the radical contingency not only of naming but of the appropriation of land?

A possible alternative can be found in the account of naming set forth by Mary Austin in the preface to her now-classic desert text, *The Land of Little Rain*. Austin follows what she calls "the Indian fashion of name-giving: every man known by that phrase which best expresses him to whoso names him."[44] This sounds in one respect very much like the descriptivist account of naming; but if names refer to what they name because they are descriptive, they are multiply descriptive. In "the Indian fashion of naming," Austin explains, each individual is described by many names: "Thus he may be Mighty-Hunter, or Man-Afraid-of-a-Bear, according as he is called by friend or enemy, and Scar-Face to those who knew him by the eye's grasp only. No other fashion, I think, sets so well with the various natures that inhabit in us."[45]

Like Austin, Powell recognizes, if he does not endorse, the multiplicity of the Indian fashion of naming. Discussing the political organization of the Indians in the Grand Canyon region in his 1874 Smithsonian report, he writes: "These Indians have no term which signifies tribe or nation – that is, a collection of people under one government, but each tribe takes the name of the land to which it is attached, and if you desire to ask an Indian to which tribe he belongs, you must say, 'how are you land-named?' or 'what is the name of your land?'"[46] Yet, as Powell concludes, with perhaps a hint of frustration, this name does not function in the same way names function in institutions like the Smithsonian: "Thus, all the tribes of this country have at least three names, one by which they know themselves, one or more by which they are known to the surrounding tribes, and a third by which they are known by white men."[47]

Austin feels, however, that this Indian fashion of naming is well-suited to the multiple natures within any individual or group. Endorsing the radical contingency of naming, she employs a practice of naming in her text that would offer an alternative to the creation and perpetuation of the myth of the absent father that can be seen to be authorizing Powell's naming practices. Declaring that "few names are written" in her text "as they appear in the geography," Austin explains: "For if I love a lake known by the name of the man who discovered it, which endears itself by reason of the close-locked pines it nourishes about its borders, you may look in my account to find it so described," for example lake of the close-locked pines.[48] Austin's naming practice challenges the authority of Powell (or other explorers) to "primally baptize" the natural features they discover. For Austin, although names should refer because of the way in which people or places express or endear themselves to the person giving the names, they should not refer permanently and without change. Thus she feels free to rename places as she will – especially those places named for their discoverers.

Because they do not operate according to a logic of discovery, however, Indian names are an exception to Austin's radical renaming practices: "But if the Indians have been there before me," she writes, "you shall have their name, which is always beautifully fit and does not originate in the poor human desire for perpetuity."[49] In relinquishing the priority of nomenclature to Indians because their names are descriptively apt, Austin is not doing anything particularly new – as evidenced by innumerable geographic names throughout the United States. But in claiming that Indian names are always beautifully fit, Austin also claims to adopt their names because (unlike explorers like Powell) Indians do not name for the purpose of perpetuating themselves. Yet in perpetuating these names for them, Austin opens the door for the law of the father and "the poor human desire for perpetuity" to creep back into her naming practices. She realizes as well that her commitment to the radical contingency of naming can only go so far: "there are certain peaks, canons, and clear meadow spaces which are above all compassing of words, and have a certain fame as of the nobly great to whom we give no familiar names."[50] Like places named by Indians, the names of these features are left unchanged by Austin, and serve as authorizing landmarks by which her reader may be "guided" to her country "and find or not find, according as it lieth in you, much that is set down here."[51] Just as people are inhabited by various natures, so is the land. For Austin, the primal baptism of naming is conceptualized like an onomastic primal scene, in which the act of naming becomes the vehicle by which the law of the (absent) father is coupled with a faithful, if seemingly polygamous, mother earth: "The earth is no wanton to give up all her best to every comer, but keeps a sweet, separate intimacy for each."[52] Indeed it is precisely the desire to contain or comprehend nature's wantonness that motivates Austin's naming practices and authorizes her own symbolic appropriation of the land: "So by this fashion of naming I keep faith with the land and annex to my own estate a very great territory to which none has a surer title."[53] Like Emerson or Thoreau, who believe that their aesthetic perception of the Concord landscape gives them a property in the land that no land owner can take away, Austin feels that her naming of the land provides her with "surer title" than that held by private or public landowners.

But curiously Austin's Indian fashion of naming also looks in many ways like the naming practices that Powell practiced in his exploration of the Grand Canyon on behalf of the United States. In the preface to his 1875 Smithsonian monograph, Powell describes his predominant strategy in naming features of the Grand Canyon: "As far as possible we have adopted the names of geographic features used by the settlers of the adjacent country, but many of the mountains, plateaus, valleys, cañons, and streams were unknown and unnamed. In such cases we have accepted the Indian names, whenever they could be determined with accuracy."[54] When he and his men discover that a "valley through which [the Colorado] runs is the home of many antelope," for example, the crew adopts the "Indian name, *Won'sits Yu-av* – Antelope Valley."[55] Not unlike Austin, Powell here relinquishes his own priority for naming, allowing the Indian name to stand rather than imposing a name of his own. Nor would Powell have been insensitive to the complexities of Native American ethnology. His surveys of the Grand Canyon involved him in ethnological as well as geological collection and description. Founder and first director of the Bureau of Ethnology in 1879, Powell was one of the motivating forces behind the federal government's interest in the institutionalization and preservation of the linguistic and cultural traditions of Western Native American peoples.

Powell's ethnological understanding is worth considering more fully, particularly as it participates in the logic of recognition that informs his naming practices. If his 1875 and 1895 monographs provide accounts of what we might call "ready-made naming," in the annual reports he sent to Smithsonian Secretary Joseph Henry, Powell provides a glimpse into the practice of "naming in action."[56] In the 1873 report, in a synoptic summary of the work performed by his survey, he provides numerous examples of the role of Indian names in his naming practice – a role that is often ignored in the 1875 and 1895 narratives. Powell offers the following derivation for the name of a formation to the north of the canyon: "In the conglomerate are found embedded many fragments, and sometimes huge tree-trunks of silicified wood . . . The Indians call this wood *Shin-ar-ump*, or the rock of *Shin-au-av*; this *Shin-au-av* is the Hercules of Ute mythology, and the fossils are said to be his arrows. The cliffs are called *Shin-ar-ump Mu-kwan-I-kunt*. It is proposed to call them *Shin-ar-ump* cliffs."[57] He also describes the role of Indian names in relation to a line of cliffs on the boundary of two great plateaus: "These plateaus are separated by the valley of the Sevier; the one on the east we call *Powns-a-gunt*, meaning Beaver Plateau; the one on the west *Mar-ka-gunt*, which signifies the plateau of flowering bushes; the escarpments forming the southern limits we have named Pink Cliffs."[58]

In 1874 Powell describes how, like Austin, he sometimes adopted Indian names in lieu of those of prior Grand Canyon explorers. In a section of the report detailing the "many new mountains [which] have been added to our geographic knowledge," including first the Henry Mountains, named "in honor of the secretary of the Smithsonian Institution," Powell explains why he adopted the name U-in-kar'-et Mountains for "a group of eruptive mountains" on the U-in-kar'-et Plateau.[59] What differentiates this act from naming hitherto unnamed features is that, rather than filling in a blank space on the official geographical map, this name requires the erasure of names already on the map, the abrogation of the mountain's primal baptism. "On New Year's day, 1854," Powell explains, "Lieutenant Whipple, from an eminence on the western flank of San Francisco Mountain, descried the summit of a peak away to the north, and on the maps of the route of the expedition he indicated the position of the mountain and called it High Mountain."[60] In addition to replacing the name "High Mountain," Powell's choice of U-in-kar'-et Mountains would also do away with the name "North-Side Mountains," given by Ives in 1858, from the official maps.[61] Powell justifies his right to name these mountains by pointing out that the position of every one of the 118 volcanic cones that make up this group "has been determined in the secondary triangulation, and the data collected to make an elaborate map of this region on a scale of two inches to the mile."[62] He concludes his justification by citing the authority of the Indians' primal baptism of this range: "The Indian name for this group is U-in-kar'-ets, by which they are known to the people of Southern Utah and Northern Arizona who live in sight of the mountains and who have daily use for some name. As the names given by Whipple and Ives were doubtless intended only as provisional, this Indian name has been adopted."[63]

Another telling example of Powell's Indian fashion of naming in action concerns the 1873 report's account of the Indian origins of the name for Vermilion Cliffs: "The Indian name for these cliffs is Un-kar Mu-kwan-Mu-kwan-I-kunt, or 'Vermilion Cliffs,' which translation we have adopted."[64] Where the 1873 report makes the name's Indian origins explicit, these origins are omitted in the 1875 and 1895 narratives: "Starting, we leave behind a long line of cliffs, many hundred feet high, composed of orange and vermilion sandstones. I have named them 'Vermilion Cliffs.' When we are out a few miles, I look back, and see the morning sun shining in splendor on their painted faces; the salient angles are on fire, and the retreating angles are buried in shade, and I gaze on them until my vision dreams, and the cliffs appear a long bank of purple clouds, piled from the horizon high into the heavens."[65] This passage is interesting for several reasons, not the least of which is Powell's transformation of the naming of Vermilion Cliffs from an act of adopting an Indian translation to an act of descriptivist naming. It is difficult not to see the excursion into the rhetoric of romantic landscape aesthetics that follows this Adamic pronouncement as an implicit, sub-conscious justification of, or compensation for, Powell's suppression of the name's Indian origins. As his romantic vision dematerializes the cliffs into an imaginary bank of clouds, so his naming dematerializes the presence of the Indian inhabitants both in and on the landscape.

But it would not be fair to portray Powell as systematically removing the signs of Indian presence from the landscape. As his ethnological interests attest, Powell's scientific project included a sustained interest in recording and preserving Indian culture, so that (like the landscape itself) it could be recognized and incorporated within such knowledge-producing government institutions as the Smithsonian. In thinking through his role as ethnologist, Powell sometimes finds himself facing the contrast between his culture's practices of knowledge-production and those of the Indians. On the day following his account of the naming of Vermilion Cliffs, after describing his desire to visit a group of Indians inhabiting a group of mountains of volcanic origin, Powell remarks:

It is curious now to observe the knowledge of our Indians. There is not a trail but what they know; every gulch and every rock seems familiar. I have prided myself on being able to grasp and retain in my mind the topography of a country; but these Indians put me to shame. My knowledge is only general, embracing the more important features of a region that remains as a map engraved on my mind; but theirs is particular. They know every rock and every ledge, every gulch and cañon, and just where to wind among these to find a pass; and their knowledge is unerring. They cannot describe a country to you, but they can tell you all the particulars of a route.[66]

This passage reveals his double stance towards the Indians. Powell clearly envies their ability to remember the landscape. Although priding himself on his topographical knowledge, "these Indians put [him] to shame." Because his "knowledge is only general," he can only remember "the more important features of a region that remains as a map engraved on [his] mind." The Indian fashion of knowledge, however, is unerring: "They know every rock and every ledge, every gulch and canyon, and just where to wind among these to find a pass." But in noting that, despite their ability to "tell you all the particulars of a route," "they cannot describe a country to you," Powell provides the basis for another, less favorable portrayal of Indian knowledge. For as we saw above, it was precisely the scientific ability to describe the geological features of the landscape that authorized Powell's replacement of the "provisional" names of Whipple and Ives. And later in the 1874 report, in detailing his ethnological accomplishments, Powell remarks on the "strange uncertainty and indefiniteness in the mind of the Indian" in regard to some details of his mythology, as well as on "how the Indian often confuses time and space."[67]

While admiring the Indians for the particularity of their knowledge, Powell is also mindful of their inability to generalize or systematize this knowledge. One reason for this seemingly double stance in relation to the

Indians might be that they provide a rhetorical problem for Powell's exploration narrative. For on the one hand the force of his narrative derives from the claim that he has penetrated an unknown region, filled in the blank spaces on the official geographical map of the United States. The narrative takes its rhetorical force from the fact that Powell was the "first" to explore the entire canyon, the one who succeeded in dispelling "uncertainty and indefiniteness" by bringing scientific knowledge back to the cultural and political centers back East. As we have seen, this knowledge is precisely knowledge as in a map – conceptual, abstract, systematic. For Powell and his contemporaries, this form of knowledge is opposed, then, and superior, to Indian knowledge, even though he can recognize that the particularity of Indian knowledge puts him to shame. These two different manifestations of Powell's stance toward Indian knowledge are not unrelated to his two different accounts of the expedition: as a scientific expedition into the unknown or a historical expedition through the land of another culture. For if we remember that the Indians were there first, then the places that Powell explores are not being cognized for the first time, but only recognized. But if this is so, then it is re-cognition without recognition – until the Indian names are adopted by Powell and brought within a system of knowledge production in which cognition can only function within a conceptual economy of recognition.[68]

The interrelation of cognition and recognition is in certain respects at the heart of ethnograhic (or other forms of descriptive) knowledge. Arguably the central epistemological question raised by anthropology is whether it is possible for an ethnographer to cognize another culture without first recognizing it within the conceptual framework of the anthropologist's own disciplinary or cultural practices of knowledge production. Interestingly this problematic is made visible in two 1872 photographs taken by Jack Hillers of Powell's interaction with the Kaibab Paiutes. In the first photograph, *Tribal Council* (see Figure 21), Powell sits in the circle of Paiutes with Jacob Hamblin, "consulting with Chuarumpeak, leader of the Kaibab Paiute band." In the second, *The Ta-vo-koki or Circle Dance of the Paiute (Winter Costume)* (see Figure 22), Powell stands off "at left observing the dance, undoubtedly staged for the camera."[69] In staging these two scenes (for surely the first is also staged), Powell and Hillers offer us two different representations of Powell as idealized ethnographer. In one he is actively engaged with the Paiutes, participating as a Paiute in a tribal council; in the other he stands off to the side, outside of the ceremonial dance, as a neutral observer, able to see and record and understand the dance as it is. As philosophers and theorists of anthropological knowledge remind us, of

21 Jack Hillers, *Tribal Council 1873*

course, the second relation represents an ideal of scientific or descriptive knowledge that can never be realized, which is in this case underscored by the "staged" quality of the photograph. But the ideal that one could participate in a tribal council, that one could "go native" (as Frank Hamilton Cushing recorded in *My Adventures in Zuni*) is equally a myth, another anthropological ideal. In other words what we have in these photographs are two different logics of ethnographic cognition, which together operate very much like the Derridean logic of the supplement. In the first case Powell completes what is incomplete; he is a necessary part of the tribal council. Furthermore, his knowledge of the council is depicted as

22 Jack Hillers, *The Ta-vo-koki or Circle Dance of the Paiute* (*Winter Costume*)

phenomenological; he experiences it as a Paiute would. In the second case Powell's presence is extraneous; he is in excess of a complete whole, the circle dance. In this instance his knowledge is structural or semiotic; he observes Paiute culture as a neutral observer from without. As the supplement to this dance he is always already making it more than whole, other than whole. The tribal council, on the other hand, is only complete when the ethnographer or anthropologist adds himself, his culture, his conceptual scheme or discursive presence, to the otherwise incomplete group.

In her attempt to challenge the authorizing law of the absent father, Austin, too, grapples with the problem of cognition without recognition, the problem of how to know the land apart from her prior conceptual frames, a form of knowledge which she sometimes describes as having a "sense" of the land. In acquiring such a sense, Austin claims a more legitimate right to appropriate the land. Faithful naming, not initial discovery or primal baptism, is what clears her title to the land. Austin's Indian fashion of naming gives her, as it implicitly gives the land's native inhabitants, a more legitimate possession of the land than does the mere act of historical discovery. Moreover her notion of owning offers an alternative means of possessing the land which does not use it up or exhaust it. Like her Indian fashion of naming, her Indian fashion of owning allows people to possess (or feel as if they possessed) the land without exhausting or consuming it, without using it up so that it is no longer available for others. Austin imagines a form of symbolic or imaginative appropriation very much like the logic of preservation informing the creation of America's national parks. By preserving a particular territory, a particular piece of land, indeed by naming that land a national park, the United States government engages in its own version of the Indian fashion of naming and owning. Or rather, as Zizek reminds us, it engages in its own fantasy of necessity. For, like Austin's or Powell's decisions to allow Indian names to stand rather than impose their own names, the federal government's decision to let certain areas remain as national parks, rather than to impose some other use on them, involves, as I have argued in relation to Yellowstone, a narrative of retroactive necessity most evident in the proliferation of interpretive materials within and about the parks. In this narrative the act of preservation, like the Indian fashion of naming, is "beautifully fit" and works counter to the "poor human desire for perpetuity." As a result there often appears to be a sublime necessity to the series of historical accidents that led to the creation of America's national parks.

SUBLIME GEOLOGY OF MIND

The relation between accident and necessity, figured mainly as design, is explicitly thematized in Clarence Dutton's *Tertiary History of the Grand Cañon District*. Moreso even than Powell, Dutton is responsible for articulating and thereby helping to perpetuate the cultural assumption of the canyon's cognitive inaccessibility. The two central features of this assumption – surprise and sublimity – are evident in almost every significant literary treatment of the Grand Canyon in the late nineteenth and early twentieth century, as is the seemingly obligatory acknowledgment of Powell and Dutton.

In 1891, for example, Charles Dudley Warner, who co-authored *The Gilded Age* with Mark Twain, writes that

Human experience has no prototype of this region, and the imagination has never conceived of its forms and colors. It is impossible to convey an adequate idea of it by pen or pencil or brush. The reader who is familiar with the glowing descriptions in the official reports of Major J. W. Powell, Captain C. E. Dutton, Lieutenant Ives, and others, will not save himself from a shock of surprise when the reality is before him.[70]

Although citing Powell and Ives as well as Dutton, Warner's account of the canyon is indebted almost exclusively to Dutton – evidenced not only by his quotations from Dutton's text but also by his commentary on the architectural quality of the canyon scenery, his comparison of seeing the canyon with seeing famous centers of Western culture like Rome or Jerusalem, and his description of the experience of the sublime as one of "an indescribable terror of nature, a confusion of mind, a fear to be alone in such a presence."[71]

Harriet Monroe expresses a similar sense of surprise and sublimity, which she characterizes as the recurrent impression that the canyon is not of this world and thus not made for humans: "For surely it was not our world, this stupendous, adorable vision. Not for human needs was it fashioned, but for the abode of gods. It made a coward of me; I shrank and shut my eyes, and felt crushed and beaten under the intolerable burden of the flesh. For humanity intruded here."[72] For Monroe, who writes about her journey to the Grand Canyon in 1899, the sublimity of the canyon does not lead to empowerment but, like much of the desert landscape, to self-effacement: "The immense and endless desolation seemed to efface us from the earth. What right had we there, on those lofty lands which never since the beginning of time had offered sustenance to man? . . . To the end it effaced me."[73]

The rhetorical trope of the canyon's cognitive inaccessibility is further articulated three years later by John Muir, who notes that "It is very hard to give anything like an adequate conception of its size, much more of its color, its vast wall-sculpture, the wealth of ornate architectural buildings that fill it, or, most of all, the tremendous impression it makes."[74] Like Warner, Muir explicitly acknowledges Dutton and Powell as his precursors: "I have just said that it is impossible to learn what the cañon is like from descriptions and pictures. Powell's and Dutton's descriptions present magnificent views not only of the cañon but of all the grand region round about it; and Holmes's drawings, accompanying Dutton's report are wonderfully good. Surely faithful and loving skill can go no further in putting the multitudinous decorated forms on paper. But the *colors*, the living, rejoicing *colors*, chanting morning and evening in chorus to heaven! Whose brush or pencil, however lovingly inspired, can give us these? And if paint is of no effect, what hope lies in pen-work? Only this: some may be incited by it to go and see for themselves."[75]

By the time the Grand Canyon was preserved as a national park, many people had indeed become incited to go there. But tourists often need fairly detailed guides to help them see for themselves. One such early and influential guide was John C. Van Dyke's *The Grand Canyon of the Colorado*, published in 1920, the year after the park's creation. Van Dyke offers tourists a guide both to the canyon's physical features and to their proper aesthetic appreciation. Beginning with its first two chapters, which are replete with expressions of the inability to recognize or comprehend the canyon's scenery, Van Dyke's book signals the institutionalization of a logic of recognition in which the creation of Grand Canyon National Park preserves it not only from social or economic development but also from cognitive accessibility. A tourist's initial response on seeing the canyon, he writes, is "bewilderment": "You cannot step out of the monotony of a railway-car and, walking a few steps, enter upon something that is the last word in grandeur and sublimity without catching your breath and gasping a bit. Some people stand and stare with their mouths ajar, some whistle or talk unconsciously to themselves, some sit down and softly swear. But all are bewildered. They cannot grasp it. Nature seems out of joint."[76] Van Dyke quickly assures his readers that time will give them a different point of view, one that will let them see that the canyon does in fact make something of a "harmonious, self-sustaining picture." His second chapter rehearses for his readers the experience of the mathematical sublime: : "At first we cannot see things here at the Canyon for their vastness. The mind keeps groping for a scale of proportion – something whereby we can mentally measure. Standards of comparison break down and common experience helps us not at all."[77] Van Dyke takes up and dismisses a series of comparisons by which one could try to comprehend the size and form of the Canyon – numerical distance; "comparisons with other scenes of huge proportions"; "the grotesqueries of the multitude," for example, imagining how small the Washington Monument or the Brooklyn Bridge would look if placed in the Canyon; architectural parallels; mythological allusions; and poetic names. None of these conceptual frames, he avers, can help visitors to make sense of the canyon. "With no adequate scale of proportion for form," he continues, "we are perhaps even worse off when it comes to color"; the coloring of the canyon, like its air and sky, "outruns all our experience."[78] We cannot recognize the canyon because we have no cognitive frames sufficient to comprehend it.

Moreso even than Warner, Monroe, or Muir, Van Dyke comes closest to suggesting the depth and richness of Dutton's articulation of the Canyon's cognitive inaccessibility. But Van Dyke's aesthetic sensibility lacks the mental habits of the natural scientist which Dutton never relinquished. A member of Powell's geographical survey, who worked mainly in the Plateau Country north of the Grand Canyon, Dutton is remembered in histories of nineteenth-century geology primarily for contributing to the decline of the contraction theory, which had attributed the creation of continents and oceans to the cooling and contraction of the earth's surface.[79] Wallace Stegner has argued, however, that it is not Dutton's "geological contributions, which were great, but his literary flair, which would seem quite irrelevant, that has kept his name fresh."[80] "The tourist and nature lover," Stegner writes, "occupied a good large corner of Dutton":

He never quite made up his mind whether he was literary traveler or sober scientific analyst: the temptations were essentially equal. He escaped his dilemma by being both, and in his reports a rich and embroidered nineteenth-century traveler's prose flows around bastions of geological fact as some of the lava coulees on the Uinkaret flow around gables of sedimentary strata . . . With hardly an apology, Dutton forsook the "severe ascetic style" of science when he came to deal with the Grand Canyon . . . The result is a scientific monograph of great geological importance which contains whole chapters as ebullient as the writing of John Muir, and deviates constantly into speculations so far from geological that they sound more like Ruskin than Lyell.[81]

Stephen Pyne offers a similar assessment of Dutton's significance for the cultural history of the Grand Canyon as lying primarily in his aesthetic vision. Where Powell, claims Pyne, would "command nature to stand front and center," Dutton writes of the view from the Aquarius Plateau "that the scene should be described 'in blank verse and painted on canvas,' for here 'the geologist finds himself a poet.'"[82] Dutton, Pyne continues "found an aesthetic meaning where Powell promoted a taxonomic order."[83] And unlike Grove Karl Gilbert, who developed the theory of fluvial erosion that informed the geological work of the Powell Survey, Dutton "measured the landscape with figures of speech rather than with numbers and reached for architectural rather than mechanical metaphors. But what organized his influential studies of the Colorado Plateau, as with his other investigations, was a commanding sense of history, one suffused with a literary sensibility."[84]

While agreeing with Stegner's and Pyne's assessment of Dutton's importance, I would take issue with their too stark accounts of the dichotomy between Dutton's literary and scientific character. This dichotomy might be more justly ascribed to Powell, whose preface to the 1895 popular edition of his exploration of the river claims that his exploration was first and foremost a scientific one, but that he was forced by political and social forces to portray it as history or adventure. In the *Tertiary History*, however, Dutton insists on seeing scientific and aesthetic knowledge as part of the same project, as sharing the same epistemological structure. In his preface Dutton explicitly defends his departure "from the severe ascetic style which has become conventional in scientific monographs." While aesthetic "stimulants" may in treatments of other regions imperil "the fundamental requirement of scientific method – accuracy of statement . . . in the Grand Cañon district there is no such danger. The stimulants which are demoralizing elsewhere are necessary here to exalt the mind sufficiently to comprehend the sublimity of the subjects. Their sublimity," Dutton concludes, "has in fact been hitherto underrated. Great as is the fame of the Grand Cañon of the Colorado, the half remains to be told."[85] Rather than support the characterization of Dutton as unable to determine whether he was a scientist or an aesthete, a follower of Lyell or Ruskin, Dutton's prefatory remarks suggest that it is the specificity of the canyon itself, its sublimity, that prompts him to incorporate aesthetic modes of representation into a scientific monograph. Indeed throughout the *Tertiary History*, Dutton sets forth elements of an almost Kantian critique, which reveals the common epistemological grounds between what might be called scientific and aesthetic judgment.

In this critique of canyon judgment the first aesthetic scheme Dutton employs is the conception of natural beauty, particularly in his repeated discussions of the way in which nature resembles art in the sculptural and architectural appearance of the "majestic walls" of the Grand Canyon region. Following a Kantian logic, which Dutton (who once described himself as "omni-biblical") would likely have been exposed to at Yale,[86] he insists that "The resemblances to architecture are not fanciful or metaphorical, but are real and vivid, so much so that the unaccustomed tourist often feels a vague skepticism whether these are truly the works of the blind forces of nature or of some intelligence akin to the human, but far mightier; and even the experienced explorer is sometimes brought to a sudden halt and filled with amazement by the apparition of forms as definite and eloquent as those of art. Each geological formation exhibits in its cliffs a distinct style of architecture which is not reproduced among the cliffs of other formations, and these several styles differ as much as those which are cultivated by different races of men."[87] In the *Tertiary History* Dutton twice returns to this same rhetorical figure of "the blind forces of nature" accidentally creating geological "forms as definite and eloquent as those of art," in what seem clearly to be allusions to Kant's idea that natural beauty is constituted precisely by the fact that such beauty appears purposive but without definite purpose. Describing the colossal scenery of the lower end of the Toroweap valley, for example, Dutton writes: "Its magnitude is by no means its most impressive feature, but precision of the forms. The dominant idea ever before the mind is the architecture displayed in the profiles. It is hard to realize that this is the work of the blind forces of nature."[88] And in depicting the sculptured architecture of the gorge he and his men call "The Transept," Dutton writes: "To many spectators the dominant thought here might be that this stupendous work has been accomplished by some intelligence akin to the human rather than by the blind forces of nature. Everything is apparently planned and cut with as much definiteness of design as a rock-temple of Petrea or Ellore."[89] These passages articulate the particular significance of architectural resemblance in the aesthetic judgment of canyon beauty. The canyon's unusual formations initially strike the spectator aesthetically as purposeful architectural designs, but this initial aesthetic apprehension is then modified by scientific deduction, which forces the mind to realize that these formations have been created by the blind forces of nature.

Dutton does not find such moments of epistemological uncertainty to be unique to the aesthetic judgment of natural beauty, but understands them as part of the scientific judgment of what might be called geological beauty. Discussing the difficulties of comprehending the role of erosion in the creation of the Grand Canyon, he explains how the Grand Canyon destabilizes the apparently more rational process of scientific cognition as well. Even in his more conventionally scientific discussions, Dutton evinces as much interest in the mechanics of the mind's scientific reasoning as in the mechanics of the earth's erosion and sedimentation. For example, he writes that the processes of land sculpture, denudation, and erosion "are operative almost everywhere, and their results in the lapse of immense periods of time attain magnitudes, the statement of which may astonish the ordinary reader and perhaps excite his incredulity, but which at length appear veritable when tested by geological research and deduction."[90] In another passage Dutton takes up in even greater detail the mechanics through which the ordinary reader's astonishment and incredulity arise, and by which geological research and deduction dispel them. After asserting that in the entire Grand Canyon district "the area of maximum denudation is from 13,000 to 15,000 square miles, and the average thickness of the strata removed from it was about 10,000 feet," Dutton notes that "The general reader will no doubt feel a strong aversion to such prodigious figures, and even the geologist may hesitate."[91] In an effort to overcome this aversion, he explains that "what the law of gravity is to astronomy," erosion and sedimentation are to geology, calling these processes "the two half phases of one cycle of causation – the debit and credit sides of one system of transactions."[92] To "know how great have been the quantities of material removed in any given geological age from the land by erosion," Dutton concludes, "we have only to estimate the mass of the strata deposited in that age. Constrained by this reasoning the mind has no escape from the conclusion that the effects of erosion have indeed been vast."[93]

But the fact that our minds have been constrained by scientific reasoning to accept the conclusion that the landscape has been produced by the workings of erosion and sedimentation does not preclude the experience of Dutton's geological version of the Kantian mathematical sublime. He writes: "our wonder is transferred to the immensity of the periods of time required" to create this landscape; "for the processes are so slow that the span of a life-time seems too small to render those results directly visible. As we stand before the terrace cliffs and try to conceive of them receding scores of miles by secular waste, we find the endeavor quite useless."[94] Even when, some thirty paragraphs of explanation later, Dutton feels confident that he has satisfactorily tested and proven "the inference of the great denudation of the Grand Cañon district," he is still unable to answer the question of "the immensity of the periods of time required to accomplish" this denudation.[95] Indeed, the report ends with this confession of the insufficiency of late nineteenth-century science to provide answers to questions of geological time:

No doubt the question will often be asked, how long has been the time occupied in the excavation of the Grand Cañon? Unfortunately there is no mystery more inscrutable than the duration of geological time. On this point geologists have obtained no satisfactory results in any part of the world. Whatever periods may have been assigned to the antiquity of past events have been assigned provisionally only, and the inferences are almost purely hypothetical. In the Plateau Country Nature has, in some respects, been more communicative than in other regions, and has answered many questions far more fully and graciously. But here, as elsewhere, whenever we interrogate her about time other than relative, her lips are sternly closed, and her face becomes as the face of the Sphinx.[96]

Dutton's geological sublime is marked less by the nineteenth-century scientist's inability to measure the canyon's immense size than by his inability to comprehend the immense periods of time required to create the canyon.

In confessing the insufficiency of the scientific mind to estimate geological time, Dutton does not mean to suggest that aesthetic judgment is more capable of comprehending the canyon than scientific reasoning. Indeed throughout the monograph he almost obsessively returns to those moments when the mind finds itself caught between one or more of a number of conceptual or epistemological schemes. His most intricate meditations on epistemological insufficiency occur in his discussions of the first-time visitor's aesthetic response to the scenery of the Grand Canyon, in passages which become the ur-texts for later literary accounts like those of Warner, Monroe, Muir, or Van Dyke. In his treatment of the scenery of the Toroweap chasm, his first description of the view of the canyon from its "brink," Dutton describes the initial "disappointment and perplexity" felt by "the observer who, unfamiliar with plateau scenery, stands for the first time upon the brink of the inner gorge." Previous representations, he explains, have been unable to describe the landscape adequately.

The fame of the chasm of the Colorado is great; but so indefinite and meager have been the descriptions of it that the imagination is left to its own devices in framing a mental conception of it. And such subjective pictures are of course wide of the truth. When he first visits it the preconceived notion is at once dissipated and the mind is slow to receive a new one. The creations of his own fancy no doubt are clothed with a vague grandeur and beauty, but not with the grandeur and beauty of Nature. When the reality is before him the impression bears some analogy to that produced upon the visitor who for the first time enters St. Peter's Church at Rome. He expected to be profoundly awe-struck by the unexampled dimensions, and to feel exalted by the beauty of its proportions and decoration. He forgets that the human mind itself is of small capacity and receives its impressions slowly, by labored processes of comparison. So, too, at the brink of the chasm, there comes at first a feeling of disappointment; it does not seem so grand as we expected.[97]

This is a remarkable passage – not only for its elaboration of the architectural quality of plateau scenery but more strikingly for what we might characterize as Dutton's epistemological uniformitarianism, his sublime geology of mind. In describing the disappointment of the first-time observer of the chasm of the Colorado, Dutton represents the mechanics of the mind as moving at almost geological speed. After the dissipation of its preconceived notion of the scenery, "the mind is slow to receive a new one"; "the human mind itself is of small capacity and receives its impressions slowly." Even after the observer finds a "standard of comparison" with which to contemplate the "real magnitudes" of the chasm's opposite wall, Dutton insists, "the mind grows restive under the increasing burden. Every time the eye ranges up and down its face it seems more distant and more vast. At length we recoil, overburdened with the perceptions already attained and yet half vexed at the inadequacy of our faculties to comprehend more."[98]

Dutton provides an even more elaborate anatomy of the seemingly geological mechanics of aesthetic judgments of sublimity in describing the difficulty of our faculties fully to comprehend the scenery as viewed from the quite self-consciously named Point Sublime, the second of his three extended descriptions of the view of the inner canyon from its brink. Calling the Grand Canyon "a great innovation in modern ideas of scenery, and in our conceptions of the grandeur, beauty, and power of nature," Dutton explains that, like all such "great innovations," the canyon's scenery

is not to be comprehended in a day, or a week, nor even in a month. It must be dwelt upon and studied, and the study must comprise the slow acquisition of the meaning and spirit of that marvelous scenery which characterizes the Plateau Country, and of which the great chasm is the superlative manifestation. The study and slow mastery of the influences of that class of scenery and its full appreciation is a special culture, requiring time, patience, and long familiarity for its consummation. The lover of nature, whose perceptions have been trained in the Alps, in Italy, Germany, or New England, in the Appalachians or Cordilleras, in Scotland or Colorado, would enter this strange region with a shock, and dwell there for a time with a sense of oppression, and perhaps with horror. Whatsoever things he had learned to regard as beautiful and noble he would seldom or never see, and whatsoever he might see would appear to him as anything but beautiful and noble. Whatsoever might be bold and striking would at first seem only grotesque. The colors would be the very ones he had learned to shun as tawdry and bizarre. The tones and shades, modest and tender, subdued yet rich, in which his fancy had always taken special delight, would be the ones which are conspicuously absent. But time would bring a gradual change. Some day he would suddenly become conscious that outlines which at first seemed harsh and trivial have grace and meaning; that forms which seemed grotesque are full of dignity; that magnitudes which had added enormity to coarseness have become replete with strength and even majesty; that colors which had been esteemed unrefined, immodest, and glaring, are as expressive, tender, changeful, and capacious of effects as any others. Great innovations, whether in art or literature, in science or in nature, seldom take the world by storm. They must be understood before they can be estimated, and must be cultivated before they can be understood.[99]

Like the process of geological research and deduction by which Dutton verified that the Grand Canyon was produced by denudation, the process of aesthetic cultivation and understanding by which he contends that one learns to estimate the scenery of the Grand Canyon is characterized by an almost Poe-like attention to detail. And like the geological processes of erosion and stratification by which nature created the canyon's innovative scenery, the aesthetic process of sublime acculturation works gradually and slowly, "requiring time, patience, and long familiarity for its consummation." Insofar as it is represented in terms that resemble the accretive operation of erosion and sedimentation, Dutton's account of the epistemology of sublime perception is finally geological. For Dutton there is no fundamental difference between his geological and his literary passages, between his scientific and his aesthetic purposes. In shifting between aesthetic and scientific frameworks, Dutton dramatizes the inability of either discourse (or both together) to comprehend the canyon. The geological and the literary, the scientific and the aesthetic, are not categorical oppositions but rather mutually supporting, if finally also competing, rhetorical or discursive technologies for recognizing the Grand Canyon, which is to say, for recognizing its cognitive inaccessibility.

RECOGNITION AND THE LIMITS OF MEDIATION

In considering the rhetorical strategies of Dutton's *Tertiary History* it is important to keep in mind the materiality of the monograph itself, to remember that Dutton's geological and literary accounts of the Grand Canyon are only the textual component of what is arguably the most stunning monograph ever produced by the Geographical and Geological Survey. Just as for Dutton the scientific and the aesthetic cannot finally be separated, so the verbal expression of his ideas cannot be treated separately from the visual images which so powerfully and plentifully supplement his prose. Dutton's ideas about the Grand Canyon are embodied in the material technologies of representation employed both in the monograph and its accompanying elephant-sized *Atlas*, whose sheets are not only listed in the monograph just following the list of plates, but are cross-referenced to the appropriate chapters. The *Tertiary History* itself is illustrated with forty-two plates, including two chromolithographs, one colored map, two geological sections, twenty wood-cuts (seven of which are credited with being drawn from photographs), nine photo-engravings, four heliotypes, and numerous diagrams and schematics (a few published as plates, but more interspersed within the text). Some of these illustrations appeared in Powell's 1875 narrative of his exploration; more reappear in his 1895 popular account. And two of the wood-cuts by Thomas Moran had already appeared in *Picturesque America*.[100] The accompanying *Atlas* has twenty-three sheets, including maps, views, geological sections, and the three-part panorama from Point

Sublime. Dutton's monograph (cum *Atlas*) is a veritable collage of verbal and visual technologies of aesthetic and scientific representation. As a material artifact, the *Tertiary History* provides an extremely interesting and complex response to the inability of individual technologies of representation or mediation adequately to comprehend or describe the landscape of the canyon.

The difficulty of representing the canyon raises interesting questions about the strategy Dutton uses in putting together the monograph, which after all has as at least one of its central purposes to provide a representation of the canyon, or an "ensemble" of representations, which will allow it to be recognized by somebody who has never seen it before. Bruno Latour has argued that such a strategy is what helps to distinguish scientific texts from other texts, through a rhetorical process which he calls "superimposition," the juxtaposition of texts, charts, graphs, diagrams, photographs, and other forms of verbal and visual mediation.[101] Clearly this strategy is consistent with Dutton's refusal to separate his scientific from his aesthetic purposes. But if, as Dutton insists, the best way to try to comprehend the canyon is first to get rid of one's preconceived notions, why would he insist on multiplying verbal and visual technologies of representation? Does he do so to overwhelm his readers, as the Canyon itself overwhelms, to convey through his text the dizzying experience of cognitive inaccessibility that would mark a first encounter with the Grand Canyon? If so, then does he hope that they will forget what they have read and seen in his monograph? Would prospective visitors to the Grand Canyon be better off not reading the *Tertiary History* at all? Or is Dutton trying to do something else in juxtaposing a number of different visual and verbal technologies of mediation?

Perhaps the best way to get at the complexity of Dutton's response to the problem of trying to represent the canyon is to consider his reasons for incorporating so many different mediating technologies and also the way in which some of these visual images function both in his monograph and in their circulation outside of Dutton's text. Unlike Holmes' images, for example, which were intended primarily to illustrate Dutton's, Powell's, and other scientific texts, the images of Hillers and Moran had a wider circulation. After his first exploration of the Colorado in 1869, which (probably for very pragmatic reasons) did not include a photographer, Powell strategically provided for an extensive photographic record of his subsequent surveys of the Grand Canyon region. Hillers was Powell's third photographer, after E. O. Beaman and James Fennemore – and clearly the best of the lot.[102] Like his predecessors' images, Hillers' photographs, particularly his stereoscopic ones, were used not only to lobby the federal government for additional funding, but also to publicize Powell's work back East. Moran, too, was invited to travel with Powell for publicity purposes, specifically for the purpose of producing his second "big picture," a painting of the Grand Canyon of the Colorado, which would complement his earlier painting of the Grand Canyon of the Yellowstone. Hillers and Moran, who travelled together on Powell's 1873 survey, developed an interesting working relationship, not unlike Moran's earlier collaborations with William Henry Jackson, both in selecting and composing scenes for Hillers to photograph in the field and in Moran's studio practice of basing his drawings for woodcuts, engravings, and etchings on Hillers' photographs. Hillers' stereographs and Moran's monumental painting of *The Chasm of the Colorado* exemplify in different artistic media the way in which the Grand Canyon's cognitive inaccessibility provided problems not only of conceptualization but also of representation.

For Hillers, one of the most interesting photographic challenges posed by the scenery in and about the Grand Canyon is the way in which the immense distances of the canyon region prevented many of his stereoscopic images from effectively producing the illusion of three-dimensionality. While it is true that many of Hillers' stereographic images work fairly conventionally, particularly those not directly of the canyon or those not depicting great distances, there are a number of stereographs in which the three-dimensional effect is striking for the near objects, but almost non-existent for the far away ones, due largely to the fact that the binocular disparity for photographs of great distances diminishes with distance. Dutton remarks on this problem of perspective in his discussion of the view from Powell's Plateau, the third destination of the three imaginary journeys he describes for his readers: "The scene here in comparison to that of Point Sublime may be likened to the vista of a grand avenue of the most stately and imposing structures viewed from the end of the street, while from Point Sublime the standpoint is analogous to one from a projecting pediment situated mid-length of the avenue, where we may with equal effect look up or down and across to noble structures on the other side. At Powell's Plateau the view is more picturesque and more systematic. In grandeur it is about equal. But the defect which usually mars all canyon scenery is here more pronounced. It is the false perspective, the flattening of objects through want of gradations in tones and shades, and the obscurity of form and detail produced by the great distances and hazy atmosphere. But under proper lights and conditions of the air these defects may, on rare occasions, be dispelled."[103]

This problem of false perspective is evident in the Hillers stereograph, *Canyon Seen from the Foot of Toroweap Valley*, where the conventional stereo effect of two-dimensional objects or representations receding in three-dimensional space only works in the foreground of the image, which takes up nearly its entire bottom half (see Figure 23). The next plane seen in the space of the stereoscopic viewer is almost entirely two-dimensional, that is, it looks like a photograph, not like a stereoscopic image. The same is true of the river and the cliffs above it (both in front and behind), where in the depicted three-dimensional space of the image, the stereoscopic effect is lost entirely. The Grand Canyon resists the technology of stereoscopic representation in much the same way as it resists the traditional conventions of picturesque landscape representation. In this image only the foreground rocks and desert shrubs and scrub can be represented by the stereoscope's three-dimensionality; the canyon itself remains as a two-dimensional backdrop.

This problem of perspective can also be seen with another Hillers stereo, *The Grand Canyon from Toroweap Valley Looking Down* (see Figure 24). Here, as in the previous image, the stereoscopic effects diminish as the viewer's vision goes back into the depicted space. But here Hillers uses that stereo effect much more dramatically. The foreground of this image is not filled with distinct, two-dimensional looking objects like rocks and trees and scrub, but with a cliff ledge onto which viewers could imagine themselves creeping. The flatness of the cliff helps accentuate the feeling of viewing a three-dimensional space. The jump or gap from this foreground plane to the cliff in the middle ground is precipitous; viewers feel as though they are on the verge of falling into the canyon. But because of the size of this middle-ground cliff on the right, the view again fails to depict the stereoscopic effect of two-dimensional objects receding into three-dimensional space. As in the previous image, by the time the viewer focuses on the river and the cliffs flanking it in the distance, the lack of binocular disparity between the two photographs makes the stereoscopic image look pretty much like a photograph, like perspectively organized and constituted two-dimensional space. With its angle of vision pointed down, this stereo is extremely effective at creating the illusion of three-dimensionality as dangerous and threatening; it produces a feeling of sublimity not unlike that described by Edmund Burke, in which to produce the experience of the sublime, a scene must be frightening or threatening but not really in a position to harm the viewer.[104] In this stereo, that feeling is offered by the precipitous foreground juxtaposed with the cliffs in the distance and the river far below. At the same time, not unlike in the Kantian sublime, this feeling is domesticated,

23　Jack Hillers, *Canyon Seen from the Foot of Toroweap Valley*

24 Jack Hillers, *The Grand Canyon from Toroweap Valley Looking Down*

like the scene itself. As the canyon comes increasingly to look like a two-dimensional photograph, it becomes less threatening or dangerous. After being overwhelmed, the judgment or imagination reasserts itself and takes control of the image, or the feeling produced by the image.

Another stereoscope that produces the effect of two-dimensionality rather than three-dimensionality is Hillers' *Cliffs* from the Grand Canyon (see Figure 25). Here the bottom foreground is filled with rocks, behind which in the middle distance is the river and shore with some low sedimentary cliffs jutting in from the left. The background is filled with large cliffs, some of which have structures that look like the "friezes" in Moran's *Chasm of the Colorado* (see below). The cliffs that make up the backdrop work to minimize the canyon's false perspective, providing a three-dimensional effect by blocking out the immense distances of the canyon, a technique Hillers employs in other pictures as well. But here they also stand as two-dimensional walls. In fact these cliffs look more two-dimensional in the stereoscopic viewer than they do in the photographs seen separately. That is, in the context of the illusion of three-dimensionality provided by the stereoscope effect, they look more two-dimensional than in the context of the conventional two-dimensional photograph.

Indeed throughout Hillers' photographs of the Grand Canyon, three-dimensional and two-dimensional effects are often reversed in the stereo and its constituent photographs. In the stereoscopic viewer the foreground is three-dimensional while the background is flattened into two dimensions. In the photographs, on the other hand, it is the distant cliffs that give the illusion of depth and distance, making the foreground look flatter, more two-dimensional. This reversal can also be seen in Hillers' *Head of the Grand Canyon* (see Figure 26), although the ratio of foreground to background space is different from *Cliffs*. *Head of the Grand Canyon* has more foreground, thus displaying more dramatic three-dimensional effects when seen in the stereoscopic viewer. The cliffs in the distance are smaller, consequently the contrast between the two-dimensionality of the cliffs in the stereo and their three-dimensionality in the photographs is less evident. Nonetheless, the basic effect, with its reversal of three-dimensional/two-dimensional and foreground/background relations is essentially the same as in *Cliffs* and other Grand Canyon stereographs.

Other challenges to photographic representation posed by the Grand Canyon region are evident in the four Hillers photographs reprinted as heliotypes in Dutton's *Tertiary History*. Three of the four heliotypes are of a piece – images of cliffs and other geological formations photographed

25 Jack Hillers, *Cliffs*

26 Jack Hillers, *Head of the Grand Canyon*

27 *Jurassic White Sandstone*, from *The Tertiary History of the Grand Canyon District*,
Clarence Dutton

at a distance across the flat foreground and middleground plane of the canyonland landscape (see Figure 27). The fourth, *Inner Gorge at Toroweap – Looking East*, uses light and shadow effectively to exemplify the way in which photographs can often surpass stereoscopic images at presenting the three-dimensionality of the Grand Canyon (see Figure 28). This image is of further interest because it served as the basis of a wood engraving made by Thomas Moran to illustrate Powell's 1875 exploration narrative in *Scribner's* and the Smithsonian monograph (see Figure 29). Like Moran's wood-cuts in Dutton's *Tertiary History*, this Hillers photograph uses the conventions of landscape composition and linear perspective to domesticate and tame the canyon scenery, thereby making it more cognitively accessible. Like Hillers' heliotypes, Moran's illustrations in Dutton's monograph stand as accessible images of Grand Canyon beauty, rather than inaccessible representations of the Grand Canyon's sublimity. As such, these images fail to convey the sense of the canyon's cognitive inaccessibility by making the canyon appear cognitively accessible through the conventions of picturesque landscape representation.

The same can hardly be said for Moran's second "big picture," *The Chasm of the Colorado*, completed eight years prior to the publication of Dutton's monograph (see Figure 30). Dated "1873 + 4," Moran's painting

28 *Inner Gorge at Toroweap – Looking East*, from *The Tertiary History of the Grand Canyon District*, Clarence Dutton

29 *Grand Canyon Looking East from Toroweap*, wood engraving by Thomas Moran from
An Exploration of the Colorado River, John Wesley Powell

did not enjoy nearly as favorable and enthusiastic a reception as did his
Yellowstone painting of 1872 – perhaps because it does not readily conform
to the accepted conventions of landscape painting. Richard Watson Gilder,
Scribner's art critic and a friend of Moran's, wrote of *The Chasm of the
Colorado*: "This later picture is a more daring attempt; it shows the growth

30 Thomas Moran, *The Chasm of the Colorado*

of the artist's mind and powers. But its subject is less fortunate, because less pleasing. It is more crowded with 'effects' and therefore, will seem to lack that firm unity which distinguishes the earlier picture."[105] Clarence Cook, art critic for *Atlantic Monthly*, was even more ambivalent about Moran's second big picture, perhaps because he more explicitly recognized the way in which the scenery of the Grand Canyon eluded established landscape conventions. "The landscape of Mr. Moran's first picture," Cook writes, "was equally awful and desolate with that shown us in the present work, but its terror was lessened by the beauty and variety of the color with which nature veiled her work of change and destruction. Here, we have no such charm. We are led into a region where the eye has hardly a resting-place, no resting-place, in fact, unless it be turned upward to the sky."[106] Interestingly Cook, with only Moran's painting as evidence, anticipates Dutton's description of the restiveness that befalls the first-time visitor to the canyon as he tries and fails to comprehend the scene. Because the scene does not conform to the landscape conventions of the time, and because Moran insists on "representing the scenes as they look to him," Cook concludes that: "The picture not only crowds too much incident into its comparatively narrow frame, but the subject it deals with is one that never should have been attempted – partly because it is impossible to do justice to it, and again because art is not concerned with it, if it were possible."[107] For both Gilder and Cook, Moran's painting is marred not so much by failures of art (although Cook does chide Moran for having "contracted a certain mannerism"), as by a failure of subject, the impossibility of the Grand Canyon to be made into art.

If this is indeed the case, it cannot be said that Moran did not fail for lack of trying. Although framed, like Moran's Yellowstone painting, in a conventional, Claudean sense, *The Chasm of the Colorado* is, unlike the earlier painting, uninhabited. But it shares with the former painting an entry-ledge or "proscenium" at almost the same spot of the painting. This proscenium is marked on the left by a small cactus with yellow flowers; to the left of the cactus is a snake slithering into the space of the picture, not unlike the way our vision itself does. Similarly the left-hand framing coulisse deliberately echoes *The Grand Canyon of the Yellowstone*, although in *The Chasm of the Colorado* the big pines on the left-hand side are much smaller, with their space on the canvas taken up by cliffs instead. The right-hand coulisse of the latter painting is much smaller than in the former; set back further in the space of the picture, it opens up the right side of the painting much more than in the former. *The Chasm of the Colorado* has more sky and horizon than the Yellowstone painting. And while the later painting provides several glimpses of the Colorado river, it is smaller and much further away than in *The Grand Canyon of the Yellowstone*. Indeed all of the distances are much greater in the second painting, making it difficult to get a firm sense of scale, to know how large, for example, the boulders perched on the rim are supposed to be.[108] This is of course the essence of the Grand Canyon, part of what makes it so difficult to contain it within conventional visual and conceptual schema.

Joni Kinsey tries to tame both the landscape and Moran's painting by offering an allegorical or symbolic reading in which "The rainbow, which appears only partially in the center of the painting, is the potential redeeming force" in a painting that has been said to be lacking in "redeeming inspirational appeal."[109] Kinsey interprets the rainbow, with the storm on the left of the painting which it accompanies, as representative of the still unfinished task of redeeming the land with irrigation and other forms of land management laid out in Powell's important 1878 *Report on the Lands of the Arid Region*. She supports her reading by noting that the storm blocks much of the scene, and can thus be seen visually to help tame and contain the landscape (not unlike the way in which obstructions work in Hillers' stereos to do the same thing, to make them more comprehensible as three-dimensional). Her impulse to read the painting symbolically or iconographically is reinforced by the presence of "what appears to be a sculptured classical frieze" highlighted by a sunbeam at the base of a tower situated underneath the storm."[110] Although unsure whether the frieze is meant to represent pictographs or petroglyphs, or, as depicted in a related wood engraving, "three bound figures, reminiscent of Michelangelo's *Slaves*," Kinsey is certain that "their presence within the natural towers of the Grand Canyon region implies that Moran was emphasizing the epic quality of the landscape, the timeless saga of transition and change he found within its formations."[III]

Rather than try to determine *what* such figures mean to Moran, however, it seems more to the point to recognize *that* they appear to mean. As Dutton repeatedly insists in the *Tertiary History*, what distinguishes the Grand Canyon from other more familiar landscapes is the way in which meaningless, accidental forms, created by "the blind forces of Nature," appear to be meaningful, appear in particular to look architectural. Moran's seemingly iconographic elements, I would argue, like the seemingly architectural forms of the canyon landscape, do not in themselves have a particular meaning, but rather dramatize the challenges of understanding or comprehending the Grand Canyon.

Moran tries to address this condition by providing a sense of the duplication and repetition of forms, suggesting the reproduction of the same geological formations all the way back to the horizon, which, as Kinsey notes, could easily be 50 or 100 miles away. By depicting only part of a landscape which extends indefinitely beyond the frame of the painting, Moran suggests the way in which this landscape is less easily contained by a single painting, by a single perceptual or conceptual act, than is, say, Yellowstone or Yosemite. Unlike Moran's *Grand Canyon of the Yellowstone*, a "great painting of the great original," as one of Moran's contemporaries described it, *The Chasm of the Colorado* doesn't seem to be a painting of a "great original" at all in the sense that it seems like an almost arbitrary portion of an endlessly repeated sameness. Less a great painting than a reproduction, Moran's picture seems to represent a scene that is the same as that which is around it, outside the picture frame. Indeed in Moran's painting, nature itself seems like a reproduction rather than an original, in that what one sees in the painting is not so much different from what one would see in the landscape around the painting. In the Yellowstone painting, on the other hand, the viewer clearly has the sense that the Grand Canyon of the Yellowstone is distinctive or unique, different from other canyons in the Yellowstone area or elsewhere. This helps explain, or perhaps contributes to, the delay in Grand Canyon becoming a national park: it is not a readily comprehensible monument to American national identity. If, as I have argued in the previous chapter, the experience of Yellowstone is about the preservation of the moment of historical discovery, then the experience of the Grand Canyon is about the resistance to discovery. The Grand Canyon both awaits discovery (it is uninhabited in Moran's picture) and thwarts discovery (since to discover something that is not unique is not really to discover anything at all). *The Chasm of the Colorado*, like the Grand Canyon itself, is about human insignificance; *The Grand Canyon of the Yellowstone*, on the other hand, with its reproduction of the moment of discovery by European Americans, a moment that brought devastating changes to the region, is about the significance of human action. When Moran paints his Grand Canyon painting, not only is the technology of preservation not in place (because the technologies of development are not in place), but there does not seem to be a strong need to preserve the Grand Canyon because (unlike the Grand Canyon of the Yellowstone, Yellowstone Lake, Mammoth Hot Springs, or Yellowstone's various geyser basins) human agency does not seem to be an immediate threat either to the canyon itself or to continued access to its features.

MEDIATING TECHNOLOGIES AT POINT SUBLIME

Unlike Moran's *Chasm of the Colorado*, his illustrations in Dutton's *Tertiary History* do not dramatize the way in which the Grand Canyon escapes or frustrates individual mediating technologies, but rather try to depict the canyon within the conventions of nineteenth-century landscape illustration. The role of dramatizing the canyon's cognitive inaccessibility is left to William Henry Holmes' remarkable *Panorama from Point Sublime*. The closest that a Moran image comes to this is his one contribution to the *Atlas*, *The Transept*, which was drawn from one of Holmes' sketches (see Figure 31). Like Holmes' *Panorama* and *Grand Cañon at the Foot of the Toroweap – Looking East*, Moran's *Transept* is shaded in browns and blacks. But Moran makes no attempt to get the geological details captured in Holmes' pictures. That is, unlike the more painterly style employed by Moran, Holmes employs the techniques of topographical drawing and geological cross-sections – he has many more *lines* in his images. While Moran still lets the reader see the geological changes from layer to layer, these changes are depicted more with shadow and color than with line-drawing. This difference has to do chiefly with Holmes' training as a scientific illustrator, his familiarity with topographical conventions which, unlike the conventions of picturesque landscape painting, can help to convey information that is not conveyable by more conventional aesthetic means. The effect of Moran's contribution to the *Atlas* is much more subjective, much

31 Thomas Moran, *The Transept*

more ideal than real – it is concerned with the effect of the view. The left-hand side of the Moran image is framed by a rock-pile structure; the right by rocks and trees and some scrub-like growth. Unlike Holmes, Moran tries more concertedly to incorporate the image within conventional landscape representations, to make the canyon cognitively accessible to readers of Dutton's monograph.

Of course, depicting a secondary formation rather than the panorama from Point Sublime makes a difference, as Dutton makes abundantly clear in his chapter entitled "The Panorama from Point Sublime." This chapter is interesting for a number of reasons, not least that it provides a striking account of the epistemological experience of cognitive inaccessibility that distinguishes the Grand Canyon from all other spectacular natural scenes. "The space under immediate view" from Point Sublime, Dutton writes, "is thronged with a great multitude of objects so vast in size, so bold yet majestic in form, so infinite in their details, that as the truth gradually reveals itself to the perceptions it arouses the strongest emotions. Unquestionably the great, the overruling feature is the wall on the opposite side of the gulf. Can mortal fancy create a picture of a mural front a mile in height, 7 to 10 miles distant, and receding into space indefinitely in either direction? As the mind strives to realize its proportions its spirit is broken and its imagination completely crushed."[112] After recounting this initial experience of what has been called the "negative sublime," Dutton goes on to describe the scene further in an attempt both to account for the spirit-breaking and imagination-crushing force of the view and to reassert some sort of control over the canyon. As Dutton continues to furnish both geological and aesthetic explanations for the scene's powerful sublimity, he employs a strategy prevalent in Powell's text: he names some of the canyon's features. Dutton's names are evocative as well as descriptive: Vishnu's Temple resembles an Oriental pagoda; The Cloisters is the name Dutton gives to two lines of characteristic butte forms; a gigantic mass of a butte is named Shiva's Temple, because "it seemed as if the fabled 'Destroyer' might find an abode not wholly uncongenial" there.[113] Most telling, though, is that the urge to name arises precisely as a way to help reestablish the mind's composure and control over what it has only partly succeeded in comprehending.

Naming also figures in Dutton's chapter insofar as it shares its name with William Henry Holmes' tri-partite panorama, the only illustrations to appear in both the monograph and the atlas. Thus in some senses the chapter title (and the chapter itself) can be seen to refer simultaneously to the panorama presented to someone on the rim of the Grand Canyon at Point Sublime and to the panorama drawn by Holmes, the reproduction of which is presented to the reader of Dutton's *Tertiary History*. Like Dutton's chapter, Holmes' panorama attempts to overcome the Canyon's cognitive inaccessibility at the same time that it dramatizes the limitations of the technologies of panoramic representation. An interesting hybrid technology of representation, the panorama is well suited to the immense scale of the canyon landscape. In part a cross between a single-point perspective drawing and a map, the panorama tries to escape some of the visual limitations built into single-point perspective, creating a representation in which the objects that make up the picture are related to one another in a more mathematical or cartographic sense, rather than being represented as they appear from a single viewing point. Indeed, the scientific and cartographic purposes of Holmes' tripartite panorama are reinforced by the key that underwrites each of the three parts – a key that unlocks both the geology and the geography of the scene by identifying the primary features of the landscape as well as the geological components of the canyon walls. This key also links Holmes' panorama to the tradition of such nineteenth-century visual technologies of representation as dioramas and panoramas, which combined painting with three-dimensional artifacts to create large-scale popular exhibitions of famous landscapes, historical events, or fictional scenes and employed the convention of "orientation maps" with numbered features to help viewers make sense of these large-scale visual exhibitions.

The individual panoramas that make up Holmes' *Panorama from Point Sublime* (*Part I – Looking East, Part II – Looking South, Part III – Looking West*; see Figures 32–34) are designed to fit together into a single, continuous panoramic view – the very view described by Dutton in his chapter. In the first image there are two figures on an overlook, conventionally understood as the overlook from which the panorama is meant to be viewed. One (apparently Holmes himself) is sketching, the other (perhaps Dutton) looking over Holmes' shoulder. If this is indeed the overlook on Point Sublime from which the entire panorama is meant to be viewed, it is interesting that the overlook itself is not present in the other two pictures. There is in each picture a foreground plateau, on which the panorama's spectators can imaginatively locate themselves, but there are no figures on the other two. The figures in the left-hand panel both look to the right, that is, not to the east (as the picture is oriented) but to the west, towards the other two parts of the panorama. Although the first panorama panel is meant to look to the east and the third to look to the west, the whole triptych is looking south – after all, Point Sublime is on the north rim. Thus while the left image is looking east, and the right image is looking west, they are not "facing" east or west but looking in that direction across to the south rim (that is, looking south-east and south-west). Despite the strong mapping impulse present in the panorama, the orientation is to the south, not to the north. In other words, unlike a map, in the depicted space of the panorama left is east and right is west. Although the top is essentially south, the bottom does not function as north, which is in fact to the back of the viewer of the panorama (or the figures on the ledge).

This orientation does some interesting things with the notion of point of view in the panorama. The fact that the viewing point is built into the picture looking east is quite interesting; perspectively speaking, the viewing point of these other two parts of the panorama is in *another picture*. Of course, practically speaking this makes no real pictorial difference; the distances represented are so great that the panoramas look virtually the same from more than one point of view. Thus each stands alone. But the fact that the three panoramas are meant to go together helps to underscore Dutton's point both about the way in which the Grand Canyon cannot be grasped or comprehended all at once and about how conventional technologies of representation cannot capture the sublime scenery of the Grand Canyon. But that is not to say that these panoramas do not try to do so. If we put the panorama together in our imagination, we can see that it is framed in

PANORAMA FROM POINT SUBLIME

32 William Henry Holmes, *Panorama from Point Sublime, Part 1 – Looking East*

PANORAMA FROM POINT SUBLIME

33 William Henry Holmes, *Panorama from Point Sublime, Part II – Looking South*

PANORAMA FROM POINT SUBLIME

34 William Henry Holmes, *Panorama from Point Sublime, Part III – Looking West*

the fairly conventional fashion of nineteenth-century landscape painting on the left and on the right by foreground coulisses – trees, rocks, brush on a kind of cliff-rim formation. In other words, the first panorama furnishes a frame on the left, the second a kind of middle ledge jutting out in its center, and the third a frame on the right. Thus on the one hand each part of the panorama stands alone, but on the other hand it does not. Each part of the panorama is simultaneously complete and fragmentary. Or to be more precise, the individual pictures stand alone when seen from the perspective of mapping or schematic or scientific representation. But when seen from the perspective of conventional landscape representation, they are incomplete fragments, insufficient individually to contain or comprehend the scenery.

Holmes' *Panorama from Point Sublime* recapitulates the tension in Dutton's prose between scientific and aesthetic representation. As in Dutton's text, the technologies of scientific representation employed by Holmes attempt to comprehend and control the initial aesthetic response both to the canyon's architectural structure and to the overwhelming immensity of the landscape itself. Keying the different geological features depicted in the panorama to the specifics of the narrative set forth in Dutton's prose, Holmes would attempt to constrain the spectator's mind to accept Dutton's scientific explanation of the landscape's origins. But this attempt at controlling or containing the landscape within the framework of scientific reasoning is counteracted by the aesthetic problems posed by the panorama's inability to represent the scene entirely within either a cartographic or a perspectival visual framework. Indeed in employing elements of a number of different technologies of representation, Holmes' panorama epitomizes the strategy of the monograph as a whole – a strategy which compensates for the inability of conventional aesthetic preconceptions to make sense of the canyon by producing a proliferation of verbal and visual representations, none of which can by itself succeed in comprehending the landscape. In saying this, I do not mean to suggest that taken all together the competing technologies of representation that make up Dutton's monograph do finally succeed in providing a unified and comprehensive understanding of the canyon; that is, they do not succeed in overcoming the experience of the canyon's cognitive inaccessibility. Rather I mean to suggest that they reproduce the feeling of cognitive inaccessibility by means of a strategy similar to that employed in the proliferation of competing representations of the canyon to this very day. And in reproducing this feeling, Dutton's monograph and its accompanying *Atlas* come close to providing what might count as a comprehensive understanding of the Grand Canyon.

REMEDIATING THE GRAND CANYON

As the variety of mediating technologies employed in Dutton's monograph and *Atlas* suggest, one way of responding to the logic of recognition associated with the Grand Canyon is to produce a multiplicity of attempts to represent it, each of which allows the Grand Canyon to be recognized at the same time that it fails to render it cognitively accessible. The aim of this response is to compensate for the impossibility of comprehending the canyon within a single representation by producing a number of different representations in a variety of genres and media. Although no individual conceptual or pictorial framework is able to comprehend the canyon in its entirety, the multiplicity of representations is able to reproduce something like the feeling of its cognitive inaccessibility. Increasingly in the past century the cultural logic of recognition associated with the Grand Canyon has manifested itself in what I have elsewhere called a double logic of "remediation," in which the inability of any single genre or medium of representation to provide a transparent experience of the canyon's "immediacy" calls forth an expression of "hypermediacy," the multiplication and juxtaposition of different forms and genres of mediation.[114] In remediating the canyon in different technologies of mediation, more recent efforts do not give up on providing an immediate experience of the Grand Canyon, but often do so in such a way as to call attention to, not conceal, the signs of its mediation. While these recent efforts operate in relation to different cultural and historical circumstances, it is interesting to note the similarities among them in their approach to the canyon's cognitive inaccessibility.

One quite dramatic effort to use a new technology to capture the immediacy of the canyon occurred in 1911, when Ellsworth and Emery Kolb attempted to capture on motion picture film the experience of running the Colorado River through the entire Grand Canyon. In the late fall of 1911 the Kolb Brothers, who had run a photographic studio on the South Rim of the Canyon since 1903, set out from Green River, Wyoming, where Powell had started in 1869. In addition to capturing their trip in photographs, stereographs, and motion pictures, Ellsworth recounted the brothers' expedition in a book, *Through the Grand Canyon from Wyoming to Mexico*. In the book's foreword, Owen Wister situates the Kolbs precisely as Powell's heirs. Noting that Kolb's book is the third of its kind (following upon those of Powell and Frederick Dellenbaugh, who accompanied Powell's second expedition in 1870), Wister nonetheless insists that "it differs from its predecessors more than enough to hold its own: no previous explorers have attempted to take moving pictures of the Colorado River with themselves weltering in its form."[115]

For Wister the new technology of moving pictures offers an immediacy of representation unavailable to still photographers. Ellsworth, too, situates the brothers' project in terms of their own prior photographic history and aspirations, noting that their river expedition comes in the context of ten years in which he and his brother have been photographing the Grand Canyon, working "in a general way," "adjacent to our home," "always in search of the interesting and the unusual." Although this ten years' work, Ellsworth acknowledges, satisfied "many of our plans" in regard to "a pictorial exploration of the Grand Canyon," it left unsatisfied their "real ambition": "to make the 'Big Trip' – as we called it; in other words, we wanted a pictorial record of the entire series of canyons on the Green and Colorado rivers."[116] For the Kolb brothers, this comprehensive photographic record is the fundamental reason for the trip: "the success of our expedition depended on our success as photographers. We could not hope to add anything of importance to the scientific and topographic knowledge of the canyons already existing; and merely to come out alive at the other end did not make a strong appeal to our vanity. We were there as scenic photographers in love with their work, and determined to reproduce the marvels of the Colorado's canyons, as far as we could do it."[117] Completing their trip safely would not in and of itself constitute a successful expedition; the only knowledge the brothers could add to what was already known about the river would be photographic. Neither scientific exploration nor heroic achievement were the aim of the trip, but the "photographic reproduction" of the "marvels of the Colorado's canyons."

In fact, what the brothers most wanted to do was to reproduce the canyon's "marvels" and "wonders" with a "motion picture":

Most important of all, we had brought a motion-picture camera. We had no real assurance that so delicate an apparatus, always difficult to use and regulate, could even survive the journey – much less, in such inexperienced hands as ours, reproduce its wonders. But this, nevertheless, was our secret hope, hardly admitted to our most intimate friends – that we could bring out a record of the Colorado as it is, a live thing, armed as it were with teeth, ready to crush and devour.[118]

This desire to capture the experience of running the river with the newly developed medium of motion picture film expresses in characteristic fashion a claim often made by new technologies of mediation or representation, to be able to provide an immediacy of experience unavailable to prior technological media. In striving to "bring out a record of the Colorado as it is, a live thing armed as it were with teeth," the Kolbs operate from the assumption that prior technologies of mediation have not yet captured or "recorded" the river "as it is." While this claim is based largely upon the capability of motion pictures to capture time and movement in a way that still photography cannot, the Kolbs also participate in a logic of recognition in which the canyon is cognitively inaccessible to any single form of technological mediation. Despite the hope that the new technology of motion pictures would enable them to capture "the Colorado as it is" on film in such a way that its mediation would be rendered transparent, and other media be rendered unnecessary, the film that the Kolbs took on their trip through the canyon was unable to stand on its own as a record of their expedition. Much like what Tom Gunning has characterized as "the cinema of attractions," the film the Kolbs took on the river never provided the experience of transparency offered by conventional Hollywood cinema.[119] On the contrary, the brothers' film was always screened as part of an ensemble of diverse and heterogeneous media, first on the lecture circuit back East and, after 1915, in the studio on the South Rim, where Emery ran something of a multimedia spectacle: "Twice every day, Emery walked to the head of the stairs at the back of the auditorium, surveyed the visitors seated below, then made his entrance quietly but regally down the stairs to a landing at the bottom. While he told his story of daring explorations of the Canyon, the projectionists ran the pictures, consisting of lantern slides alternating with movie film depicting the famous 1911 river trip."[120] Not only was the motion picture film juxtaposed with still slides and supplemented with Emery's lecture, but the studio itself, with its upstairs gift shop, offered photographs, Navajo rugs, petrified wood, and Indian jewelry for sale. In addition, for those who wanted an even closer look at the canyon, a telescope was available for viewing at the studio window.[121] In the film's social and material presentation, the desire to capture the immediacy of the experience of running the river, "the Colorado as it is," is replaced by an experience of hypermediacy, in which the motion picture film is only one of a number of competing media that come (directly or indirectly) to represent the Grand Canyon.

Although the Kolb Studio finally closed in 1976, the year Emery Kolb died, the experience it offered tourists of viewing a film made by men who were weltering in the foam of the Colorado was resurrected in 1984, with the release of the IMAX film *Grand Canyon: The Hidden Secrets*. The aim of the film, as expressed in the companion piece *Making of Grand Canyon: The Hidden Secrets*, is similar to that of the Kolb Brothers: to provide the "ninety-five percent of people, who only see the South Rim . . . an extraordinary extension of their experience," by putting cameras "where very few people ever go" and providing "perspectives very few people ever get." The challenge posed by IMAX technology is not insignificant: "Filming in areas few tourists ever reach proved to be a test of endurance." *Making of Grand Canyon* emphasizes the heroism of the filmmakers, opening with a voice-over narrative that makes a claim very much like that made by both Wister and Ellsworth Kolb about the limitations of prior media technologies: "The Grand Canyon, a masterpiece of nature formed by 6,000,000 years of erosion, a chasm over 270 miles long and one mile deep – so epic, its wonder and majesty have never successfully been recorded, until now." Like their effort to use new motion picture technology to capture "the Colorado as it is," the voice-over continues, the Academy Award-winning director of the film, Kieth Merrill, is using "the most advanced motion picture format in existence" to try to capture the Grand Canyon's "hidden secrets." Not only does the oversized IMAX technology make it difficult to "put that camera in places people have never seen before," but the IMAX format posed formal cinematographic problems as well. "Although experienced in conventional 35 mm film production, the filmmakers had to reeducate themselves to the unique requirements of the IMAX format." One of the main differences, according to David Douglas, veteran cinematographer, is that "with IMAX . . . we have tried to fill the field of view completely with the image so that you have no terms of reference except for the screen and the pictures on the screen."[122]

Unlike the experience of viewing the Kolbs' film of their expedition, with its juxtaposition to still images projected by lantern slides, the experience of viewing the IMAX film is designed to be totally immersive. As with most new advances in mediation technologies, however, IMAX bears with it the claim to eliminate signs of mediation at the same time that it participates in a proliferation of media technologies. Like the film of the Kolb brothers running the Colorado, the IMAX film *Grand Canyon: Hidden Secrets* is presented in an environment filled with other "terms of reference." Employing "the world's largest motion picture format in one of the world's largest locations," the film is currently shown 365 days a year, hourly at half past the hour, in the National Geographic Theater in Grand Canyon, Arizona, "Arizona's Number One Tourist Attraction."[123] Just as the IMAX film is significantly more immediate than the Kolbs' film, so the National Geographic Theater is significantly more hypermediated than the Kolb Studio. Like the Kolb Studio gift shop, which "offered photographs, Navajo rugs, petrified wood, and Indian jewelry for sale," the National Geographic Theater has two gift shops "offer[ing] an excellent selection of

Native American arts and crafts." But the theatre, which is home to the Arizona Tourist Information and Visitor Center, also offers a food court featuring Taco Bell, Pizza Hut, and the Canyon Cappuccino and Cafe; ATM and Phoneline USA machines; postage stamps and a mailbox; and a courtesy desk where visitors can make reservations for airplane and helicopter tours of the Grand Canyon.[124] The experience of the Grand Canyon as mediated through IMAX is simultaneously claimed (by the film's voice-over) to allow us to "discover a consciousness of our own immortality" through feelings of "reverence, appreciation, and kinship," at the very same time as we are invited to enmesh our experience of the National Park in a post-industrial network of commodification, communication, transportation, and commerce.

The IMAX film and its exhibition space epitomize how, in today's media-saturated environment, the logic of recognition invoked by the sublimity of the Grand Canyon takes the form of a double logic of remediation – the simultaneous attempt to erase and to proliferate signs of mediation.[125] I want to conclude with another late-twentieth-century remediation of the canyon's sublimity within a cultural logic of recognition: Lawrence Kasdan's 1991 film *Grand Canyon*. Despite its title, the film only incidentally concerns the canyon. It does, however, serve to remediate the Grand Canyon through two different but related accounts of its sublimity. The first, a version of Kant's mathematical sublime, is that the immediacy of the canyon makes people feel small. This is the gist of a speech by Danny Glover's character early in the movie, after he "rescues" Kevin Kline's character from the clutches of a gang of LA teenagers. Talking about a trip he had made to the canyon, Glover's character explains how the Grand Canyon makes humans feel insignificant. When he visited the canyon, he says, he realized that because the rocks were so old, because they took so long "to happen" (indeed because they are still happening), they could not care less about human worries or accomplishments. The canyon makes us feel that we and our concerns are insignificant, he continues, and that it is laughing at us. In this account the canyon seems perfectly comprehensible; there is no problem with our ability (or inability) to understand it. Rather we understand it fine, and in understanding it we understand our own insignificance. The canyon is immediately present to us, independent not only of any signs of mediation, but (as Harriet Monroe had implied) of all signs of humanity. For Glover's character this feeling of insignificance is empowering. The sublimity he experienced at the canyon enables him to accommodate himself to the social and economic inequities of late-twentieth-century Los Angeles, a point underscored later in the film when Steve Martin's character uses the Grand Canyon as a social metaphor of the abyss or chasm between the haves and have-nots in late-twentieth-century America. In this account of the canyon's sublimity, it is immediately comprehensible, so comprehensible that it can stand as the vehicle of a metaphor of class division in Los Angeles.

There is, however, a second sense in which the canyon is represented as sublime, which comes at the end of the film and precisely concerns our inability fully to represent or comprehend it. This version of the dynamic, or epistemological, sublime evokes a crisis of representation or knowledge, in which our concepts, our conventional modes both of knowledge and of representation, are unable to control or subsume, to apprehend or comprehend, the canyon. This cognitive inaccessibility is marked by the fact that the only images that Kasdan provides of the Grand Canyon occur in an approximately two-and-a-half minute sequence at the end of the film, just prior to and then under the final credits. As the film nears its conclusion, the narrative takes us to the edge of the canyon, to the brink of the abyss, where the camera shows the faces of the film's central characters as they look in varying degrees of awe at the canyon (which we have not seen and do not know is the object of the characters' gaze). The camera then does a 180-degree pan and presents the canyon in an approximately 20-second sequence from behind the characters, framed (or grounded) by them in the bottom of the shot. This is followed by about a 15-second sequence of the canyon unmediated by people or text, after which the camera swoops out over the canyon in an approximately two-minute sequence shot from a helicopter and presented almost entirely underneath the closing credits. Kasdan's suggestion in doing this is that the experience of looking at the canyon is so sublime that we need the credits as a filter or mediation in order to be able to see the canyon at all. A related point is made in a Sony commercial from 1992, which was airing during the time the movie would have been available on video. In this commercial we see an image of the Grand Canyon and hear the voices of a family apparently looking at the canyon and proclaiming in amazement about how huge it is and how clear it looks. As the camera pulls back, we see that, although the family is indeed standing on the rim of the Grand Canyon, what they are marvelling at is not the canyon itself but its image on a big-screen Sony TV.[126]

In both the Sony commercial and the closing credits of *Grand Canyon*, the canyon is represented as so difficult to comprehend that it can only be understood in terms of an arbitrary social, formal, or technological frame (whether the physical frame of the TV screen or the conventional cinematic frame of the closing credits). But this also proves true of the film's first sense of the canyon's sublimity in which the canyon proves comprehensible enough to serve as a metaphorical frame with which Kasdan and his characters make sense of race and class division in LA. In each sense, then, the sublimity of the canyon is ultimately empowering when the canyon's incomprehensibility is framed for us by some conceptual or technological mediation. Like the classical structure of Kant's dynamic sublime, our inability to comprehend, which produces our feeling of insignificance, is followed by the assertion of some attempt at comprehension, at framing or representation, which makes us (or at least our concepts) greater or more powerful than the canyon in a way that the initial form of the sublime would at first deny. As evidenced in the logic of recognition that has been affiliated with the Grand Canyon since its exploration by Powell in 1869, such limiting frames make it possible for us to recognize the canyon at the same time that they preserve its cognitive inaccessibility. Paradoxically, the more the canyon escapes our comprehension, the more we attempt to comprehend it by proliferating technologies of representation which remediate our experience of the canyon by reproducing themselves in response to the failure of any single technology (or "unmediated" experience) to comprehend and thus tame the Grand Canyon.

Remediating nature: national parks as mediated public space

At the beginning of the twenty-first century it is now possible to watch Old Faithful erupt on America Online. Indeed, courtesy of two webcams linked to the Yellowstone National Park website, anybody with an internet connection can monitor the activity of Yellowstone's best known geyser or check on the grazing elk herds in the parking area in front of the park's Mammoth Hot Springs (see Figure 35). In addition to the opportunity of monitoring nature's fidelity by means of the fidelity of digital technology, Yellowstone's official website also invites visitors to take any number of virtual tours of the park, choosing from a menu comprised of history and nature tours, as well as QTVR (Quick-Time Virtual Reality) panoramas.[1] Initially, such technologically mediated phenomena might appear antithetical to the kinds of experience that national parks were established to provide for American citizens and other visitors. Parks, it would seem, should get people out from behind their computers, not encourage them to stay there. Isn't at least one of the purposes of America's national parks to preserve and protect nature from the encroachment of technology, to provide opportunities for individuals to encounter nature or the wilderness face to face, without the perceptual or conceptual mediations of society or culture? Well, yes and no.

As I have argued throughout this book, national parks have functioned from their inception as technologies for reproducing nature according to the scientific, cultural, and aesthetic practices of a particular historical moment – the period roughly between the Civil War and the end of the First World War. In this brief conclusion I want to extend the book's treatment of the origins of the national parks to today's media-saturated environment, in order to suggest some of the ways in which the concept of nature as public space continues to be "remediated" into the first decade of the twenty-first century.[2] At a moment when the explosive growth of new digital technologies has enabled nature to be mediated in an arguably unprecedented variety of aesthetic forms, it is important to understand the often contradictory

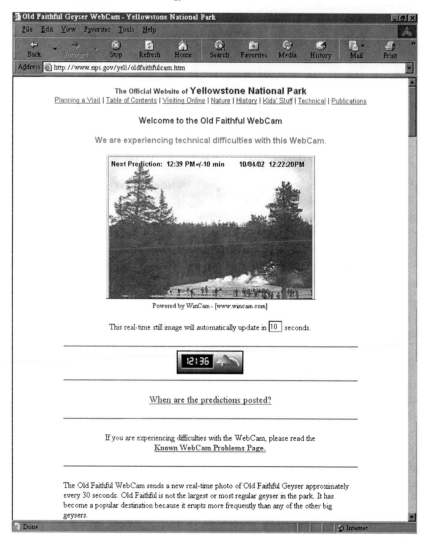

35 Old Faithful Webcam, October 4, 2002

ways in which these new media technologies claim to improve upon prior
forms of representing place, environment, and landscape. On the one hand,
through their liveness and interactivity, new media technologies like stream-
ing video or virtual reality claim to offer us a more immediate, authentic
experience of nature than prior media forms, an experience in which all

signs of cultural mediation have vanished. The goal of these technologies is to make possible the experience of unmediated nature anywhere in the world, that is, anywhere within the extensive networks of global telecommunication. On the other hand, through their self-acknowledgment and ubiquity, networked technologies, like portable information appliances or the world wide web, claim to offer us a more highly mediated experience of nature than has been possible before. The goal of these technologies is to make possible the experience of digital mediation anywhere in the natural world, which simultaneously produces and destabilizes the distinction between nature and its mediation.

This conclusion takes up some examples of how the National Park Service transforms nature into a public space where the boundary between the natural world and the mediated one has become increasingly open and permeable. Of the major American parks, Yellowstone, recognized as the world's first national park, has the most extensively developed web apparatus for cybertourists, evident in its on-line tours, webcams, and QTVR panoramas – not to mention its own IMAX film and theatre. Grand Canyon, the most visited park in the West, has the most extensively developed media apparatus for tourists who travel to the park seeking to experience the mysteries of the canyon. As I argued in the previous chapter, Grand Canyon National Park is a heterogeneous cultural and technological network for reproducing nature as cognitively inaccessible. The seeming impossibility of capturing the canyon within a single representational form has brought forth a proliferation of different representations in a variety of genres and media. Although no individual conceptual or pictorial framework may let a visitor comprehend the Grand Canyon in its entirety, the multiplicity of representations can reproduce something like the feeling of nature's cognitive inaccessibility that lies at the heart of the Grand Canyon's appeal to tourists. In remediating the canyon in different technologies of mediation, more recent efforts do not give up on the goal of capturing an experience of the canyon's immediacy, but often do so in such a way as to call attention to, while at the same time seeking to obscure, the signs of nature's mediation. The aim of this process is not only to mediate nature in another form, but to reform nature, to remedy the damage we have done to it.

In environmental waste management, "remediation" refers explicitly to the clean-up of contaminated sites, the process of rehabilitating or restoring soil and groundwater to a healthy condition, if not to its natural state. Without getting into the interesting philosophical and ecological questions about what would constitute a "healthy" or "natural" state for any particular site, it is worth noting the way in which the National Park Service itself employs a rhetoric of remediation that functions both in this ecological sense as well as in terms of mediation. Indeed to "remediate" a contaminated site it is necessary to re-fashion or remediate that site in another form in order to remedy or reform it. This process of environmental remediation resembles what Carolyn Merchant has characterized as the "recovery narrative" at the heart of American environmentalism,[3] a narrative that is at work across the Park System, as I will illustrate in brief discussions of Cumberland Island National Seashore, Dinosaur National Monument, and the "virtual" Bravo 20 National Park.

Each of these parks adopts different strategies for remediating something that has gone wrong in nature as a result of human action. In the interpretive materials on Cumberland Island, for example, the National Park Service presents two competing accounts of the island's history, one which relies on the linear metaphor of time's arrow, the other which relies on a metaphor of time's cycle.[4] Cumberland Island was established as a national seashore in 1972, to preserve the scenic, scientific, and historical values of the largest and most southerly island off the coast of Georgia. The story that the Park Service tells is essentially a teleological one. In this, narrative nature has fallen from its original Edenic state; the goal of the Park Service is to restore it to its natural condition, which can only be preserved and maintained by the authority of the Park Service itself. The Park Service narrates the history of Cumberland Island as a series of prior historical appropriations, each of which has left some mark upon the island both of its own culture and of the damage it has done to the island's coastal ecosystem. The earliest human inhabitants were American Indians, followed by Spanish missionaries, English colonial military personnel, antebellum plantation owners, Confederate soldiers, and the wealthy industrialists of the Gilded Age. That is to say, on first blush the Park Service offers a version of the island's history as a linear progression from a prehuman state of nature through a succession of human appropriations of the island. As such, this narrative presents the current island, the island as national seashore, as the latest in a series of human occupations, human developments, this time for the purposes of preservation and recreation.

But at the same time, there is another way to read this narrative about the ecological state of the park. In preserving the island for recreation, the Park Service is also protecting its natural qualities, that is, protecting it from yet more of the kind of human misappropriations detailed in the official interpretive history. Rather than take the current state of the island as the latest in a series of cultural appropriations, this reading takes Cumberland Island National Seashore as an escape from any human appropriation whatsoever, in other words, as a return to what it was prior to any human acquisition of the island. This constitutes a kind of typological reading evident elsewhere in the literature of the parks, in which the natural, pre-human state of the island prefigures the coming of the Park Service – a kind of preservationist typology in which not Jesus but the National Park Service represents the culmination or fulfillment of the history of human interaction with nature.

Cumberland Island manifests two competing visions of what it means to remediate nature, one which acknowledges the National Seashore as the latest historical occupation, the product of American ecological imperialism, and one which imagines the island as independent of historical occupation, human appropriation, or cultural mediation. Indeed, it is the coexistence of these two different accounts of remediating nature that marks today's national parks. The return of Cumberland Island to nature has been made possible by the (ongoing) intervention of the Park Service, which aims both to preserve a record of prior interventions and to return nature to self-sufficiency (as defined and authorized by the institutional practices of the Park Service itself). Thus not only does the Park Service tell the history of the island as a series of remediations, in which nature is mediated differently according to the cultural practices of its different owners, but it also seeks to remedy the detrimental ecological effects brought about by its prior inhabitants.

The idea that national parks should seek to present nature as it was prior to its first encounter by European-Americans obtains from Yellowstone to the state parks of Florida. Cumberland Island presents a more radical version of this idea in that its official goal is to return the national seashore to a coastal ecosystem independent even of its earliest human inhabitants. An even more extreme remediation of nature can be found in Dinosaur National Monument, which tries in some senses to return visitors to an ecosystem prior to the appearance of humans on the planet. As on Cumberland Island, Dinosaur National Monument attempts to return to some originary state of nature. But where that ur-nature for Cumberland is placed in the context of human interaction with landscape, in Dinosaur this ur-nature exists prior to humans completely, as the park in some sense tries to return visitors to a natural world before dinosaurs went extinct.

Perhaps the more significant remediation of nature in Dinosaur National Monument is the attempt to remedy the thoughtless and selfish activities of nineteenth-century explorers, discoverers, and even early museum curators, all of whom participated in plundering sites for profit rather than preserving them for scientific purposes or for human appreciation and observation. This threat to the site's natural resources is not unlike the activities of early developers who sought to privatize or profit from Yosemite Valley, Grand Canyon, Mesa Verde, or other spectacular natural or cultural features. In aiming to remediate the site, the museum that constitutes the heart of Dinosaur National Monument is built into a hillside containing undisturbed dinosaur fossils (see Figures 36 and 37). This intriguing design preserves for visitors the experience of the moment of scientific discovery, as well as preserving the fossils themselves – similar to what was done at Yellowstone more than a century earlier. Through interpretive exhibits, the museum also situates the monument in relation to the history of the early discoverers and provides a genealogy of the museums and collections to which notable fossils have gone, as well as records of when they were found. Thus in Dinosaur National Monument the interpretive materials primarily concern not (as in Cumberland or other traditonal parks) the appropriation of the land or landscape, but rather the appropriation of the fossils of extinct dinosaurs, whose extinction could (at least in the imagination of the monument's visitors) be remediated.

Where Dinosaur National Monument exists in part to preserve a record of both the extinction of dinosaurs and the destruction of their remains, Bravo 20 National Park would (if it were ever actually to be established) preserve the devastation of a desert landscape by the United States Navy, which has used it as a bombing range since 1952. Currently existing only as a virtual park on the world wide web, Bravo 20 National Park is the brainchild of Richard Misrach, a photographer known for his images of devastated natural landscapes. As set forth in a book published in 1990, Bravo 20 National Park would "serve as a permanent reminder of how military, government, corporate, and individual practices can harm the earth. In the spirit of Bull Run and the Vietnam Memorial, it would be a national acknowledgment of a complex and disturbing period in our history."[5] Andrew Ross has criticized the proposal for its lack of radical edge, for running the risk of "being viewed more as an example of conceptual art" than as a political statement. Ross laments: "This would be unfortunate, since it promises to be an entirely novel way of presenting an environmental critique: rather than celebrate the preservation of an environment, Bravo 20 would be a park whose purpose is to preserve a record of environmental destruction."[6] But as my discussion of Cumberland and Dinosaur has suggested, Ross here misses the point of contemporary National Park Service ideology and practice. Although Bravo 20's remediation of nature is only at this point a proposed one, it is of a piece with the logic of remediation informing present-day national parks. Misrach remediates the site aesthetically by photographing it (see Figure 38) and reproducing these photographs as a book and on the web, as well as displaying them as a museum exhibit

36 Dinosaur National Monument (exterior)

37 Dinosaur National Monument (interior)

and as individual prints. The proposal for the national park also remediates the site by memorializing it in terms of the history of nuclear and other armed air warfare. That is, the national park remediates not only the effect of these practices on our own landscape, but in an even larger sense, the practices themselves. So, the remediation in Bravo 20 is not only formal (as in the photographs, the book, the exhibit, the web-site, and even the proposed park), but also reformative, in that it is meant to improve the landscape but also somehow to remediate our practices of military testing or our militaristic posture towards nature in the twentieth century.

Most importantly, what Misrach's proposal for Bravo 20 National Park recognizes is the way in which national parks function as technologies for the reproduction of nature. The book concludes with a series of architectural drawings and illustrations depicting the proposed park, commissioned from Burton and Spitz, a Santa Monica landscape architecture firm, with help from Matthew Miller and Rico Solinas (see, for example, Figures 39 and 40). What these architectural drawings and illustrations remind us is that national parks are constituted not as Ross naively suggests by "the celebration of a natural environment," but by the cultural and technological reproduction of nature. Because he does not understand that national parks have always been constituted by the network of technological, cultural, and

38 Richard Misrach, *Crater and Destroyed Convoy,* from *Bravo 20: The Bombing of the American West*

aesthetic practices for the reproduction of nature at a particular historical moment, Ross has difficulty imagining "visitors incorporating Bravo 20 into the tourist circuit of the West which includes the likes of Yosemite, King's Canyon, Lake Mead, the Grand Canyon, Grand Teton, Yellowstone, and the great national parks of Utah."[7] Although it may be difficult to imagine Bravo 20 as part of the vacation plans of nature-loving tourists, it is less difficult to imagine such a park as part of a circuit including Hoover Dam, Mesa Verde, and other more historical parks, monuments, and battlefields.

In any case, what Misrach understands and Ross does not is the way in which, just as Yellowstone and Yosemite were created as national parks in accordance with late-nineteenth-century assumptions about landscape and representation, so a national park today (whether scenic or historic) must be created according to present-day assumptions about media, culture, and technology. Consequently, his proposal for Bravo 20 National Park is presented as complete with all of the technologies of a national park circa 1990. "In accordance with the 'interpretive programs' of all national

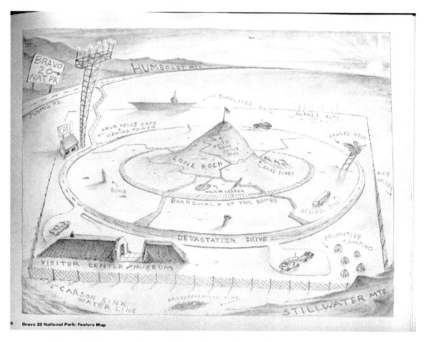

39 Richard Misrach, *National Park: Feature Map*, from *Bravo 20: The Bombing of the American West*

parks," Misrach writes,"Bravo 20 will serve an educational function." The park will have a "Visitor Center and Museum, devoted to the history of military abuse in peacetime, which will include "a film and video archive" and a "library [which] will collect relevant material for the public's edi-fication" (see Figure 41).[8] "To put the consequences and implications of the Navy's actions into perspective," Misrach continues, "the geological, archaeological, environmental, religious, economic, and cultural (Indian) significance of the area will be highlighted." The park proposal also includes a cafe, primitive camping sites, viewing towers, a scenic drive, a boardwalk for viewing "the rough terrain of craters and shrapnel," a walk-in crater, and a trail to the top of Lone Rock, the sacred Northern Paiute mountain at the center of the park. Noting that "no national park is complete without a gift shop," he writes that "as in all national park gift shops, the Bravo 20 items will range from the meaningful to the tacky," from serious books, maps, and art reproductions to "imprinted clothing such as camouflage-style caps, t-shirts, pants; 'Nevada is not a Wasteland' and 'Bombs Away' mugs,

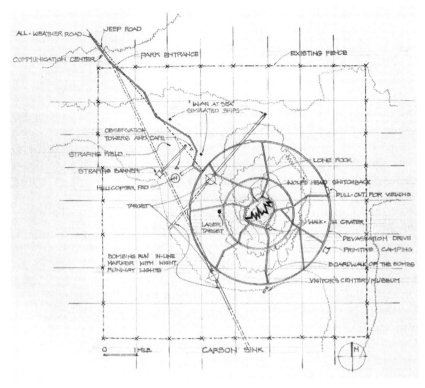

40 Richard Misrach, *National Park: Site Plan*, from *Bravo 20: The Bombing of the American West*

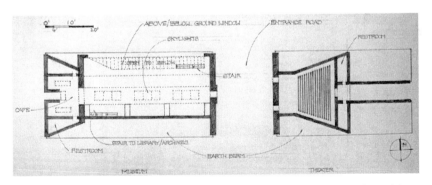

41 Richard Misrach, *Visitors' Center and Museum*, from *Bravo 20: The Bombing of the American West*

tote-bags, and bumper stickers; and for the kids, Mattel models based on the most advanced, top-secret military designs – up-to-date delivery systems and Stealth bombers."[9]

Although the book's dramatic photographs and narrative of environmental "monkey reclamation" are meant in part to create the impetus for preserving the "Bravo 20 landscape [as] a poignant and sobering symbol of the military's destruction of the environment" and "a powerful warning for future generations," Misrach's work is also important for its self-conscious recognition of the way in which national parks are cultural practices for re-mediating nature as mediated public space. While today Bravo 20 National Park can only be read about in a book or visited on the world wide web, access to the web is now readily available at parks like Yosemite, Yellow-stone, and Grand Canyon, not only for tourists but for the parks' native inhabitants as well. Indeed, since September 2000, the Havasupai reser-vation on the floor of the Grand Canyon (along with Navajo and Hopi reservations in New Mexico and Utah) has been linked to the Internet via two-way, high speed wireless satellite connections furnished by an alliance between Starband Communications, Northern Arizona University, and the Southwest Navajo Nation Virtual Alliance.[10] At a moment when we can not only watch Old Faithful erupt on America Online, but also access America Online from the site of Old Faithful, a firm distinction between natural and mediated public space becomes increasingly difficult to maintain. And just as national parks were created in postbellum America as technologies for reproducing nature according to the aesthetic forms and practices of nineteenth-century landscape representation, so they will increasingly be created and maintained in the century to come as technologies for remedi-ating nature according to the aesthetic forms and practices of digital media today.

Notes

INTRODUCTION

1 Aldo S. Leopold *et al.*, "Wildlife Management in the National Parks" (March 4, 1963), in *Compilation of the Administrative Policies for the National Parks and National Monuments of Scientific Significance (Natural Area Category)* (Washington, DC: US Department of the Interior, rev. 1968), 92.

2 The "locus classicus" for the idea of America as "nature's nation" is Perry Miller, "Nature and the National Ego," in *Errand into the Wilderness* (Cambridge, Mass.: The Belknap Press of Harvard University Press, 1956), 204–216. For a revisionary interpretation of Miller's essay, see Myra Jehlen, *American Incarnation: The Individual, the Nation, and the Continent* (Cambridge, Mass.: Harvard University Press, 1989), and Cecelia Tichi, *Embodiment of a Nation: Human Form in American Places* (Cambridge, Mass.: Harvard University Press, 2001).

3 In *Uncommon Ground: Toward Reinventing Nature*, ed. William Cronon (New York: W.W. Norton & Co., 1995), this position can be found not only in Cronon's lead essay ("The Trouble with Wilderness; or, Getting Back to the Wrong Nature," 69–90), but also in the essays by Anne Whiston Spirn ("Constructing Nature: The Legacy of Frederick Law Olmsted," 91–113) and Kenneth Olwig ("Reinventing Common Nature: Yosemite and Mount Rushmore – A Meandering Tale of a Double Nature," 379–408). In *Sacred Places: American Tourist Attractions in the Nineteenth Century* (New York: Oxford University Press, 1989), John Sears detailed the way in which Yosemite and Yellowstone are constructed as culturally sacred places for American tourists. More recently Mark Spence has treated the cultural politics of Indian removal in the founding of America's national parks, *Dispossessing the Wilderness: Indian Removal and the Making of the National Parks* (New York: Oxford University Press, 1999).

4 Cronon's paper was drawn from the essay "The Trouble with Wilderness; or, Getting Back to the Wrong Nature," published in *Uncommon Ground*, 69–90. Cronon's argument, indeed the entire three-year project from which the book emerged, provoked a rather lively response from two University of California-Santa Cruz ecologists, Michael Soulé and Gary Lease, who sponsored a counter-conference, the proceedings of which were published in a collection of essays meant to challenge the increasing acceptance of arguments for the cultural

construction of nature in environmental studies, *Reinventing Nature? Responses to Postmodern Deconstruction* (Washington, DC: Island Press, 1995).

5 Lawrence Buell, *The Environmental Imagination: Thoreau, Nature Writing, and the Formation of American Culture* (Cambridge, Mass.: The Belknap Press of Harvard University Press, 1995), 35.

6 In "The Trouble With Wilderness," William Cronon angered many environmental historians and ecocritics alike with his claim that wilderness is a cultural construction: "Far from being the one place on earth that stands apart from humanity. It is quite profoundly a human creation – indeed, the creation of very particular human cultures at very particular moments in human history" (*Uncommon Ground*, 69). Cronon's appeal to the particularity of history and culture goes precisely in the direction I set out to pursue in this book. Unfortunately the essay itself takes an overly broad approach to cultural history, citing as an example of this particularity the fact that Wordsworth, Thoreau, and Muir participated in the same "cultural tradition" of "mountain as cathedral," without even acknowledging, for example, the very real differences among the three men's religious upbringings. Nonetheless, Cronon's expressed desire to historicize and particularize such notions as nature, wilderness, or national parks is one that I share in this book.

7 N. Katherine Hayles, the only author to appear both in Cronon's *Uncommon Ground* and in Soulé's and Lease's *Reinventing Nature?* offers the position of "constrained constructivism" as her attempt to preserve the insights of cultural constructivism while simultaneously accounting for the materiality and particularity of nature; "Searching for Common Ground," in *Reinventing Nature?* 47–63.

8 "Organic machine" is the term coined by Richard White in *The Organic Machine: The Remaking of the Columbia River* (New York: Hill and Wang, 1995) to describe "the remaking of the Columbia River" in the Pacific Northwest as "an energy system which, although modified by human interventions, maintains its natural, its 'unmade' qualities"; ix. Although White's approach differs from mine in that he focuses more on the human and technical labor involved in remaking the river, while I focus more on the logic and practices of representation through which national parks reproduce nature, we are both engaged in trying to find a way to talk about nature as simultaneously constructed and unmade.

9 Bruno Latour, *Science in Action: How to Follow Scientists and Engineers through Society* (Cambridge, Mass.: Harvard University Press, 1987), 201.

10 Thomas Cole, "Essay on American Scenery," in *Atlantic Monthly* 1 (January 1836), rpt. *American Art: Readings from the Colonial Era to the Present*, ed. Harold Spencer (New York: Scribner's, 1980), 82–90; 85.

11 Asher Durand, "Letters on Landscape Painting: Letter II," *The Crayon*, January 17, 1855, rpt. *American Art: Readings from the Colonial Era to the Present*, ed. Harold Spencer (New York: Scribner's, 1980), 93–94.

12 Angela Miller, *The Empire of the Eye: Landscape Representation and American Cultural Politics, 1825–1875* (Ithaca, N.Y.: Cornell University Press, 1996), 39.

13 Ibid., 129.

14 Ibid., 137.

15 Angela Miller, "Everywhere and Nowhere: The Making of the National Land-scape," *American Literary History*, vol. 4, no. 2 (Summer 1992), 209.

16 Ibid., 209.

17 Marguerite Shaffer, "Negotiating National Identity: Western Tourism and 'See America First,'" *Reopening the American West*, ed. Hal K. Rothman (Tucson: University of Arizona Press, 1998), 122.

18 Ibid., 123.

19 William G. Robbins, *Colony and Empire: The Capitalist Transformation of the American West* (Lawrence: University of Kansas Press, 1994), 84.

20 It is generally accepted that the major figures of the new Western history are William Cronon, Patricia Nelson Limerick, Richard White, and Donald Worster. The paradigmatic works of this intellectual movement include *Under an Open Sky: Rethinking America's Western Past*, ed. Cronon, George Miles, and Jay Gitlin (New York: Norton, 1992); Limerick's *The Legacy of Conquest: The Unbroken Past of the American West* (New York: Norton, 1987); White's *"It's Your Misfortune and None of My Own": A New History of the American West* (Norman: University of Oklahoma Press, 1991); and Worster's *Under Western Skies; Nature and History in the American West* (New York: Oxford University Press, 1992).

The works of these and other new Western historians are by no means univocal. In a special issue of *Arizona Quarterly* devoted to the new Western history (vol. 53, no. 2, Summer 1997), Jerome Frisk maps out some of the differences among these historians. Frisk argues in part that these differences are made possible only within a horizon of shared assumptions, including the assumption that environmentalism and preservationism do not escape, but replicate, the ideological categories and the discriminatory or exploitative practices of nineteenth-century American culture. Although my work has been influenced by the new Western history, my book does not address the issue of the West as a central problematic. My reasons for doing so are at least partly because I take seriously the claim that the West is not an exceptional region but rather part of the development of the nation as a whole. Consequently I proceed from the assumption that the origins of America's national parks need to be understood in relation to the "discourse networks" of the nation as a whole, rather than in relation to a particular regional history.

21 Robbins, *Colony and Empire*, 62–63.

22 Shaffer, "Negotiating National Identity," 122.

23 "Introduction," *Configurations* 3 (1995): 349–351.

24 Alan Trachtenberg, *The Incorporation of America: Culture and Society in the Gilded Age* (New York: Hill and Wang, 1982).

25 White, *Organic Machine*.

26 Robbins, *Colony and Empire*, 86.

27 For further discussion of Bierstadt and Watkins in relation to Yosemite, see Chapter 1. Throughout the book I take up the question of photography's

representational and ontological status. In the Yosemite chapter, I deal with the question of photographic agency; the Yellowstone chapter focuses more on the mimetic fidelity of the photograph in relation to other technologies of representation.

28 As such, the purified space of a national park is in some senses analogous to the purified space of the scientific laboratory, whose freedom from the interference of social, economic, or political forces is made possible precisely by its participation in (and protection by) a heterogeneous network of linguistic, social, and economic practices. See Bruno Latour, *Science in Action*, Chapter 2.

29 It is true that in their early years America's national parks, like museums themselves, were most often patronized by members of an elite class. This practice is not only the result of the fact that early park tourism operated according to a particular class model, but also because the inexpensive technologies of transportation and accommodation envisioned by early park advocates did not begin to develop in earnest until early in the twentieth century. Nonetheless, it is important that Frederick Law Olmsted, for example, interpreted the creation of the parks as fundamentally democratic, aimed precisely at preventing them from falling into private hands, thus being only available to a wealthy, privileged class. For a contrary view of Olmsted, and of the national parks in general, as deploying nature primarily as an instrument of class, race, and gender inequities, see Stephen E. Germic, *American Green: Class, Crisis, and the Deployment of Nature in Central Park, Yosemite, and Yellowstone* (Lanham, Mass.: Lexington Books, 2001).

30 Bruno Latour, *We Have Never Been Modern*, trans. Catherine Porter (Cambridge, Md.: Harvard University Press, 1993).

31 Michel Foucault, *The Archaeology of Knowledge*, trans. A.M. Sheridan Smith (New York: Pantheon Books, 1972), 47.

32 Ibid., 47.

33 Ibid., 72.

1 RECREATING YOSEMITE

1 US, *Statutes at Large*, 13 (1864): 325.

2 *Congressional Globe*, 38th Congress, 1st session, 1310. All subsequent citations from the *Globe* will be noted in the text as (*Globe* pp.).

3 *Wilderness and the American Mind* (3rd ed.; New Haven: Yale University Press, 1982), 106.

4 According to Roderick Nash the precedent set by Yosemite's preservation was one which "completely countered dominant American purposes. For the pioneer, wilderness preservation was absurd, and even those who recognized the advantages of reservoirs of wildness had to admit the force of civilization's claims"; *Wilderness and the American Mind*, 96. While more recent scholarship recognizes the difficulty of escaping prevailing ideological formations, preservationism is still seen chiefly as an attempt to oppose these formations. Thus Alan Trachtenberg, although lamenting that preservationism did not emerge

until "the apparatus of exploitation was already in place," nonetheless contends that the preservation movement ran counter to the nation's "massive conversion of nature into the means and ends of industrial production"; *The Incorporation of America: Culture and Society in the Gilded Age* (New York: Hill and Wang, 1982), 22.

5 *National Parks: The American Experience* (2nd ed., Lincoln, Nebr.: University of Nebraska Press, 1987), 48.

6 Nash, *Wilderness and the American Mind*, 96.

7 To see contestatory ideological positions as part of dominant American purposes is not to say that ceding land for the preservation of a park is identical to ceding land for the construction of a railroad. But it is equally the case that these two examples of federal land-use policy are not motivated by diametrically opposed purposes. In granting land for the construction of the Osage and Cottonwood Valley Railroad, Congress increases the value of land that is not being used for public purposes, land that has no special value to the government because it is no different from any of the other land surrounding it. In ceding Yosemite to California for recreational purposes, on the other hand, Congress both converts into valuable property land that is ostensibly of no value to the government (because it cannot be converted into a mine, railroad, or homestead), and re-produces this land as nature by preserving it as a park, thereby preventing its appropriation for other economic, industrial, or cultural purposes.

8 By framing the question of Yosemite's preservation in this way, I mean to offer an alternative to a line of argumentation developed in the past couple of decades by environmental historians, who generally agree that despite its historical significance the 1864 preservation of Yosemite by Congress was not an expression of genuine environmental concerns because it was not founded upon the recognition of an intrinsic value in nature, a value inalienable and un-able to be converted into something else. Thus, despite considering Yosemite's preservation a significant legal precedent, for example, Nash minimizes its sig-nificance for the origins of the American environmentalist movement because it was motivated not by biocentric ideas of wilderness but by the anthropocentric values of tourism. Nash, *Wilderness and the American Mind*, 106; *The Rights of Nature: A History of Environmental Ethics* (Madison, Wis.: University of Wisconsin Press, 1989), 35. Similarly, Runte has characterized "the park act of 1864" as "a model piece of legislation," even while faulting Congress for failing to measure up to a twentieth-century idea of ecology: "Monumentalism, not environmentalism, was the driving impetus behind the 1864 Yosemite Act." Al-fred Runte, *Yosemite: The Embattled Wilderness* (Lincoln, Nebr.: University of Nebraska Press, 1990), 21. Writing environmental history as if the value of these oppositions was culturally and temporally stable, Nash and Runte illustrate a crucial limitation of much contemporary environmental history, the inability to come to terms with the way in which ideas like environmentalism or actions like wilderness preservation did obtain in the early years of the national parks movement, even if these earlier ideas and actions cannot measure up to current standards.

9 George Catlin, *Letters and Notes on the Manners, Customs, and Conditions of the North American Indians Written during Eight Years' Travel (1832–1839) amongst the Wildest Tribes of Indians in North America*, 1844; rpt. in two volumes (New York: Dover Publications, Inc., 1973), I, 260–264; Henry David Thoreau, "Walking," *Excursions: The Writings of Henry David Thoreau*, vol. IX, Riverside edition, 11 vols. (Boston: Houghton Mifflin, 1893); George Perkins Marsh, *Man and Nature; or, Physical Geography as Modified by Human Action* (New York: Charles Scribner, 1864), 328–329.

10 John Muir, *The Yosemite* (1892; rpt. San Francisco, Calif.: Sierra Club Books, 1988), 196–197.

11 Much ink has been spilled over the struggle for Hetch Hetchy. A standard Whig account (from the preservationist point of view) of the Hetch Hetchy controversy is Holway R. Jones, *John Muir and the Sierra Club: The Battle for Yosemite* (San Francisco, Calif.: Sierra Club Books, 1965). See, as well, Nash, *Wilderness and the American Mind*, 161–181. For a more nuanced account, see Michael L. Smith, *Pacific Visions: California Scientists and the Environment, 1850–1915* (New Haven: Yale University Press, 1987), 172–185.

12 Elizabeth Stevenson, *Park Maker: A Life of Frederick Law Olmsted* (New York: Macmillan, 1977), 263.

13 The suppression of Olmsted's report is passed over in a sentence in what is nonetheless the best, most recent biography of Olmsted: Witold Rybczynski, *A Clearing in the Distance: Frederick Law Olmsted and America in the Nineteenth Century* (New York: Scribner, 1999). In her earlier biography of Olmsted, Roper has suggested that his Yosemite report was sabotaged by two of his fellow commissioners, Ashburner (who attended the meeting in the valley) and Whitney (who didn't). As members of the California Geological Survey the two men apparently felt that the funds which Olmsted had requested for managing the park would come out of the state's appropriations for the Survey, *FLO: A Biography of Frederick Law Olmsted* (Baltimore: Johns Hopkins University Press, 1973), 287. For whatever reason, Olmsted's report was lost from sight until Roper resurrected it for publication in 1952. For further discussion of the report's suppression, see Runte, *Yosemite*, 28–31 and "Introduction," *The Papers of Frederick Law Olmsted*, vol. V: *The California Frontier, 1863–1865*, ed. Victoria Post Ranney (Baltimore: Johns Hopkins University Press, 1990), 22–23. For the history of the report's reconstruction, see Roper, "The Yosemite Valley," 12–13.

14 Alfred Runte, for example, sees Olmsted as possessing an early environmental consciousness lacking both in Congress and throughout the history of Yosemite's management, calling Olmsted's report an uncompromising demand for "preservation of the park for its own sake"; Runte, *Yosemite*, 31. John Sears, who considers Yosemite "a turning point in the history of American tourism and in the search for an adequate cultural monument," reads Olmsted's report quite differently, arguing that Olmsted articulates the "view that Yosemite should be developed as a public park, that roads and railroads be built to it and facilities constructed for the accommodation of tourists" (Sears, *Sacred Places*,

123, 133). Despite these differing estimations of the report, it is generally agreed that the report is, in Runte's words, "a classic, a statement that literally anticipated the ideals of national park management" (Runte, *Yosemite*, 28). Runte is not alone in this assessment. Albert Fein credits the report with the articulation of "a philosophy and a set of working principles for the creation of state and national parks"; *Frederick Law Olmsted and the American Environmental Tradition* (New York: George Braziller, 1972), 40. The editors of the Olmsted papers call his report "the first comprehensive statement on the preservation of natural scenery in America." *The Papers of Frederick Law Olmsted*, vol. V, 3. All quotations from Olmsted's report will come from this edition. All subsequent references to the Olmsted Papers will be cited in the text, with volume and page numbers, as (*FLO* vol.: pp.). Laura Wood Roper makes a similar claim, arguing that "With this single report, in short, Olmsted formulated a philosophic base for the creation of state and national parks"; "The Yosemite Valley and the Mariposa Big Trees: A Preliminary Report (1865)," *Landscape Architecture* 43 (1952): 13. Roper elaborates this claim in her biography of Olmsted, contending that "Olmsted's report was the first systematic exposition of the right and duty of a democracy to take the action that Congress had taken in reserving the Yosemite Valley and the Mariposa Big Tree Grove from private preemption for the enjoyment of all the people"; *FLO: A Biography*, 283. And in her biography Elizabeth Stevenson concurs, asserting that "it was Olmsted who honorably instigated the movement of preservation to be followed, abandoned, and then re-adopted here and elsewhere in the national park system and later in the wilderness system" (Stevenson, *Park Maker*, 271).

15 Shortly after the war had ended, while still in San Franciscso, Olmsted declined the position of General Secretary of the American Freedmen's Aid Union. His plans instead involved becoming associate editor of William Godwin's weekly newspaper, *The Nation*, and resuming his landscape architecture in collaboration with Calvert Vaux.

16 *FLO* 5: 488.

17 Abraham Lincoln, *Annual Message to Congress, December 1, 1862*.

18 Although conceptualizing the space of the canvas as a map worked primarily to underscore East–West iconography, it occasionally worked to depict an iconographic point about the relation between North and South as well. This can be seen in Durand's *Progress* and Jasper Cropsey's *Autumn on the Hudson River*, both of which are seen by Angela Miller as invoking pictorial depth as the mark of civilization. That is, the further you go back into the depicted space of these paintings, the more you move toward progress or civilization, which is marked by light-filled distance, factories, and farms. This marks, in some sense, a North–South axis as well – that is, if we map cartographic space onto the canvas, to move back in space is also to move up on the canvas, i.e., to the civilized North, which contrasts with the barbarism and savagery of the South, depicted by Olmsted in his *Cotton Kingdom*; Angela Miller, *The Empire of the Eye: Landscape Representation and American Cultural Politics, 1825–1875* (Ithaca, N.Y.: Cornell University Press, 1996), 160–162.

19 Marguerite S. Shaffer, "Negotiating National Identity: Western Tourism and 'See America First,'" in Hal Rothman, ed., *Reopening the American West* (Tucson: University of Arizona Press, 1998), 122.

20 The alliance between Eastern and Western interests, of course, preceded the war, particularly insofar as the states of the Northeast were aligned politically with Western states like California in opposition to slavery. The war itself shifts the nation's attention from the East–West axis in favor of a focus on the division between Northern and Southern States. As Olmsted's report already foresees, the end of the war helps recreate the East–West axis as the basis of the nation's orientation in the cultural imagination, which then gets recreated after the war; cf. Miller, *Empire of the Eye*, 182–190.

21 Olmsted's conviction that the preservation of Yosemite could help reunite the nation after the Civil War was also shared by Frederick Billings, who "saw in Yosemite and other scenic locales in the West a powerful symbol for a nation in the midst of the Civil War"; Mark David Spence, *Dispossessing the Wilderness: Indian Removal and the Making of the National Parks* (New York: Oxford University Press, 1999), 36–37.

22 This cliché is exemplified in the following passage from Samuel Bowles, who travelled in August 1865 from Mariposa to Yosemite in a party that included Olmsted among its number: "The Yosemite! As well interpret God in thirty-nine articles as portray it to you by word of mouth or pen. As well reproduce castle or cathedral by a stolen frieze, or broken column, as this assemblage of natural wonder and beauty by photograph or painting." Bowles was the editor of the influential *Springfield Republican*, one of the few newspapers that Olmsted admired (*FLO* 5: 380). Bowles' travel letters to the *Republican* were collected in *Across the Continent: A Summer's Journey to the Rockey Mountains, the Mormons and the Pacific States, with Speaker Colfax* (Springfield, Mass.: Samuel Bowles & Co., 1865), 223.

23 Albert D. Richardson, a correspondent for the *New York Daily Tribune*, travelled to Yosemite with the party that included Bowles and Olmsted in August 1865; Richardson records his trip in letters to the *Tribune*, collected as *Beyond the Mississippi From the Great River to the Great Ocean. Life and Adventure on the Prairies, Mountains, and Pacific Coast* (Hartford, Conn.: American Publishing Company, 1867). Fitz-Hugh Ludlow recorded his travels West with Albert Bierstadt in a series of articles for the *Atlantic Monthly*; their 1863 trip to Yosemite is described in "Seven Weeks in the Great Yo-Semite," *Atlantic Monthly* 13 (1864): 739–754. Thomas Starr King reported his 1860 trip to Yosemite in a series of travel letters in the *Boston Evening Transcript*; these letters have been reprinted as *A Vacation Among the Sierras: Yosemite in 1860* (San Francisco, Calif.: Book Club of California, 1962). Like Olmsted's Yosemite report, all of these journalistic accounts participate in the reorientation of national unity from the North–South axis of the Civil War to an East–West axis of tourism and economic development.

24 "The Relation of Photography to the Fine Arts," *Philadelphia Photographer* 2 (1865), 3. John Moran was the younger brother of Thomas "Yellowstone"

Moran, whose paintings and lithographs of the Yellowstone region were (with William Henry Jackson's photographs), like Bierstadt's paintings and Watkins' photographs in the case of Yosemite, influential in persuading Congress to pass the legislation establishing the nation's first official national park.

25 Ibid., 3.

26 Stanley Cavell describes this relinquishment of agency as satisfying "the human wish, intensifying in the West since the Reformation, to escape subjectivity and metaphysical isolation": "Photography overcame subjectivity in a way undreamed of by painting, a way that could not satisfy painting, one which does not so much defeat the act of painting as escape it altogether: by *automatism*, by removing the human agent from the task of reproduction"; Stanley Cavell, *The World Viewed: Reflections on the Ontology of Film*, enlarged edition (Cambridge, Mass.: Harvard University Press, 1979), 21, 23. What twentieth-century commentators ascribed to mechanism or automatism, nineteenth-century commentators ascribed to the laws of nature. Thus in *The Pencil of Nature* (London, 1844–1846; rpt. New York: Da Capo Press, 1969), the first published book of photographs, H. Fox Talbot assured his readers that his photographs were "impressed by Nature's hand" "without any aid whatever from the artist's pencil": "and what they want as yet of delicacy and finish of execution arises chiefly from our want of sufficient knowledge of [Nature's] laws." For Fox Talbot as for Moran, photography is distinguished from painting precisely because in order to realize his intention the photographer must at the moment of exposure, a "moment" which in the early days of photography could sometimes take over an hour, relinquish artistic control to "Nature's hand."

27 This passage initially appeared in Olmsted's first book, *Walks and Talks of an American Farmer in England*, published in 1852 and written, as he would later say, "before [Central] Park was dreamed of, . . . and with no more idea that I should ever be a professional landscape-designer than that I should command a fleet"; Olmsted, "The Spoils of the Park," in *Landscape into Cityscape: Frederick Law Olmsted's Plans for a Greater New York City*, ed. Albert Fein (Ithaca, N.Y.: Cornell University Press, 1967), 427. The centrality of this double logic to Olmsted's aesthetics of landscape architecture is evinced by his resurrection of this passage at pivotal moments in his career – like the 1858 letter accepting the position of Architect-in-Chief of Central Park, or *The Spoils of the Park*, a pamphlet written in 1882 to save the Park's original design from political mismanagement.

28 From an undated fragment in the Olmsted papers, qtd. Irving D. Fisher, *Frederick Law Olmsted and the City Planning Movement in the United States* (Ann Arbor, Mich.: University of Michigan Press, 1986), 30.

29 Miller, *Empire of the Eye*, 87. As Miller later notes, "transparent representation" is also the ideal of the mid-nineteenth-century "Sister Arts" theory; ibid., 95.

30 Asher Durand, "Letters on Landscape Painting," *Crayon* I: 274 (1855); qtd. Lisa Fellows Andrus, "Design and Measurement in Luminist Art," in *American Light: The Luminist Movement, 1850–1875*, ed. John Wilmerding (Washington,

DC: Princeton University Press/National Gallery of Art, Washington, 1980), 56 n. 13.

31 Durand, "Letters on American Landscape Painting," Letter 5, *Crayon* 1 (1855), in *American Art: Readings from the Colonial Era to the Present*, ed. Harold Spencer (New York: Charles Scribner's Sons, 1980), 95.

32 James Jackson Jarves, *The Art-Idea* (Cambridge, Mass., 1864, rpt. 1960), 205. The aesthetics of "high art" that Jarves ascribes to the landscapes of Inness are similar to the aesthetics of absorption that Michael Fried has so compellingly detailed in *Absorption and Theatricality: Painting and Beholder in the Age of Diderot* (Berkeley: University of California Press, 1980). There are particularly striking parallels between Jarves' account of Inness' landscapes and Diderot's descriptions of Vernet's landscapes in the Salon of 1767, which (like Inness' paintings) invite the spectator to enter into and inhabit them; see Fried, *Absorption and Theatricality*, 122–132.

33 Jarves, *The Art-Idea*, 205–206. The formal basis of Jarves' evaluation is not always evident to present-day observers. Angela Miller, for example, sees landscape artists after Cole as using natural conflicts in their compositions to display nationalist ideas, to minimize "human and social agency": "One result of this rhetoric of natural conflict was to blunt any notion of historical causality, and to substitute compelling natural dramas for human and social agency"; *Empire of the Eye*, 110. For Miller, Church is the major figure for this overcoming of human and social agency in his "naturalization of national allegory." It is not unlikely that Jarves' evaluation of Church and Bierstadt was in part a response to the way in which they exhibited their paintings. Both employed a hypermediated optical and tactile experience which reminded spectators of the mediation of their paintings, rather than concealing the signs of it; see Jay David Bolter and Richard Grusin, *Remediation: Understanding New Media* (Cambridge, Mass.: MIT Press, 1999). In displaying *The Heart of the Andes* in 1859, for example, Church employed "a level of organized showmanship that he never surpassed. The painting was shown in a darkened room, lit by gasjets, and surrounded by tropical plants. An almost endless series of newspaper reviews and commentaries discussed the picture, and the pamphlets of Louis Noble and [Theodore] Winthrop interpreted it to eager readers"; Franklin Kelly, *Frederic Edwin Church and the National Landscape* (Washington, DC: Smithsonian Institution Press, 1988), 98. Following the example of Church, Bierstadt displayed his Yosemite paintings in a studio filled with "sketches, photographs, Indian artifacts, and stuffed animal heads secured on his overland journey"; Nancy K. Anderson and Linda S. Ferber, *Albert Bierstadt: Art and Enterprise* (Brooklyn, N.Y.: Hudson Hills Press, 1990), 31. Cook, too, sees the appeal of Bierstadt as precisely and primarily theatrical – see page 31 for Cook's description of Bierstadt's exhibition style, and pages 73–74, 83, and 90 for similar practice regarding Bierstadt's Yosemite paintings.

34 *Landscape into Cityscape*, 74. Here, ownership and property rights are both involved in letting us see that the park is also a technology for producing and

eliding the ownership of nature. The ideal of the national parks (and of all parks for Olmsted) is that the visitor is in the best sense the true owner of the park.

35 *Frederick Law Olmsted, Landscape Architect, 1822–1903*, ed. Frederick Law Olmsted, Jr., and Theodora Kimball, 2 vols. (New York: Benjamin Blom, Vol. I 1922, Vol. II 1928; rpt. as single vol. 1970), 309–10.

36 Ibid.

37 Ibid., 427 n.

38 Although Mountain View Cemetery was laid out along the lines of Olmsted's design, neither of Olmsted's other two designs were ever implemented – in fact it was a number of years before Olmsted even received payment for his design for the Berkeley campus. Olmsted's correspondence with Vaux was quite involved and often bitter, focusing not only on the continuation of the partnership but on who should receive what kind of credit and how much for their work on Central Park; *FLO* 5: 358–445.

39 Olmsted Papers; qtd. Fisher, *Frederick Law Olmsted and the City Planning Movement*, 29.

40 Olmsted offered a more vexed definition of landscape architecture in a letter written to Calvert Vaux from Bear Valley, California, the town in which Olmsted lived while managing the Mariposa Mining Company. Dated August 1, 1865, the letter is mostly concerned with the problems Olmsted has with the term "landscape architecture." "I am all the time bothered with the miserable nomenclature of L.A. *Landscape* is not a good word, *Architecture* is not; the combination is not. *Gardening* is worse. I want English names for ferme and *village* ornée – street &c ornée – but ornée or decorated is not the idea – it is artified & rural artified – which is not decorated merely. The art is not gardening nor is it architecture. What I am doing here in Cal[ifornia] especially, is neither. It is the sylvan art, *fine-art* in distinction from Horticulture, Agriculture or Sylvan *useful* art. We want a distinction between a nurseryman and a market gardener & an orchardist, and an artist. And the planting of a street or road – the arrangement of village streets – is neither *Landscape* Art, nor *Architectural* Art, nor is it both together, in my mind – of course it is not, & it will never be in the popular mind. Then neither park nor garden, nor street, road, avenue or drive, nor boulevard, apply to a sylvan bordered and artistically arranged system of roads, sidewalks and public places, – playgrounds, parades etc. There is nothing of park, garden or architecture, or landscape in a parade ground – not necessarily, though there may be a little of any or each and all. If you are bound to establish this new art – you don't want an old name for it. And for clearness, for convenience, for distinctness you do need half a dozen new technical words at least" (*FLO* 5: 422–423). Despite Olmsted's unhappiness with calling this new art "landscape architecture," the name stuck. And his concern that "the popular mind" would not accept the name proved ultimately to be unfounded.

41 Fisher, *Frederick Law Olmsted and the City Planning Movement*, 27.

42 Immanuel Kant, *Critique of Judgment*, trans. J. H. Bernard (New York: Hafner Publishing Company, 1951). Subsequent references cited in the text as (Kant pp.).

43 This discourse has been elaborated in two recent books: William A. Gleason, *The Leisure Ethic: Work and Play in American Literature, 1840–1940* (Stanford: Stanford University Press, 1999); and Bill Brown, *The Material Unconscious: American Amusement, Stephen Crane, and the Economies of Play* (Cambridge, Mass.: Harvard University Press, 1996).

44 Olmsted's Prospect Park report, like many of his reports (including the original "Greensward" proposal for Central Park), was co-authored with Calvert Vaux. It is generally accepted by Olmsted scholars, however, that there was a division of labor between them in which Olmsted did the writing and Vaux (a professionally trained architect) did the maps and designs. That the philosophy of recreation set forth in the Prospect Park report was primarily Olmsted's is confirmed by its fundamental agreement with the philosophy of recreation that Olmsted set forth in the landscape reports he wrote on his own in California.

45 *Landscape into Cityscape*, 100. All further citations from the Prospect Park Report are cited in the text from this edition as (*Landscape* pp.).

46 The idea of "productive labor" is elaborated in James Livingston, *Pragmatism and the Political Economy of Cultural Revolution, 1850–1940* (Chapel Hill: University of North Carolina Press, 1994), 43–45, 95–97, 166–172, 181–183. In Livingston's account of nineteenth-century political economy, the urban park itself represents a form of capital or wealth.

47 Cf. Brown, *Material Unconscious*, 29; this quotation comes from Crane's 1869 text, *Popular Amusements*.

48 For an interesting and informative cultural history of neurology, see George Frederick Drinka, *The Birth of Neurosis: Myth, Malady, and the Victorians* (New York: Simon & Schuster, 1984). For a more conventional medical history, see Russell DeJong, *A History of American Neurology* (New York: Raven, 1982).

49 DeJong, *History of American Neurology*, 4, 14.

50 Shortly before he resigned from the Commission, Olmsted supported Mitchell's attempt to improve the conditions at the Fort Delaware prison depot; *FLO* 4: 684–685. His involvement with Hammond was more extensive. Not only did Olmsted lobby for Hammond's appointment as Surgeon General of the United States Sanitary Commission but "the two men worked together in August 1862 planning a campaign to secure an independent ambulance corps" and Olmsted consulted with and received pledges of support from Hammond regarding the weekly journal that Olmsted and Edwin Godkin were planning to edit; *FLO* 4: 96–99. Although his relationship with Hammond has been characterized as "cordial though never particularly intimate," it seems likely that the two men would have had more than one occasion to share medical and other opinions (*FLO* 4: 98).

51 For a good discussion of Olmsted's positioning amidst the physiological and hygienic arguments for recreation and urban parks, see David Schuyler, *The*

New Urban Landscape: The Redefinition of City Form in Nineteenth-Century America (Baltimore: Johns Hopkins University Press, 1986).

52 DeJong finds that although Beard "was actually more closely allied to psychiatry than neurology," his works on electrotherapy, including his establishment of the short-lived *Archives of Electrology and Neurology*, were influential both in the United States and in Europe; DeJong, *History of American Neurology*, 49. In addition he "made many important contributions to our understanding of the functional disorders of the nervous system"; ibid., 39. And despite the fact that the paper he delivered at the second meeting of the American Neurological Association in 1876 prompted Hammond to accuse Beard of "humbuggery," contending that "if Beard's doctrine [of the emotional basis of disease] was accepted, he 'should feel like throwing his diploma away and joining the theologians,'" Beard remained an active member of the Association until his death in 1883 at the age of 46; ibid., 38–39. For a more extended and engaging discussion of Beard's theories, see Drinka, *Birth of Neurosis*, 20–22, 182–197.

53 That Beard considered the habit of forethought central to his account of the causes of neurasthenia as a particularly American disease is underscored by the fact that when Herbert Spencer made a similar claim in "The Gospel of Recreation," a "farewell address to his American friends," published in the January 1883 issue of *Popular Science Monthly*, Beard was moved to defend his priority in "his own article, entitled 'A Scientific Coincidence'"; Drinka, *The Birth of Neurosis*, 191–192. In advocating the gospel of recreation, Spencer had accused Americans of being too civilized, contrasting civilization with savagery on the basis of the habit of forethought. "The savage thinks only of present satisfactions, and leaves future satisfactions uncared for. Contrariwise, the American, eagerly pursuing a future good, almost ignores what good the passing day offers him; and when the future good is gained, he neglects that while striving for some still remoter good"; Herbert Spencer, "The Gospel of Recreation," *Popular Science Monthly* (1883): 355–356. In *American Nervousness* (New York, 1881), 128–133, Beard had set forth a similar contrast, noting that "This forecasting, this forethinking, discounting the future, bearing constantly with us not only the real but imagined or possible sorrows and distresses, and not only of our own lives but those of our families and of our descendants, which is the very essence of civilization as distinguished from barbarism, involves a constant and exhausting expenditure of force."

54 Although uninterested in the structure of agency that I have been discussing here, T. Jackson Lears treats the emergence of neurology in post-Civil War America as participating in the creation of the "therapeutic world view" characteristic of what he calls "antimodernism," a resistance to the industrialization and modernization endemic in late capitalist culture; *No Place of Grace: Antimodernism and the Transformation of American Culture, 1880–1920* (New York: Knopf, 1981), 47–58.

55 *The Collected Works of Ralph Waldo Emerson* (Cambridge, Mass., 1871), vol. I, 13. Emerson makes a similar claim in "The Young American," where in conjunction with calling for the creation of public parks and gardens, he contends

that "we must regard the *land* as a commanding and increasing power on the American citizen, the sanative and Americanizing influence, which promises to disclose new virtues for ages to come"; ibid., 229.

56 In making this distinction between Olmsted and Emerson I do not mean to reinstate the traditional reading of the disembodied Emerson. Indeed, as I have argued elsewhere, Emerson's transcendentalism is not so much a rejection of the body as it is a sustained meditation on questions of embodiment; Richard A. Grusin, *Transcendentalist Hermeneutics: Institutional Authority and the Higher Criticism of the Bible* (Durham, N.C.: Duke University Press, 1991). Rather I mean mainly to emphasize that Olmsted's understanding of the therapeutic value of natural scenery is more explicitly involved with the discourse of nineteenth-century medical science than is Emerson's.

57 Frederick Law Olmsted, *Public Parks and the Enlargement of Towns* (New York: Arno Press, 1870; rpt. 1970), 32.

58 The three articles Holmes wrote on photography were: "The Stereoscope and the Stereograph," *Atlantic Monthly* 3 (1859): 738–748; "Sun-Painting and Sun-Sculpture, with a Stereoscopic Trip across the Atlantic," *Atlantic Monthly* 8 (1861): 13–29; and "Doings of the Sunbeam," *Atlantic Monthly* 12 (1863): 1–15. As the titles of the last two articles make clear, Holmes participated in the mid-century discourse of photography as a form of representation in which the laws of nature (through the artistry of the sun) are seen as the agents of artistic reproduction. Although I have not found any indication that Holmes himself ever drew a connection between the logic of photography and the "nature-trusting heresy," his own participation in both discourses seems from our vantage point to be (at the least) logically consistent.

59 For an excellent discussion of Holmes and the "nature-trusting heresy," see J. H. Warner, "'The Nature-Trusting Heresy': American Physicians and the Concept of the Healing Power of Nature in the 1850s and 1860s," *Perspectives in American History* 11 (1977–1978): 291–324.

60 Two important cultural histories of nineteenth-century therapeutics are: Charles E. Rosenberg, "The Therapeutic Revolution: Medicine, Meaning, and Social Change in Nineteenth-Century America," in *The Therapeutic Revolution: Essays in the Social History of American Medicine*, ed. Morris J. Vogel and Charles E. Rosenberg (Philadelphia: University of Pennsylvania Press, 1979), 3–25; and Martin Pernick, *The Calculus of Suffering: Pain, Professionalism, and Anesthesia in Nineteenth-Century America* (New York: Columbia University Press, 1985).

61 Rush's remark is quoted in John W. Jones, "Vis Medicatrix Naturae and Antistasis," *Atlanta Medical and Surgical Journal* 1 (1855): 69; qtd. Warner, "'Nature-Trusting Heresy,'" 294.

62 Ibid., 295–296.

63 Elisha Bartlett, *An Essay on the Philosophy of Medical Science* (Philadelphia, 1844), 288–289; qtd. Warner, "'Nature-Trusting Heresy,'" 298.

64 Holmes, *Homeopathy and Its Kindred Delusions: Two Lectures Delivered Before the Boston Society for the Diffusion of Useful Knowledge* (Boston, 1842), 50–54; qtd. Warner, "'Nature-Trusting Heresy,'" 299.

65 Although Olmsted's understanding of the therapeutic value of natural scenery parallels the "nature-trusting heresy," in treating his own illnesses he followed the not uncommon practices of using quinine as a prophylactic and of relying on alcohol as a tonic. On the train trip across the Isthmus of Panama on his way to Mariposa, for example, Olmsted prescribed as a nightly prophylactic against malaria three grams of quinine to each member of his travelling party and reminded his wife Mary not to "despise the prophylactic" when she came to join him the following year; *FLO* 5: 82–84. Similarly he described a course of medical treatment in a letter to Vaux from Bear Valley, dated September 28, 1865: "We have an epidemic of fevers here, typhoid in the highlands, congestive remittent below. One of our clerks has died, and several of us have been threatened, but by timely care & quinine & brandy have escaped any severe attack. I was the last & kept my bed yesterday, am living on port wine today"; *FLO* 5: 443. Insofar as these passages represent a discrepancy between his theory and his practice (and it's not entirely certain that they do), Olmsted's therapy is nonetheless consistent with the behavior of even the most heretical "nature-trusting" physicians. As Charles Rosenberg has argued, "Practice changed a good deal less than the rhetoric surrounding it would suggest; . . . older modes of therapeutics did not die, but, as we have suggested, were employed less routinely, and drugs were used in generally smaller doses"; "Therapeutic Revolution," 17–18. Interestingly Rosenberg also notes that "the decades between 1850 and 1870" saw "a vogue for the use of alcoholic beverages as stimulants"; 17.

66 To note Olmsted's participation in the culture of industrial capitalism is not to deny, as critics have often contended, that the urban park movement participates in an ideology of Jeffersonian agrarianism. Rather it is to insist with Philip Fisher "that modern capitalism, however much Jefferson feared it, turned out to be the very means to a Jeffersonian America"; "Democratic Social Space: Whitman, Melville, and the Promise of American Transparency," *Representations* 24 (1988): 65. Insofar as Olmsted seeks to extend Jefferson's agrarian vision to the late-nineteenth-century city, he seeks to design parks not as pastoral sanctuaries in which agrarian virtues can reside as in a drawer or cabinet but as aesthetic systems of circulation and exchange that serve both to reproduce and elide the difference between urban and agrarian ideals.

67 Olmsted approaches this design problem in Prospect Park not by striving for "a perfect compromise at all points" but by seeing that each design objective "should be carried out at certain points in high degree"; *Landscape* 101. Unlike providing therapeutic recreation through the creation of natural scenery (which, by concealing the signs of art, allows the mind to occupy itself without purpose), in providing opportunities for people to see each other, Olmsted must attract attention away from the scenery by employing such purposeful signs of "the application of art to inanimate nature" as "architectural objects" or "festive decorations"; *Landscape* 104. In obeying the double imperative of urban park design – providing natural scenery while also accommodating the movements of the public through the park – Olmsted must devise a system of traffic circulation in which both his own agency as artist and the parkgoer's agency as viewer can be successively produced and elided.

68 This is equally true of Central Park's network of trails, but is even more interesting in Prospect Park, where, for example, the circulation of water in the landscape functions both as streams within the park (features of a scenic or picturesque landscape) and as a source of water in the park's kitchen and power plant to provide natural resources for the infrastructure of the park. Prospect Park is of course even more of a built technology than Yosemite, which has the unusual benefit of appearing already designed.

69 The phrasing of this passage is indicative of the persistence in Olmsted's habit of mind of the logical structure of agency that I have been outlining here. In saying that "the Commissioners *propose to cause to be constructed* a double trail," Olmsted reveals the way in which he sees being a commissioner, like being a doctor or a photographer or a landscape architect, to involve relinquishing agency or control to others for one's intentions to be realized.

70 Olmsted's concern that artificial constructions work as parts of an overall scenic composition is evident in the plan he drew up for the design of the neighborhood surrounding the Berkeley campus, a plan that (though never implemented) provides a good indication of his design principles around the time of the Yosemite report. In describing "the view from the window or balcony" of a Berkeley house, he writes that it should "be artistically divisible into the three parts of; first, the home view or immediate foreground; second, the neighborhood view or middle distance, and third, the far outlook or background. Each one of these points should be so related to each other one as to enhance its distinctive beauty, and it will be fortunate if the whole should form a symmetrical, harmonious and complete landscape composition"; *FLO* 5: 556. In designing individual homes, Olmsted insists that their participation as elements of the "middle distance" of others' views be always kept in mind.

71 Jacques Derrida, *The Truth in Painting*, trans. Geoff Bennington and Ian McLeod (Chicago: University of Chicago Press, 1987), 73.

72 For a more extended discussion of the establishment of this park, see Runte, *Yosemite*, 45–56.

73 John Muir, *A Thousand-Mile Walk to the Gulf* (Boston: Houghton Mifflin, 1916), 212.

74 John Muir, *The Mountains of California* (1894; rpt. New York: Penguin, 1985), 90.

75 Ibid., 91.

76 Although King describes the experience of relinquishing one's agency to nature in terms very similar to Muir's, his account of the relation of such an aesthetic experience to scientific observation is almost diametrically opposed to Muir's. King sees such relinquishment as little more than a welcome respite from his more scientific habits of mind, as in the following passage: "I was delighted to ride alone, and expose myself, as one uncovers a sensitized photographic plate, to be influenced; for this is a respite from scientific work, when through months you hold yourself accountable for seeing everything, for analyzing, for instituting perpetual comparison, and as it were sharing in the administering of the physical world. No tongue can tell the relief to simply withdraw scientific

observation, and let Nature impress you in the dear old way with all her mystery and glory, with those vague indescribable emotions which tremble between wonder and sympathy"; *Mountaineering in the Sierra Nevada* (1874; rpt. New York: Penguin, 1989), 108.

77 Muir did receive support from Joseph LeConte, Professor of Geology and Natural History at the University of California. In 1873, LeConte published an essay on Sierra glaciers, which built upon Muir's earlier findings, "On Some of the Ancient Glaciers of the Sierras," *American Journal of Science and the Arts*, 3rd ser., vol. 5, no. 29 (May 1873): 324–342. For an extended discussion of Muir's participation in the debate over the origins of Yosemite valley, see Dennis R. Dean, "John Muir and the Origin of Yosemite Valley," *Annals of Science* 48 (1991): 453–485; see also Smith, *Pacific Visions*, 100–103.

78 Muir's essays from *The Overland Monthly* were compiled in *Studies in the Sierra*, introd. by William E. Colby, foreword by John P. Buwalda (San Francisco, Calif.: Sierra Club Books, 1950); all citations in the text refer to this edition and are cited as (*Sierra* pp.).

79 Muir's idea of the ongoing metamorphosis of nature is a more scientifically based version of Emerson's account of nature. For a discussion of Emerson's notion of metamorphosis and change in nature, see Richard Grusin, "'Monadnoc': Emerson's Quotidian Apocalypse," *ESQ* 31 (1985): 149–163.

80 The interest in preserving watersheds as a way of regulating the action of nature goes back at least to George Perkins Marsh, whose 1864 publication *Man and Nature* emphasized not only the importance of protecting the watershed but also the relation between human agency and the agency of forests and other natural features.

81 Stephen Greenblatt presents a similar account of the pleasures that Yosemite offers visitors today in "Towards a Poetics of Culture," in *The New Historicism*, ed. H. Aram Veeser (New York: Routledge, 1993), 1–14.

2 REPRESENTING YELLOWSTONE

1 In thinking of the idea of "wonder" as a fundamental aesthetic response to discovery, I am indebted to Stephen Greenblatt's account of Columbus' "discovery" of America in *Marvelous Possessions: The Wonder of the New World* (Oxford: Clarendon Press, 1991), esp. 52–85.

2 Owen Wister, "Old Yellowstone Days," *Harper's* 172 (March 1936): 471–480.

3 Owen Wister, "Bad Medicine," in *When West Was West* (New York: Macmillan, 1928), 1–48.

4 "Old Yellowstone Days," 476.

5 Robert B. Keiter, "An Introduction to the Ecosystem Management Debate," in *The Greater Yellowstone Ecosystem: Redefining America's Wilderness Heritage*, ed. Robert P. Keiter and Mark S. Boyce (New Haven: Yale University Press, 1991), 4–5. Although some critics of Park Service policy have charged that one consequence of this management philosophy was to create the environmental conditions that led to the devastating fires of 1988, I introduce the Leopold

report not because it provides the philosophical basis for the current ecosystem-based management paradigm but because it employs a twofold notion of the fidelity to nature that both derives from and can help to illuminate the cultural discourse surrounding the establishment of Yellowstone as the world's first national park in 1872.

6 Aldo S. Leopold *et al.*, "Wildlife Management in the National Parks" (March 4, 1963), in *Compilation of the Administrative Policies for the National Parks and National Monuments of Scientific Significance (Natural Area Category)* (Washington, DC: US Department of the Interior, rev. 1968), 92.

7 Ibid., 93. The Leopold report's recommendation that Yellowstone should be managed to represent an "illusion of primitive America" was not a new idea, but one that has manifested itself in a number of different contexts in the history of Yellowstone. See James A. Pritchard, *Preserving Yellowstone's Natural Conditions: Science and the Perception of Nature* (Lincoln, Nebr.: University of Nebraska Press, 1999).

8 Leopold *et al.*, "Wildlife Management," 95.

9 Ibid., 96. Attempting to incorporate recent developments in population ecology in order to devise a management plan based not on human but on natural needs, the committee based its recommendations on the assumption that the aim of the national parks was to preserve or re-create an unpeopled North American landscape as it might have existed prior to the arrival of Europeans. In urging the preservation of the biotic associations that obtained within each park "when the area was first visited by the white man," the committee relies upon a conception of nature that minimizes the significance of humans, particularly native peoples, in creating and maintaining biotic associations. By choosing to define as "natural" the biotic associations that prevailed when Europeans first arrived in Yellowstone, however, the committee employs a very human-centered standard to determine the "natural" state of the Yellowstone ecosystem. Seeking to re-create the biotic associations that prevailed when Europeans first encountered Yellowstone, the committee sets forth a management philosophy that defines nature both biocentrically (as prior to or independent of humans) and anthropocentrically (in terms of human history, particularly the history of the Euro-American encounter with the "wilderness").

10 Aubrey L. Haines, *The Yellowstone Story: A History of Our First National Park*, 2 vols. (Yellowstone National Park, Wyo.: Yellowstone Library and Museum Associaton, 1977), vol. I, 35.

11 Ibid., 101.

12 Indeed, *Scribner's* was so interested in Langford's narrative that they published it, in two parts, as the lead article in consecutive issues; [Nathaniel Pitt Langford], "The Wonders of Yellowstone," *Scribner's Monthly*, vol. 2, no. 1 (May 1871), 1–17 and vol. 2, no. 2 (June 1871): 113–128.

13 *Scribner's Monthly*, vol. 1, no. 1 (November 1870): 106.

14 Haines, *Yellowstone Story*, pp. 151–153.

15 Peter B. Hales, *William Henry Jackson and the Transformation of the American Landscape* (Philadelphia: Temple University Press, 1988), 68.

16 Ferdinand V. Hayden, *Preliminary Report of the United States Geological Survey of Wyoming and Portions of Contiguous Territories (Being a Second Annual Report of Progress* [1870 Survey] (Washington, DC: Government Printing Office, 1871), 3; qtd. in Hales, *William Henry Jackson*, 69.

17 Ferdinand V. Hayden, "On the Geology and Natural History of the Upper Missouri," *Transactions of the American Philosophical Society*, n.s., 12 (1862); qtd. Hales, *William Henry Jackson*, 68.

18 Latour describes this representational economy as one in which to represent nature faithfully is to reproduce it in the form of inscriptions that can "bring things back to a place for someone else to see it for the first time so that others might be sent again to bring other things back"; *Science in Action* (Cambridge, Mass.: Harvard University Press, 1987), 220.

19 For many years Hayden worked closely with William Blackmore, a British capitalist actively engaged in the extension of European capital to the American West. For the role of European capital in incorporating undeveloped American wilderness into established social and political networks, see the Introduction pp. 10–11. For a discussion of how Olmsted's Yosemite report works rhetorically to reorient the nation's attention from the North–South divide of the war to the East–West axis of the postbellum era, see the previous chapter.

20 Joni Kinsey, *Thomas Moran and the Surveying of the American West* (Washington, DC: Smithsonian Institution Press, 1992), 43.

21 Ibid., 44.

22 Kinsey cites one of the two letters in which Moran refers to these figures, asking Hayden for a photograph from which to draw one of the two figures on horseback in the foreground, the figures which Kinsey identifies as Moran and Jackson; March 11, 1872, National Archives, Record Group 57, mfm. 623, roll 2. While these figures are not strictly on horseback (they are standing and seated next to horses), it is clear from Moran's letter to Hayden of April 6, which Kinsey does not mention, that the figures in the left foreground are meant to be Hayden and James Stevenson, his chief assistant: "I received your note on March 28th but this morning. I have been expecting you along this way for a week past. I wrote to Jim [Stevenson] in the early part of the week & received a reply from him this morning. He sent his pictures, & I think I have now all that I require for the figures in the Big picture"; April 6, 1872, National Archives, Record Group 57, mfm. 623, roll 2.

23 Mark Spence argues persuasively that the history of the national parks is marked by an almost systematic removal of Indians and of all signs of their presence from an idealized natural landscape: "uninhabited wilderness had to be created before it could be preserved, and this type of landscape became reified in the first national parks"; Mark David Spence, *Dispossessing the Wilderness: Indian Removal and the Making of the National Parks* (New York: Oxford University Press, 1999), 5. In addition to being the first national park, "Yellowstone also provides the first example of removing a native population in order to 'preserve' nature"; 69–70. Native peoples, Spence argues, were "hardly a key component of the wilderness condition" in Yellowstone, but rather "the one great flaw in the

western landscape"; 62. In this respect Moran is idiosyncratic in that he places the encounter with Indians at the center of his first large Yellowstone painting; in addition he uses this motif throughout his artistic career, particularly in the many versions of the cliffs of Green River which he continued to paint long after his initial encounter with that landscape in 1871.

24 Ferdinand V. Hayden, "The Yellowstone National Park," *American Journal of Science and the Arts*, 3rd ser., 3.15 (1872): 295.

25 Robert V. Bruce, *The Launching of Modern American Science, 1846–1876* (Ithaca, N.Y.: Cornell University Press, 1987).

26 Despite Hayden's claim, Richard Sellars argues that the corporate emphasis on tourism prevented national parks from being managed according to truly scientific, ecological principles: "Except perhaps for Muir's efforts to understand the natural history of California's High Sierra, the advances in ecological knowledge taking place by the late nineteenth century had little to do with the national park movement. Busy with development, the parks played no role in leading scientific efforts such as the studies of plant succession by Frederic Clements in Nebraska's grasslands, or by Henry C. Cowles along Indiana's Lake Michigan shoreline. Once national parks became more numerous and more accessible, an ever-increasing number of scientists would conduct research in them. But within national park management circles, awareness of ecological matters lay in the distant future, and genuine concern in the far-distant future." (Richard West Sellars, *Preserving Nature in the National Parks: A History* [New Haven and London: Yale University Press, 1997], 15.) My interest in unpacking the logic of Hayden's and others' claims about the scientific value of preserving Yellowstone is not in how these claims were implemented in park management but in how they participated in the widespread cultural articulation of the concept of representational fidelity to nature that helped enable Yellowstone's preservation.

27 Theodore B. Comstock, "The Yellowstone National Park: I. Its Scientific Value," *American Naturalist*, vol. 8, no. 2 (February 1874): 65–79; "The Yellowstone National Park: II. Its Improvement," *American Naturalist*, vol. 8, no. 3 (March 1874): 155–166.

28 Comstock, "The Yellowstone National Park: I," 71–72. James A. Pritchard, who does not mention Comstock's article, places the origin of arguments for the scientific benefits of preservation in the early twentieth century. Clearly, as Hayden's concern with the scientific progress of America also demonstrates, this argument goes back to the establishment of Yellowstone National Park.

29 Ibid., 78.

30 Comstock's most Darwinian argument is that Yellowstone's preservation constitutes it as "a really valuable laboratory and conservatory of science," in which answers to "momentous questions . . . bearing upon the process of natural selection" can be pursued. Because of "the obliterating influences of modern civilization," Comstock writes, the "experiment and observation" of "animals in a state of nature" is "daily becoming less possible." Consequently, "one of the most important uses to which the park can be put" is "*the preservation*

from extinction of at least the characteristic mammals and birds of the west, as far as they can be domiciled in this section." Although Comstock stops short of "question[ing] the right of a nation to decide as to whether it will utilize its wild productions or supply their waste by the laborious and costly processes of civilization," he insists that, "unless prompt and vigorous measures are instituted to check the wholesale slaughter, now in progress in our western wilds, the *zoological record of to-day must rapidly pass into the domain of the paleontologist.*" (Ibid., 72–73.)

31 Ferdinand V. Hayden, "The Hot Springs and Geysers of the Yellowstone and Firehole Rivers," *American Journal of Science and the Arts*, 3rd ser., vol. 3, no. 14 (1872): 106–107.

32 Michel de Certeau, *The Practice of Everyday Life*, trans. Steven Rendall (Berkeley: University of California Press, 1984).

33 Hayden, "The Hot Springs and Geysers of the Yellowstone and Firehole Rivers," 108.

34 Ibid., 174–175.

35 In the next chapter, I argue that the cultural conception of the Grand Canyon is marked by a logic of recognition that responds in large part to the canyon's "cognitive inaccessibility." To characterize the Grand Canyon in this fashion is not to deny or minimize the fact that Yellowstone, too, was often described as cognitively inaccessible. Nor should characterizing Yellowstone as being marked by a logic of representational fidelity to nature suggest that such a concern is absent from depictions of Yosemite or Grand Canyon. But I would point out that the "inexpressibility" that Hayden remarks most often refers to his emotional response to Yellowstone, not to the features of the park itself.

36 Hayden, *Preliminary Report* [1870 Survey], 5.

37 Ferdinand V. Hayden, *Preliminary Report of the United States Geological Survey of Montana, and Portions of Adjacent Territories, (Being a Fifth Annual Report of Progress)* [1871 Survey] (Washington, DC: Government Printing Office, 1872), 5.

38 Hayden, *Preliminary Report* [1870 Survey], 6–7. Hayden's detailed account of the survey's scientific and nationalistic purposes takes on added significance in light of the fact that his letter of transmission, although not published until 1872, was written at the same time (the winter of 1870–1871) that he was lobbying the Secretary of the Interior for an increased appropriation for the upcoming summer's exploration of Yellowstone. In articulating his survey's dual commitment to the faithful representation of the book of nature and the faithful reproduction of American expansionism, he is also making a case for funding his proposed expedition to Yellowstone. Hayden's case proved to be successful: in the Sundry Civil Act of March 3, 1871, the Hayden Survey was provided with $40,000 (up from $20,000 the previous year) to explore the sources of the Missouri and Yellowstone rivers, and Hayden's salary as government geologist was increased to $4,000 (up from $3,000). While the survey's increased funding is indicative of the interest in Yellowstone created by the previous summer's Washburn and Doane expeditions, it also registers the

confidence of Congress and Interior in Hayden's fidelity both to natural and to national purposes.

39 See Chapter 2, p. 24.

40 George A. Crofutt, *Crofutt's New Overland Tourist and Pacific Coast Guide* (Chicago: Overland Press, 1878–1879), qtd. Patricia Hills, "Picturing Progress in the Era of Westward Expansion," in *The West as America: Reinterpreting Images of the Frontier*, ed. William H. Truettner (Washington, DC: Smithsonian Institution Press, 1991), 134.

41 Hayden, *Preliminary Report* [1870 Survey], 7–8.

42 James Dwight Dana, "*Photographs of the Hot Springs, Geysers and Scenery in the Region of the Yellowstone National Park*, Illustrating the Geological Survey of the Territories under the Department of the Interior," in *American Journal of Science and the Arts*, 3rd ser., 5.25 (1873): 79–80; qtd. in Ferdinand V. Hayden, *Sixth Annual Report of the United States Geological Survey of the Territories, Embracing Portions of Montana, Idaho, Wyoming, and Utah: Being a Report of Progress of the Explorations for the Year 1872* (Washington, DC: Government Printing Office, 1873), 5.

43 Ibid.

44 Don DeLillo, *White Noise* (New York: Viking, 1985).

45 "*Application of Photography to Illustrations of Natural History. Bulletin of the Museum of Comparative Zoology*, 3, no. 2, by Alexander Agassiz," in *American Journal of Science and the Arts*, 3rd ser., vol. 3, no. 14 (1872): 156; emphasis added.

46 "Stellar Photography," in *American Journal of Science and the Arts*, 3rd ser., vol. 3, no. 14 (1872): 157.

47 In *Philosophy and the Mirror of Nature* (Princeton: Princeton University Press, 1979), Richard Rorty argues that the idea of representation as a faithful mirror of nature is an old one in the history of Western thought. In the Cartesian model, for example, which Rorty characterizes as "the basis for modern epistemology," "it is *representations* which are in the mind. The Inner Eye surveys these representations hoping to find some mark which will testify to their fidelity," even though, as Descartes skeptically concludes, there is no way finally to know whether "anything which is mental represents anything which is not mental"; 45–46.

48 James T. Gardner, quoted in Hayden, *Sixth Annual Report of the United States Geological Survey of the Territories*, 10.

49 Jonathan Crary, "Techniques of the Observer," *October* 45 (Summer 1988): 24.

50 Hales, *William Henry Jackson*, 124–126.

51 For the idea that nineteenth-century artists thought of landscape photographs not as pictures but as "views," see Rosalind Krauss, "Photography"s Discursive Spaces: Landscape/View," *Artjournal* (Winter 1982): 311–319.

52 Crary, "Techniques," 30.

53 Krauss, "Photography's Discursive Spaces," 314.

54 Crary, "Techniques," 28.

55 Krauss, "Photography's Discursive Spaces," 314.

56 Hales, *William Henry Jackson*, 95–111.

57 Alan Trachtenberg, *Reading American Photographs* (New York: Hill and Wang, 1989), 127–132; quotation on 128.
58 Michel Foucault, *The Archaeology of Knowledge*, trans. A.M. Sheridan Smith (New York: Pantheon, 1972), 129.
59 Ibid.
60 Roland Barthes, *Camera Lucida: Reflections on Photography* (New York: Hill and Wang, 1981).
61 For a comprehensive discussion of the reception of Moran's painting, see Kinsey, *Thomas Moran*, 64–67. For Ruskin's influence on Moran, see Kinsey, 12–16, and William H. Truettner, "'Scenes of Majesty and Enduring Interest': Thomas Moran Goes West," *The Art Bulletin* 58 (June 1976): 241–249.
62 Ruskin is arguably the most significant nineteenth-century commentator on this and other aesthetic issues. His aesthetic theory addresses most of the aspects of fidelity to nature that this chapter has discussed; indeed Roger Stein finds "a distinct difference, if not an outright contradiction, between Ruskin's assertion that the test of truth in landscape art was a literal fidelity to the particular truths of rock and leaf and his assertion that greatness in art was to be measured by the number and quality of the ideas involved"; Roger Stein, *John Ruskin and Aesthetic Thought in America, 1840–1900* (Cambridge, Mass.: Harvard University Press, 1967), 113. In characterizing Ruskin's aesthetics as embodying a contradiction between realism and idealism, Stein points out that Asher Durand had strived to reconcile this Ruskinian contradiction in his eighth "Letter on Landscape Painting," where he describes the real in Emersonian terms as a "disciplinary stage" on the way to the ideal: "'The term Realism signifies little else than a disciplinary stage of Idealism . . . and is misapplied when used in opposition to it, for the ideal is, in fact, nothing more than the perfection of the real'" (qtd. in Stein, *John Ruskin*, 115). But in describing Ruskin's aesthetics in terms of a contradiction between a "literal fidelity" to nature and something else, Stein fails to recognize that Ruskin consistently refused to accept a strict opposition between realism and idealism, a point I discuss below in more detail.
63 Sanford Gifford, for example, who served as the artist on Hayden's survey in 1870, wrote Hayden that he had heard that Moran's painting was "excellent not only for local truth, but as a work of fine art"; Gifford to Hayden, May 16, 1872, National Archives, Record Group 57, mfm. 623, roll 2. Richard Gilder, editor of *Scribner's* and a childhood friend of Moran who helped sponsor his trip west with Hayden's Yellowstone survey, praised the painting both for its "truthfulness" in "render[ing] nature with firm mastery of technical detail" and for its greatness as "a glorious and inspiring poem" in pigments, rivalled only by Church's *Niagara*; "Thomas Moran's 'Grand Cañon of the Yellowstone,'" *Scribner's Monthly* 4 (June 1872): 251–252. And Clarence Cook, a founding member of the American Pre-Raphaelites, who also sees Moran's painting as second only to Church's, repeatedly describes the painting in terms of the opposition between realistic truth and ideal beauty. After praising the painting's "truthfulness" in his review for the New York *Tribune*, Cook notes that truthfulness alone is not

enough: "the artist seeks for other satisfactions in a picture; scientific accuracy he can find in photographs and surveyors maps; here in a work of art he asks for the added charm of beauty, the light of life"; *New York Tribune*, May 3, 1872, Archives of American Art, roll N730, frame 62; qtd. Truettner, "Scenes of Majesty and Enduring Interest," 246. Similarly in his review for the *Atlantic Monthly*, Cook characterizes the painting as "a work of real artistic and scientific importance," which is both "faithful to the facts of the place" and "above all and before all, a work in which the imagination has its part, and in which the artist has revealed his love of beauty and his desire to communicate to others what he knows or feels of beauty"; "Art," *Atlantic Monthly* 30 (August 1872): 246–247.

64 Moran to Hayden, March 11, 1872, Record Group 57, National Archives, mfm. 623, roll 2.

65 George Sheldon, *American Painters* (New York: D. Appleton and Co., 1881), 122–128.

66 Interestingly, Moran characterizes Turner in such a way as to suggest that it is he, not Turner, who should inherit Ruskin's mantle. In contending that Turner "generalizes Nature always," Moran invokes Ruskin's consistent effort to distinguish himself from idealists like Johua Reynolds, particularly Ruskin's conviction that "generalization, as the word is commonly understood, is the act of a vulgar, incapable, and unthinking mind." Although Ruskin goes on to distinguish Turner's "right, true, and noble" generalization, "which is based on the knowledge of the distinctions and observance of the relations of individual kinds," from that generalization which is "wrong, false, and contemptible, which is based on ignorance of the one, and disturbance of the other," Moran is less effusive about the quality of Turner's later works, "in which realism is entirely thrown overboard"; Sheldon, *American Painters*, 123–124.

67 Ibid., 126.

68 John Ruskin, *Modern Painters* (Boston: Estes and Lauriat Publishers, n.d.), vol. IV, 34.

69 Ibid., 37–38.

70 Ibid., 39.

71 In the first volume of *Modern Painters*, Ruskin had set forth a similar distinction between "the two great and distinct ends" of the landscape painter: "the first, to induce in the spectator's mind the faithful conception of any natural objects whatsoever; the second, to guide the spectator's mind to those objects most worthy of its contemplation, and to inform him of the thoughts and feelings with which these were regarded by the artist himself"; 121. "In attaining the first end," Ruskin continues, "the painter only places the spectator where he stands himself; he sets him before the landscape and leaves him. . . But in attaining the second end, the artist not only *places* the spectator, but talks to him; makes him a sharer of his own strong feelings and quick thoughts; hurries him away in his own enthusiasm; guides him to all that is beautiful; snatches him from all that is base, and leaves him more than delighted"; pp. 121–122. Although these two ends of landscape painting require different subjects, Ruskin concludes,

and "it is possible to reach . . . the first end of art, the representation of facts, without reaching the second, the representation of thoughts, yet it is altogether impossible to reach the second without having previously reached the first"; 124.

72 Ruskin, *Modern Painters*, vol. IV, 41–42.

73 Ruskin's discussion of Turner's "topographical truth" takes up the question of mimesis in terms very similar to those that Jacques Derrida uses to discuss the notion of mimesis in Kant: "*Mimesis* here is not the representation of one thing by another, the relation of resemblance or of identification between two beings, the reproduction of a product of nature by a product of art. It is not the relation of two products but of two productions. And of two freedoms. The artist does not imitate things in nature, or if you will, in *natura naturata*, but the acts of *natura naturans*, the operations of the *physis*. But since an analogy has already made *natura naturans* the art of an author-subject, and one could even say, of an artist-god, *mimesis* displays the identification of human action with divine action – of one freedom with another . . . all that presupposes a commerce between the divine artist and the human one. And indeed this commerce is a *mimesis*, in the strict sense, a play, a mask, an identification with the other on stage, and not the imitation of an object by its copy. 'True' *mimesis* is between two producing subjects and not between two produced things. Implied by the whole third *Critique*, even though the explicit theme, even less the word itself, never appears, this kind of *mimesis* inevitably entails the condemnation of imitation, which is always characterized as being servile"; "Economimesis," *Diacritics* 11 (1981): 9. For Ruskin, in seeking to reproduce in the spectator of a work of art the feeling or impression produced upon the artist by a scene in nature, the artist strives not to imitate or copy the scene but to imitate what Derrida characterizes as "the acts of *natura naturans*, the operations of the *physis*."

74 Sheldon, *American Painters*, 125–126.

75 Ferdinand V. Hayden, *The Yellowstone National Park, and the Mountain Regions of Portions of Idaho, Nevada, Colorado and Utah* (Boston: L. Prang and Co., 1876), prefatory pages.

76 Hayden, *Preliminary Report* [1871 Survey], 84. By the time that Hayden's survey reached the canyon in 1871, the sentiment that the scenery of the canyon was beyond the reach of human representation had almost become a truism. In the diary from his 1869 journey with Charles Cook, David Folsom recorded that the men's response to the falls of Yellowstone's Grand Canyon impressed them with the limitations of being human: "we return to camp realizing as we never have before how utterly insignificant are man's mightiest efforts when compared with the fulfillment of the Omnipotent Will. Language is inadequate to convey a just conception of the awful grandeur and sublimity of this masterpiece of nature's handiwork . . . We have seen many phases of mountain scenery but nothing that could compare with this for variety; it is pretty, beautiful, picturesque, magnificent, grand, sublime, awful, terrible"; Charles W. Cook, David E. Folsom, and William Peterson, *The Valley of the Upper Yellowstone*,

ed. Aubrey L. Haines (Norman: University of Oklahoma Press, 1965), 25. Nathaniel P. Langford employed a similar rhetoric of the sublime in describing the canyon on the public lecture tour he undertook in the winter of 1870–1871, a tour designed both to publicize the Washburn expedition of the previous summer and to promote the development of a northern trans-continental route for Jay Cooke's Northern and Pacific Railroad. "The great cataracts of the Yellowstone, are but one feature in a scene composed of so many of the elements of grandeur and sublimity, that I almost despair of giving you the faintest conception of it. The immense cañon or gorge of rocks through which the river descends, perhaps more than the falls, is calculated to fill the observer with feelings of mingled awe and terror"; "Notes of Lectures given by N.Langford During the Winter of 1870–71," Yellowstone National Park Reference Library. And Hayden himself notes in the 1871 report that although he will attempt to describe the scenery of the Grand Canyon, "it is only through the eye that the mind can gather anything like an adequate conception of them[;] . . . no language can do justice to the wonderful grandeur and beauty of the canon below the Lower Falls"; 82–83.

77 William Blackmore, Personal Diary No. 7, Yellowstone National Park Reference Library. For Ruskin, color, too, must be true to nature. In a footnote in the fifth volume of *Modern Painters*, Ruskin places a great deal of importance on accurate color, arguing that because "color is sacred," "a type of love," unfaithful color can bring about the artist's "fall": "Violate truth wilfuly in the slightest particular, or, at least, get into the habit of violating it, and all kinds of failure and error will surround and haunt you to your fall"; Ruskin, *Modern Painters*, vol. V, 401–404 n. Among the reasons that Moran is so concerned about fidelity to color is the crucial role it plays in Ruskin's aesthetics.

78 Ruskin, *Modern Painters*, vol. IV, 39–40.

79 For a comprehensive explanation of the way in which Moran's painting combines views from several different Jackson photographs to create an imaginary point of view that does not exist at the Canyon itself, see Joni Kinsey, *Thomas Moran*, 54–58.

80 Ibid., 57.

81 Hayden, *Preliminary Report* [1871 Survey], 81. Hayden further explains: "Hot springs, geysers, &c., are so intimately connected with what we usually term volcanoes that their origin and action admit of the same explanation. Both undoubtedly form safety-valves or vents for the escape of the powerful forces that have been generated in the interior of the earth since the commencement of the present period; the true volcanic action has ceased, but the safety-valves are the thousands of hot springs all over this great area. I believe that the time of the greatest volcanic activity occurred during the Pliocene period – smoke, ashes, fragments of rock, and lava poured forth from thousands of orifices into the surrounding waters. Hundreds of cones were built up, fragments of which still remain; and around them were arranged by the water the dust and fragments of rock, the *ejactementa* of these volcanoes in the form of the conglomerate or breccia as we find it now'; ibid., 180–181.

82 Ibid., 81.

83 Ibid., 82.

84 Hayden, *The Yellowstone National Park*, 295–96.

85 For an interesting discussion of the story in the context of visual culture and Western tourism, see John D. Dorst, *Looking West* (Philadelphia: University of Pennsylvania Press, 1999), 68–74.

86 Wister, "Bad Medicine," 4.

87 Ibid., 14.

88 Ibid., 2–3.

89 Ibid., 26–27.

90 Ibid., 27–28.

91 Ibid., 30.

92 Ibid., 31.

93 Ibid., 31–32.

94 Ibid., 32.

95 Ibid., 33.

96 Ibid., 33–34.

97 Ibid., 34.

98 Ibid., 34–35.

99 Ibid., 35.

100 Ibid., 37.

101 Ibid., 38.

102 Ibid., 38–39.

103 Barthes, *Camera Lucida*, 10–11.

104 Ibid., 12.

105 Wister, "Bad Medicine," 41.

106 Barthes, *Camera Lucida*, 14.

107 Wister, "Bad Medicine," 42.

108 Ibid., 42.

109 Ibid., 44.

110 Ibid.

111 Ibid., 45–47.

112 Slavoj Zizek, *The Sublime Object of Ideology* (London: Verso, 1989), 56.

113 Ibid., 56.

114 Ibid., 57–58.

3 RECOGNIZING THE GRAND CANYON

1 Powell never repeated this accomplishment, although he did survey the region from the Green River Station to the Kanab with different sets of crew members in 1871 and 1872. These surveys, sponsored by the Smithsonian, were much better equipped than the original journey, with the men being furnished with supplies carried down the canyon at key points along the way.

2 This quotation comes from the back cover of the Dover edition of Powell's 1895 narrative of the exploration; J. W. [John Wesley] Powell, *The Exploration of the Colorado River and Its Canyons* (New York: Dover Publications, 1961; reprint of *Canyon of the Colorado* [Flood & Vincent, 1895]). The rhetoric, however, is Powell's own. Summarizing the work done by his survey in the 1873 report to Joseph Henry, Secretary of the Smithsonian, Powell notes: "On the general map of the 'Territory of the United States,' prepared at the War Department, a copy of which I herewith transmit, the entire district of country is left as a blank, it having previous to this expedition been unexplored . . . When that is done [the work proposed under the present appropriation], all that blank can be filled with the proper topographical delineations"; US Congress, House of Representatives, "Report of the Survey of the Colorado of the West. Letter from the Secretary of the Smithsonian Institution, Transmitting a Report of the Survey of the Colorado River of the West, and its Tributaries." H. Misc. Doc. 76, 42nd Cong., 3rd sess., January 31, 1873, 8. The following year, Powell makes the point more dramatically: "As before stated, the greater part of the country embraced in this survey was an unknown region in geographic science. An examination of the map prepared by the War Department from data collected up to 1868, being a compilation of all knowledge of this class concerning the territory of the United States west of the Mississippi River accessible to geographers, will show that this region is left an entire blank. We have filled this blank and completed the survey of the last unexplored region, mapping minutely the unknown portions of the Green and Colorado Rivers"; US Congress, House of Representatives, "Professor Powell's Report on the Survey of the Colorado of the West; Letter from the Secretary of the Smithsonian Institution, Transmitting a Report of Professor Powell on the Survey of the Colorado River of the West and its Tributaries, &c., &c." H. Misc. Doc. 265, 43rd Cong., 1st sess., May 2, 1874, 6.

3 For more detailed accounts of the early preservation history of the Grand Canyon region, see John Ise, *Our National Park Policy: A Critical History* (Baltimore: Johns Hopkins University Press, 1961); J. Donald Hughes, *In the House of Stone and Light: A Human History of the Grand Canyon* (Grand Canyon, Ariz.: Grand Canyon Natural History Association, 1978); and Barbara J. Morehouse, *A Place Called Grand Canyon: Contested Geographies* (Tucson: University of Arizona Press, 1996).

4 For a thorough discussion of the context and motivations for the Congressional purchase of Moran's *Chasm of the Colorado*, see Joni Kinsey, *Thomas Moran and the Surveying of the American West* (Washington, DC: Smithsonian Institution Press, 1992), Chapter 6.

5 Stephen Pyne argues that from its initial exploration by the Spanish in the sixteenth century, there was no conceptual framework even to understand what it was. Before the canyon was even cognitively inaccessible, it was cognitively invisible; Stephen J. Pyne, *How the Canyon Became Grand: A Short History* (New York: Viking Penguin, 1998), 4–10.

6 Ibid., 1–2.

7 Ibid., 6–7.
8 Ibid., 4.
9 Lieutenant Joseph C. Ives, *Report upon the Colorado River of the West*, Senate Ex. Doc., 36th Cong., 1st sess. (Washington, DC: Government Printing Office, 1861), 110. For a more detailed discussion of the Ives expedition, see Pyne, *How the Canyon Became Grand*, 38–50.
10 Although Powell only made one complete exploration of the Colorado River, from Green River Station to the end of the Grand Canyon, he wrote several different accounts of this journey (and subsequent partial explorations). Having obtained support from the Smithsonian Institution after his initial 1869 exploration, Powell wrote reports to Joseph Henry, Secretary of the Smithsonian, as a condition of this support, in 1872, 1873, and 1874. As a condition of further support, Powell was requested to write a book-length account of his work, including a journal account of the original exploration, supplemented with geological and other information gathered on the Smithsonian-sponsored surveys. In 1875, the Smithsonian published this book, which was lavishly illustrated with illustrations by Thomas Moran and others. In January, February, and March of 1875, Powell published a three-part narration of the 1869 trip in *Scribner's*, illustrated by many of the same illustrations used in the Smithsonian book; John Wesley Powell, "The Cañons of the Colorado," *Scribner's Monthly* 9 (January 1875): 293–310, 394–409, 523–537. In October of that same year, *Scribner's* published an account of Powell's overland trip of 1870; John Wesley Powell, "An Overland Trip to the Grand Cañon," *Scribner's Monthly* 10 (October 1875): 659–678. Finally, in 1895, Powell published a popular account, which reprinted almost verbatim the journal account of the original 1869 edition, but added many more illustrations and geological and ethnological chapters more suitable than those in the 1875 Smithsonian monograph for the broader-based popular audience he aimed to reach in 1895. The stylistic, rhetorical, and substantive differences between these accounts indicate that Powell was clearly aware of his audience. The *Scribner's* articles, for example, are in the form of a past-tense historical narrative – not the present-tense journal style used in the two book-length versions. Similarly, in *Scribner's* Powell omits virtually all of the accounts of naming and selects his illustrations to emphasize the heroic achievements of his crew. All references to Powell's narrative of his exploration will be to the 1875 Smithsonian edition, except where otherwise noted.
11 [John Wesley Powell,] *Exploration of the Colorado River of the West and Its Tributaries: Explored in 1869, 1870, 1871, and 1872, Under the Direction of the Secretary of the Smithsonian Institution* (Washington, DC: US Government Printing Office, 1875), 37. Unless otherwise noted, all subsequent quotations from Powell's narrative of his exploration come from this edition, which will be noted as Powell, *Exploration* (1875).
12 Powell, *The Exploration of the Colorado River and its Canyons*. Subsequent citations from this edition will be cited as Powell, *Exploration* (1895).
13 Powell, *Exploration* (1875), 38.

14 John R. Searle, "Proper Names and Descriptions," *The Encyclopedia of Philosophy* (New York: Macmillan, 1967), 491.

15 Saul A. Kripke, *Naming and Necessity* (Cambridge, Mass.: Harvard University Press, 1972), 106.

16 Powell, *Exploration* (1875), 18, 51, 39, 112.

17 Ibid., 38, 53, 67.

18 Ibid., 14, 54.

19 Ibid., 54–55.

20 In addition to his 1875 government report and the 1895 popular edition of this report, Powell also published a series of illustrated essays drawn from these reports in *Scribner's* in 1875. Unlike both of the book-length versions, the *Scribner's* essays leave out most of the debates about naming, like this one and the Whirlpool Creek debate, presenting instead a more black-boxed or ready-made image of Powell's exploration.

21 Powell, *Exploration* (1875), 14–15.

22 Ibid., 19; 15.

23 Ibid., 65; 72.

24 Ibid., 76.

25 Ibid., 28; 29; 56; 61.

26 Kripke, *Necessity and Naming*, pp. 96–97.

27 Powell, *Exploration* (1875), 28.

28 Ibid., 67.

29 Ibid., 86.

30 Ibid., 17.

31 Ibid., 23; 27; 32–33; 71.

32 Ibid., 38; 46; 76.

33 Kripke, *Naming and Necessity*, 96.

34 Ibid., 93.

35 Ibid., 106–107.

36 Powell, *Exploration* (1895), iii.

37 Ibid., iii.

38 Ibid., iv.

39 Ibid., iv. Powell's account of the genealogy of his published narratives in the 1895 preface may not be entirely accurate. Joni Kinsey notes that he had negotiated in 1873 with Riverside Press to publish an illustrated book account of his exploration; *Thomas Moran*, 104; 201 n. 34. What is important for my argument, however, is not the historical accuracy of this account, but Powell's representation of the relationship between historical adventure and scientific exploration.

40 Slavoj Zizek, *The Sublime Object of Ideology* (London: Verso, 1989), 95.

41 Ibid.

42 Powell, *Exploration* (1875), 46.

43 Ibid., 196.

44 Mary Austin, *The Land of Little Rain* (Albuquerque: University of New Mexico Press, 1974; rpt. of 1903 edition), xv.

45 Ibid.

46 US Congress, House of Representatives, "Professor Powell's Report on the Survey of the Colorado of the West; Letter from the Secretary of the Smithsonian Institution, Transmitting a Report of Professor Powell on the Survey of the Colorado River of the West and its Tributaries, &c., &c." H. Misc. Doc. 265, 43rd Cong., 1st sess., May 2, 1874, 20.

47 Ibid., 21.

48 Austin, *Land of Little Rain*, xv. Austin's text is full of such descriptive nominative phrases, which serve precisely as names for her. The title "Land of Little Rain" is only the most prominent example of this practice.

49 Ibid., xv.

50 Ibid.

51 Ibid.

52 Ibid., xvi.

53 Ibid.

54 Powell, *Exploration* (1875), x.

55 Ibid., 44.

56 I borrow these terms from Bruno Latour, who applies them to science, not naming, in *Science in Action* (Cambridge, Mass.: Harvard University Press, 1987).

57 US Congress, House of Representatives, "Report of the Survey of the Colorado of the West. Letter from the Secretary of the Smithsonian Institution, Transmitting a Report of the Survey of the Colorado River of the West, and its Tributaries." H. Misc. Doc. 76, 42nd Cong., 3rd sess., January 31, 1873, 10.

58 Ibid.

59 US Congress, House of Representatives, "Professor Powell's Report on the Survey of the Colorado of the West; Letter from the Secretary of the Smithsonian Institution, Transmitting a report of Professor Powell on the survey of the Colorado River of the West and its tributaties, &c., &c." H. Misc. Doc. 265, 43rd Cong., 1st sess., May 2, 1874, 10.

60 Ibid.

61 Ibid.

62 Ibid.

63 Ibid.

64 US Congress, House of Representatives, "Report of the Survey of the Colorado of the West. Letter from the Secretary of the Smithsonian Institution, Transmitting a Report of the Survey of the Colorado River of the West, and its Tributaries." H. Misc. Doc. 76, 42nd Cong., 3rd sess., January 31, 1873, 10.

65 Powell, *Exploration* (1875), 112–13.

66 Ibid., 113.

67 US Congress, House of Representatives, "Professor Powell's Report on the Survey of the Colorado of the West; Letter from the Secretary of the Smithsonian Institution, Transmitting a Report of Professor Powell on the Survey of the Colorado River of the West and its Tributaries, &c., &c." H. Misc. Doc. 265, 43rd Cong., 1st sess., May 2, 1874, 23–24.

68 But this of course is also true in some sense of Indian geographical knowledge, where the particularization of knowledge means that it can only be cognized after one has already experienced these particular features. At least ideally, the systematic knowledge of Western science/culture suggests that a knowledge of particulars can be derived from general systems or theories (or maps) or concepts.

69 These photographs and their captions can be found in Don D. Fowler, *The Western Photographs of John K. Hillers: Myself in the Water* (Washington, DC: Smithsonian Institution Press, c. 1989), 45.

70 Charles Dudley Warner, "The Heart of the Desert," *The Grand Canyon: Early Impressions* (Boulder, Colo.: Pruett Publishing Co., 1989), 35; reprinted from *Our Italy* (New York: Harper & Brothers, 1891), 177–200.

71 Ibid., 42.

72 Harriet Monroe, "The Grand Canyon of the Colorado," *The Grand Canyon: Early Impressions* (Boulder, Colo.: Pruett Publishing Co., 1989), 52; reprinted from *Atlantic Monthly* (December 1899): 816–821.

73 Ibid., 49; 54.

74 John Muir, "Our Grand Canyon," *The Grand Canyon: Early Impressions* (Boulder, Colo.: Pruett Publishing Co., 1989), 74; reprinted from *Century Illustrated Monthly Magazine* (November 1902): 107–116.

75 Ibid., 80.

76 John C. Van Dyke, *The Grand Canyon of the Colorado: Recurrent Studies in Impressions and Appearances* (1920; rpt. Salt Lake City: University of Utah Press, 1992), 9.

77 Ibid., 11.

78 Ibid., 19.

79 Following the work of earlier nineteenth-century geologists, Dutton championed the idea of (and coined the term) "isostasy," which he defined as the "condition of equilibrium of figure . . . to which gravitation tends to reduce a planetary body irrespective of whether it is homogeneous or not"; qtd. Mott T. Greene, *Geology in the Nineteenth Century: Changing Views of a Changing World* (Ithaca, N.Y.: Cornell University Press, 1982), 249. Dutton held that the earth's surface floated on a fluid layer and that its "isostasy was perpetually disturbed by erosion and sedimentation"; ibid. According to this theory, variations in the thickness of the earth's crust, including the creation of continents, oceans, and mountain ranges, could be explained by "the slow sinking of sea bottoms loaded with sediment and the corresponding rise of eroded land masses, with bending and fracturing along the margins or coastlines"; Wallace Stegner, *Beyond the Hundredth Meridian: John Wesley Powell and the Second Opening of the West* (Lincoln, Nebr.: University of Nebraska Press, 1953), 160.

80 Stegner, *Beyond the Hundredth Meridian*, 161.

81 Ibid., 164–165.

82 Pyne, *How the Canyon Became Grand*, 75.

83 Ibid., 75.

84 Ibid., 75–76.

85 C[larence]. E. Dutton, *The Tertiary History of the Grand Canyon District*, US Geological Survey Monograph 2 (Washington: Government Printing Office, 1882), xvi.

86 Pyne, *How the Canyon Became Grand*, 72; Stegner, *Beyond the Hundredth Meridian*, 159. For a brief biography of Dutton, see Wallace E. Stegner, *Clarence Edward Dutton: An Appraisal* (Salt Lake City: University of Utah Press, 1935).

87 Clarence E. Dutton, "The Physical Geology of the Grand Cañon District," in *United States Geological Survey 2nd Annual Report, 1880–1881* (Washington, DC: Government Printing Office, 1881), 51–52.

88 Dutton, *Tertiary History*, 86.

89 Ibid., 172.

90 Dutton, "Physical Geology," 49.

91 Dutton, *Tertiary History*, 61.

92 Ibid., 62.

93 Ibid.

94 Ibid.

95 Ibid., 75.

96 Ibid., 260. Dutton's invocation of the Sphinx to describe the inscrutability of nature is consistent with an Orientalism that he employs in naming some of the canyon's features.

97 Ibid., 89.

98 Ibid., 90.

99 Ibid., 141–142.

100 William Cullen Bryant, ed., *Picturesque America; or, The Land We Live In*, 2 vols. (New York: D. Appleton and Co., 1874).

101 See, for example, "Drawing Things Together," *Representation in Scientific Practice*, ed. Michael Lynch and Steve Woolgar (Cambridge, Mass.: MIT Press, 1990), 19–68.

102 For accounts of how Hillers became Powell's photographer, see Fowler, *Western Photographs of John K. Hillers*, 20–23; Kinsey, *Thomas Moran*, 101–103.

103 Dutton, *Tertiary History*, 164.

104 Edmund Burke, *A Philosophical Enquiry into the Origin of Our Ideas of the Sublime and Beautiful*, ed. J. T. Boulton (1958; rpt. Notre Dame, Ind.: University of Notre Dame Press, 1968).

105 "Culture and Progress: 'The Chasm of the Colorado,'" *Scribner's Monthly* 8 (July 1874): 374.

106 "Art," *Atlantic Monthly* 34 (September 1874): 375.

107 Ibid., 376.

108 Joni Kinsey makes this point in her perceptive discussion of this painting in *Thomas Moran*, 95–99.

109 Ibid., 114–115.

110 Ibid., 97.

111 Ibid., 98; 123.

112 Dutton, *Tertiary History*, 145.

113 Ibid., 148; 148; 150. Similar to his earlier comparison of nature to the Sphinx, Dutton here invokes the cultural affiliation of an Eastern religion with a sense of mystery or the unknown.

114 Jay David Bolter and Richard Grusin, *Remediation: Understanding New Media* (Cambridge, Mass.: MIT Press, 1999).

115 Owen Wister, "Foreword," in E. L. Kolb, *Through the Grand Canyon from Wyoming to Mexico* (1914; rpt. Tucson: University of Arizona Press, 1989), xi.

116 E. L. Kolb, *Through the Grand Canyon from Wyoming to Mexico*, 1–2.

117 Ibid., 3–4.

118 Ibid., 4.

119 Tom Gunning, "An Aesthetic of Astonishment," in Linda Williams, ed., *Viewing Positions: Ways of Seeing Film* (New Brunswick, N.J.: Rutgers University Press, 1995), 114–133.

120 William C. Suran, *The Kolb Brothers of Grand Canyon* (Grand Canyon, Ariz.: Grand Canyon Natural History Association, 1991), 7.

121 Ibid.

122 Quotations taken from *Making of Grand Canyon: The Hidden Secrets*, on *Grand Canyon: The Hidden Secrets*, produced by Kieth Merrill and O. Douglas Memmott, filmed in IMAX, (Grand Canyon Theatre Venture, Distributed by Destination Cinema, Inc., 1994).

123 Quotations from IMAX brochure for National Geographic Theater in Grand Canyon, Arizona.

124 Airplane and helicopter flights also serve as technologies of mediation by providing perceptions of or perspectives on the Grand Canyon landscape which are different from, and unavailable from, other media. Of course, these rides, too, provide a kind of immediacy and a kind of hypermediacy epitomized by the pilots' narrative, the established air routes, the ubiquitous automatic cameras and videocams, and so forth. The canyon flights interface with, surpass, and claim to erase other cultural technologies of mediation.

125 Bolter and Grusin, *Remediation*, 2–15.

126 David Nye offers a similar reading of both the Kasdan film and the Sony commercial in a working paper published in 1996 by the Man and Nature Research Center at Odense University in Denmark. Nye's *American Technological Sublime* (Cambridge, Mass.: MIT Press, 1994) also has a relevant discussion of the Grand Canyon.

CONCLUSION

1 Yellowstone National Park's Official 'Online Tours' Page (http://www.nps.gov/yell/tours/index.htm), December 12, 2000.

2 Jay David Bolter and Richard Grusin, *Remediation: Understanding New Media* (Cambridge, Mass.: MIT Press, 1999).

3 Carolyn Merchant, "Reinventing Eden: Western Culture as a Recovery Narrative," in *Uncommon Ground: Rethinking the Human Place in Nature* (New York: W.W. Norton & Co., 1996), 132–159.

4 These terms and concepts are borrowed from Stephen Jay Gould, *Time's Arrow, Time's Cycle: Myth and Metaphor in the Discovery of Geological Time* (Cambridge, Mass.: Harvard University Press, 1987).

5 Richard Misrach, with Myriam Weisang Misrach, *Bravo 20: The Bombing of the American West* (Baltimore: Johns Hopkins University Press, 1990), 95.

6 Andrew Ross, *The Chicago Gangster Theory of Life: Nature's Debt to Society* (New York: Verso, 1994), 199–200.

7 Ibid., 198.

8 Misrach, *Bravo 20*, 95.

9 Ibid., 96.

10 *New York Times* (Thursday, September 21, 2000), D11 (Circuits Section).

Index

Lightning Source UK Ltd.
Milton Keynes UK
UKOW052358090312

188692UK00001B/76/P